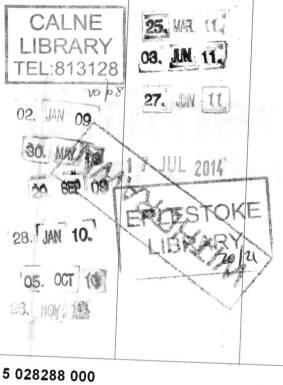

Ultimate
Cover Letters

A guide to job search letters, online applications and follow-up strategies

2nd edition

Martin Yate

KOGAN
PAGE

Publisher's note
Every possible effort has been made to ensure that the information contained in this book is accurate at the time of going to press, and the publishers and authors cannot accept responsibility for any errors or omissions, however caused. No responsibility for loss or damage occasioned to any person acting, or refraining from action, as a result of the material in this publication can be accepted by the editor, the publisher or the author.

First published in the United States in 1992 as *Cover Letters that Knock 'em Dead* by Adams Media Corporation

First published in Great Britain in 2003 as *The Ultimate Job Search Letters Book* by Kogan Page Limited
Reprinted in 2007
Second edition published in 2008 as *Ultimate Cover Letters*

Published by arrangement with Adams Media Corporation, 57 Littlefield Street, Avon, MA 02322, USA

Kogan Page Limited
120 Pentonville Road
London N1 9JN
United Kingdom
www.koganpage.com

British Library Cataloguing in Publication Data

A CIP record for this book is available from the British Library

ISBN 978 0 7494 5328 2

Typeset by Jean Cussons Typesetting, Diss, Norfolk
Printed and bound in India by Replika Press Pvt Ltd

Contents

Read this first   1

1 What is a job search letter?   6
Step one 7; Step two 7; Step three 8; Step four 9

2 The four types of job search letters   12
The executive briefing 15; The broadcast letter 17;
Recruitment agencies and executive recruiters 20

3 What goes in, what stays out   22
Desirable professional behaviours 22; Brief is beautiful 27;
A question of money 28; Telephone and e-mail 29; Ingredients:
a basic checklist 29

4 Assembling your job search letter   31
Gather information 31; Creating punchy sentences 35;
Length 40; Your checklist 41

5 The final product   44
Layout 44; How to brighten the page 44; Proofing and
printing 45; Envelopes send messages too 47; Appearance 48

6 The plan of attack   50
Online job postings 50; Job advertisements 51; Networking 53;
Direct-research contacts 56; Recruitment agencies 59; Business
magazines 60; Sending out your job search letter 60;
Do you need to compose more than one letter? 62;
The plan 62; Following up: a cautionary tale 64; Follow-up
calls work 65

7   How the internet can help in your job search   67
What you need to start an online job search 68; Online privacy
and organization 68; Privacy is a concern for everyone 69; Rules
to protect your online privacy 69; Free e-mail accounts 70; How
to organize your job-hunting e-mail account 71; Job search
letters and online job-hunting 73; Differences between electronic
and paper job search letters 74; The need for multiple electronic
search letters 77; Make sure your job search letter templates are
electronic transmission compatible 78; E-mail subject lines 81;
How to customize and send your e-mail job search letter and
CV 82; Reaching the right person 87; Electronic signatures and
'fake' real stationery 87; Accuracy is essential 88

8   Sample letters   **89**
Responses to online job postings
E-mails:
Technical sales representative   90
Investment banker   91
Legal administrator   92
Manufacturing   93
Production supervisor   94

Responses to newspaper advertisements
Letters:
Health care management   95
Speech therapist   96
Hydrogeologist   97
Customer service representative   98
Sales associate   99
Skilled labourer   100
Assessment coordinator   101
Office administrator   102
Legal secretary   103
Accounting manager   104
International sales manager   105
Executive assistant   106

Power phrases   107

'Cold' enquiries to potential employers
Letters:
Entry-level network administrator   112
Entry-level librarian   113

Manager   114
Mental health   116
Senior customer service specialist   117
Research professional   118
Personal trainer   119
Registered nurse   120
Entertainment industry   121
Management   122
Radiation safety officer   123
Veterinary surgeon   125
Work placement   126
Teacher   127
Production supervisor   128
Sales professional   129
Credit account specialist   130
Sales   131
Media   132
Director   133
Pharmaceutical sales   134
Recruiter   135
Project management   136
Publishing   137
International sales   138

E-mails:
Banking   139
Software development   140
Work experience   141

Power phrases   142

'Cold' enquiries to employment industry professionals
Letters:
Health care   145
Senior network control technician/administrator   146
Accountant   148
Quality assurance   149
Executive computer specialist   150
Director   151
Senior manager   152
International operations   153

E-mails:
IT professional   154
Computer professional   155
Programmer/analyst   156
IT management   157
Systems integration   158
Systems administrator   159

Power phrases   160

Broadcast
Letters:
Teaching position   163
Assistant director of student housing   165
Financial planning professional   166
Heavy equipment operator   167
Executive chef/hotel restaurant manager   168
Maintenance mechanic   169
Database engineer   170
Senior technical sales   171
Telecommunications   172
Senior R&D engineer   174
Multilingual sales manager   176
Management   178
HR generalist   180
Operations manager   182
Information technology programme manager   183
Pharmaceutical sales   184
Director of operations   185
Consultant   186
Project manager   188

E-mails:
Senior buyer/purchasing agent/purchasing manager   189
Logistics   190
New product marketing   191
Senior marketing executive   192
Director, asset liquidation   193

Power phrases   194

Networking
Letters:
Managerial/administrative position   197
Administrative assistant   198
Creative media   199
Management   200
Computer and information systems manager   201
Chief financial officer   202
General   203
Accounting   204

E-mails:
HR administration   205
Publishing   206

Power phrases   207

Follow-up (after telephone contact)
Letters:
Fundraising consultant   210
Adult education   211
Legal assistant   212
Purchasing   213
Manager   214

E-mails:
General   215
Arts management   216

Power phrases   217

Follow-up (after face-to-face meeting)
Letters:
Library system director   219
Sales   220
Loan processor   221
Hospitality manager   222
Merchandise manager   223
Manufacturer representative   224
General   225
Librarian   226
Construction manager   227
Executive assistant   228

Assistant   229
Management information systems   230
Sales   231

E-mails:
General   232
Sales manager   233
Management   234
Senior counsellor   235
Graphic design   236
General   237
Entry-level   238
Auditing   239

Power phrases   240

'Resurrection'
Letters:
HR position   244
Stevedore   245
Social worker   246
Wholesale market manager   247
Construction manager   248
Entry-level   249

E-mails:
Account executive   250
Programmer   251
Product manager   252

Power phrases   253

Rejection of offer
Letters:
Head librarian   254
Team supervisor   255
General   256

E-mail:
Department manager   257

Power phrases   258

Acceptance
Letters:
Marketing research manager   259
Director   260
Managing consultant   261

E-mail:
General   262

Power phrases   263

Negotiation
Letters:
General   265
Sales   267
Senior lab specialist   268
Product specialist   269

Resignation
Letters:
ITU nurse   270
Care coordinator   271
Management   272
Sales representative   273
Director   274

E-mail:
General   275

Power phrases   276

Thank-yous (after appointment)
Letter:
General   278

E-mail:
Software manager   279

Power phrases   280

Appendix: How to jump-start a stalled career search   282

Index   289

Read this first

We strive to excel in our professions, spending our energies to become top-notch accountants, lorry drivers, brain surgeons ... and we spend little or no time learning to promote ourselves on the printed page. When our livelihood suddenly depends on our ability to compose a compelling professional profile we find ourselves in dire straits.

In the technological revolution that brought us computers and e-mail we all started writing once more, but at the same time we found our writing skills have long since rusted. Although packaging our professional selves for evaluation by others has such an enormous impact on all aspects of the quality of our lives, most of us have simply never made the development of adequate written communication skills a top priority. This task is made the more difficult because, when writing a cover letter, we are creating a sales document, and a document where we are the subject. If you are like most people, packaging and pitching yourself to others is both an uncomfortable and difficult prospect.

Sometimes, more senior professionals hire others to craft these messages. As for the rest of us... well, we just send these all-important sales documents out into the world far weaker than they could be. The result? We stay longer in that dead-end job, or unemployed for longer.

If you find yourself short of writing and self-presentation skills at the most inopportune time imaginable – during your job search – take heart. This book has helped millions of people around the world craft personal, unique, and hard-hitting job-hunting letters of all types, and it can do the same for you. Use it exactly as I recommend in the pages that follow. If you do, you will reap a number of benefits, the most important of which is this:

- Your job hunt will get a tremendous boost, because your letters will look great, pack a punch, get read, and position you as a mover and shaker worth interviewing, and worth remembering.

This book will enable you to have templates on hand for all kinds of useful letters which you can use in a productive job hunt – not only cover letters of every conceivable type, but letters for every situation, including follow-up letters, acceptance letters, and those oh-so-happy letters of resignation. These letters were all designed to keep your candidacy forefront in the minds of employers. They are real letters written by real job hunters, and also by professional CV and letter writing professionals. They will give you that extra edge in a highly competitive job market, as you will have the advantage of proven tools, customized to your own needs.

There are other advantages:

- You won't waste a moment of precious time conceiving letters from scratch, because you will have a wide selection of templates to rework for your own needs.
- You'll have the satisfaction of having made a tough, intricate and vitally important professional challenge a little easier and more enjoyable than it is for most people in your shoes (your competitors, for example).
- Once settled in a new position you will be able to adapt the techniques you learn here to other on-the-job written communications that are part of the underpinnings of any successful career.

Employers go through four distinct stages in reaching a hiring decision:

1. Longlist development. Advertising and other sources develop the biggest possible field of qualified candidates.
2. Shortlist development. The long list is screened to rule out also-rans. Those who make the cut are invited in for an interview.
3. Shortlist prioritization. Through a series of two or three interviews, candidates are weeded out. Those still standing are ranked according to various criteria.
4. Shortlist review. After the dust settles, each candidate's strengths and weaknesses are reviewed for one last time before the final decision. The information in the dossier created for every short-

listed candidate plays a key role here. This dossier will contain all the knowledge the company has about you. This will include your CV, job search letter, and any follow-up letters you have been smart enough to send during the interview process.

In each of these steps, letters have a role to play in taking you to the next level. For example, a CV without a covering letter rarely gets any further than the waste-paper basket. The reader feel you are obviously not interested enough in their specific job to write a cover letter while, on the other hand, your competition is providing concrete evidence of commitment and communication skills.

A 'To whom it may concern' letter fares little better. A letter with a salutation by names gets read and kept, as will follow-up letters on meetings that make comments on the discussions and issues addressed.

It's estimated that the average piece of business correspondence initially gets less than 30 seconds of the reader's attention, just a quick scan to reject or save for more careful consideration. A great cover letter will get you much more; it will get you a second, more careful reading, and it will get your CV read with serious attention. In crafting your job search letter, you are not aiming to win a place next to a favourite novel on the reader's bedside table. A powerful letter will win that momentary flash of genuine interest and get your CV read carefully. Once that's accomplished, you can use the models for the follow-up letters in this book to help you step up on the four-tiered ladder to the job offer.

Letters help you move through each phase of the cycle by supporting your candidacy and reminding employers of your relevant skills, continued existence and interest in the job, all the way to the offer. It's a well-known fact in head-hunting circles that when there is no difference between two top candidates, the offer will always go to the most enthusiastic; professional follow-through with your letters makes that enthusiasm clear.

In the fourth step (the shortlist review) the interviewer recalls what happened in each phase of the interview cycle. All notes and documentation in the applicant dossier are reviewed for each candidate. This means that as you pass through each step of the cycle, you are presented with a heaven-sent opportunity to advance your candidacy when the moment of truth finally arrives. You can seize the opportunity to include all manner of pertinent information that will identify you as the unquestioned prime choice when that last, most critical evaluation is taking place.

Your written record (all the different types of letters you can create during the interview cycle to advance your candidacy) demonstrate writing skills, attention to detail, professionalism and that all-important enthusiasm; each letter adds yet another meaningful plus to your candidacy. And remember that these pluses are being made when you aren't there to speak for yourself.

I took a common-sense approach to putting this book together: I collected over 4,000 successful job-search letters from the most cynical professionals in the country, corporate human resources people and professional headhunters. I approached over a thousand of these people and asked them to provide the truly impressive letters they came across – the letters that grabbed attention, advanced someone's candidacy against tough competition and made a real difference. The cream of the crop can be found within these covers.

Over the years, this book has become the standard against which the others in the field are judged, and it is updated on a regular basis to add to its breadth, depth and efficacy.

From these letters, and from my discussions with professionals in the field, I learnt about certain things that work and don't work when putting together a job search letter. These are explored in detail later on in the book, but there is one overriding factor that virtually all the successful letters shared. It's worth exploring here. All but a handful of the letters were only one page long. Yours probably should be too. Why is brevity so important? My sources on the hiring side of the desk, where I spent a number of years myself, feel that:

1. They don't have time to wade through dense patches of text, and they view those who can't get to the point in a dim light.

2. Second pages get detached and often lack sufficient contact information. (For that matter, first pages often fall short in the same category.)

A strong mail dimension to your job hunting campaign can double or triple your effectiveness. Throughout this book whenever you read the word 'mail' it has a double meaning – regular mail and e-mail. The most effective job-hunting campaign will always use the two media in tandem. For maximum impact you will want to follow up each letter with a telephone call to the recipient.

If you use the letters simply as non-customized templates, you may open a few doors. But the 'real' you will be so different from the letters that the interviewers will eventually be left with a nagging doubt that you aren't all you appear to be. Besides, when it's so easy to customize these samples, why not make the effort as a gift to your career? Then, with small changes, you'll be able to use them again and again throughout your career.

Browse through the wide variety of letters in the second half of this book. Not all of them will fit your needs at this moment, but take a look anyway. You will see, on every page, proven methods of getting the good word across to potential employers.

This book will also highlight key phrases and wording techniques that caught the eyes of people whose eyes are usually tough to catch. You will discover a 'rhythm' to the words and phrases that have real impact. Then you'll be able to incorporate them into your own original work. By sampling a few phrases from this letter, and a few from that letter, you will be able to create powerful communications that reflect the real you.

In choosing the examples for this book, I was pleased to see that the ones that rose to the top were all businesslike, with no gimmickry or cuteness. Some may even seem a little dry to you, but remember: they worked. This collection of successful job-search letters includes the best of the best as determined by line managers, human resource professionals, head-hunters and career management professionals who know a winner when they see one. It is just such people who will be evaluating your efforts, and the drawbridge of opportunity will be raised (or lowered) for you depending on their evaluation.

1

What is a job search letter?

Junk mail never gets the attention a properly focused letter does.

We all receive junk mail, and either bin it without reading or after a quick glance; junk mail never gets the attention a properly focused letter does because it's formulaic. Because we put too little thought into our job search letters, most of them end up being treated in the same way.

Your job search letter is the personalized factor in the presentation of an otherwise essentially impersonal document, your CV. A good letter sets the stage for the reader to accept your CV as something worth serious attention. Only if your job search letter and CV work together and do their job will interviews and ultimately job offers result.

When the envelope is opened, your letter is the first thing seen. It can make an indelible first impression, it can set the tone for your candidacy and it can earn your CV the careful examination it deserves.

The higher up the professional ladder you climb, the more important job search letters and the other letters we write become. For the candidate who must demonstrate written communication skills in the execution of daily duties (and that's just about all of us), these letters become a valuable vehicle for demonstrating critical job skills. If you mess up here, the door to opportunity could well slam shut. On the other hand, if you do a good job here it will help you stand out from the competition.

Step one

There are four basic building blocks to creating a productive cover letter, and the underlying rules of effective written communication embodied in these four steps can be applied to any memo or business letter you ever write.

Your first step is to grab your reader's ATTENTION. You do this with the appearance of your letter: the type is large and legible enough for others to read; it is free of misspellings and it is well laid out so that it is easy on the eye; and if that letter is going by mail rather than e-mail you grab attention by using quality stationery, and matching envelopes. This way your letter and CV will match and give an impression of balance and continuity (see Chapter 5, 'The Final Product', for details on paper choice). When your message is crafted with this attention to detail, and convenience for the reader, it reflects the kind of professional who just might have something to say.

Step two

Your second step is to generate INTEREST with the content. The first opportunity you have to do this is by addressing the letter to someone by name. The first couple of sentences grab attention, and the rest of the paragraph introduces your candidacy. The secret is to introduce yourself with conviction. Think about it – if you don't believe in the professional product that is you, how can you expect anyone else to?

Use research to get your letter off to a good start; with Google and other search engines, anyone can search the web for articles and visit the employer's own site. For example:

> *'I came across the enclosed article in* Newsweek *magazine and thought it might interest you. It encouraged me to do a little research on your company. I am now convinced of two things: You are the kind of people I want to be associated with, and I have the kind of qualifications you can use.'*

On a company's website you will find lots of eye-opening information, including news and press clippings. You can also use search engines to find interesting info about the company by typing in the company name as a keyword. Once you find a relevant article, you can use it in the following ways:

- with an e-mail, you paste the article and attach it;
- with a traditional letter, you enclose a copy of the article.

Of course, not every company you approach will have been mentioned in *Newsweek*. Even if there is no mention in the press, though, the chances are still good that the company's website (or your other research) can give you some insight that can be turned to your advantage. Here are some real-life examples that you can adapt to your own needs.

> *'I have been following the performance of your fund in the* Financial Times. *The record over the last three years shows strong portfolio management. With my experience working for one of your competitors, I know I could make significant contributions ...'*

> *'Recently I have been researching the local _____ industry. My search has been for companies that are respected in the field and which pride a commitment to professional development. I am such an individual and you are clearly such a company.*

> *'Within the next few weeks I will be moving from London to _____ . Having researched the companies in my field in my new home town, I know that you are the people I want to talk to ...'*

> *'The state of the art in _____ changes so rapidly that it is tough for most professionals to keep up. I am the exception. I am eager to bring my experience to bear for your company.'*

Step three

Now having built a bridge between you and the reader turn that INTEREST into DESIRE to know more. First, tie yourself to a specific job category or work area. Use phrases like:

> *'I am writing because ...'* or *'My reason for contacting you ...'*

> *'... should this be the case, you may be interested to know ...'*

> *'If you are seeking a _____, you will be interested to know ...'*

'I would like to talk to you about your personnel needs and how I am able to contribute to your department's goals.'

'If you have an opening for someone in this area, you will see that my CV demonstrates a person of unusual dedication, efficiency and drive.'

You might next, call attention to your merits with a short paragraph that highlights one or two of your special contributions or achievements:

'I have an economics degree from London and a quantitative analysis approach to market fluctuations. This combination has enabled me consistently to pick the new technology flotations that are the backbone of the growth-oriented technical fund.'

Similar statements applicable to your area of expertise will give your letter more personal punch. Include any qualifications, contributions and attributes that prove you are someone with professional commitment and talent to offer. If an advertisement (or a conversation with a potential employer) reveals an aspect of a particular job opening that is not addressed in your CV, you can use the letter to fill in the gaps. For example:

'I notice from your advertisement that audio- and video-training experience would be a plus. In addition to the qualifications stated in my enclosed CV, I have over five years of experience writing and producing sales and management training materials in both these media.'

It is through this third step that you want the reader to say 'Wow, this man/woman really understands the job. I need to read on and learn more.'

Step four

Here's where your letter turns that DESIRE into ACTION. The action you're aiming for is that the reader will move straight on to your CV, then call you in for an interview. You achieve this action with brevity – leave the reader wanting more. Offer too much information and you may be ruled out of consideration, so whet the reader's appetite but leave them asking questions.

Make it clear to the reader that you want to talk. Explain when, where, and how you can be contacted. You can now be proactive by telling the reader that you intend to follow up at a certain time if contact has not been established by then.

Just as you worked to create a strong opening, make sure your closing carries the same conviction. It is the reader's last impression of you; make it strong, make it tight and make it obvious that you are serious about entering into meaningful conversation.

Useful phrases include:

'It would be a pleasure to give you more information about my qualifications and experience ...'

'I look forward to discussing our mutual interests further ...'

'While I prefer not to use my employer's time taking personal calls at work, with discretion I can be reached on _____ .'

'I will be in your area around the 20th, and will ring you prior to that date. I would like to arrange ...'

'I hope to speak with you further and will ring the week of _____ to follow up.'

'The chance to meet you would be a privilege and a pleasure, so to this end I shall ring you on _____.'

'I look forward to speaking with you further and will ring in the next few days to see when our schedules will permit a face-to-face meeting.'

'May I suggest a personal meeting where you can have the opportunity to examine the person behind the CV.'

'My credentials and achievements are a matter of record that I hope you will examine in depth when we meet ...'

'I look forward to examining any of the ways you feel my background and skills would benefit [name of organization]. I look forward to hearing from you.'

'CVs help you sort out the probables from the possibles, but they are no way to judge the calibre of an individual. I would like to meet you and demonstrate that I have the personality that makes for a successful _____.'

'I expect to be in your area on Tuesday and Wednesday of next week and wonder which day would be best for you. I will ring to determine. In the meantime, I would appreciate your treating my application as confidential, since I am currently employed.'

'With my training and hands-on experience, I know I can contribute to _____, and want to talk to you about it in person. When may we meet?'

'After reading my CV, you will know something about my background. Yet, you will still need to determine whether I am the one to help you with current problems and challenges. I would like an interview to discuss my ability to contribute.'

'You can reach me at _____ to arrange an interview. I know that your time investment in meeting me will be repaid amply.'

'Thank you for your time and consideration; I hope to hear from you shortly.'

'May I ring you for an interview in the next few days?'

'A brief phone call will establish whether or not we have mutual interests. Recognizing the demands of your schedule, I will make that call within the week.'

Some people feel it is powerful in the closing to state a date – 'I'll ring you on Friday if we don't speak before' – or a date and time – 'I'll ring you on Friday morning at 10 am if we don't speak before' when they follow up with a phone call. The logic is that you demonstrate that your intent is serious, that you are organized, and that you plan your time effectively (all desirable behavioural traits).

On the other hand, at least one 'authority' has said that the reader would be offended by being 'forced' to sit and await your call. Frankly, in 20 years of being involved in the employing process, I have never felt constrained by such statements; I guess I'm just not the sensitive type. What I look for is the person who doesn't follow through on commitments as promised. Therefore, if you use this approach, keep your promises.

2

The four types of job search letters

Practically speaking, there are four types of job search letters that together address most of the situations you will run into in a job search. The following examples will appeal to you partly based on their relevance to a particular situation, and partly based on your personal preferences.

To show the nuts and bolts of building effective job search letters, we'll start with an example of a general letter. It was created using the sample phrases from the last chapter. You can create powerful job search letters of all types with this same technique, taking a sentence from one sample and a phrase from another, then all you have to do is make the necessary changes to personalize each document.

The following two examples have underlined text to show where I have cut and pasted a phrase from the last chapter. This is the kind of letter you would send with your CV when you do not know of a specific job opening.

James Swift
18 Park Street ● London X1 0BB
020 8123 4567

2 October, 20–

Jackson Bethell, Head of Operations
ABC Ltd
Industry Square
London X2 2EF

Dear Jackson Bethell,

Recently I have been researching the leading local companies in data
communications. My search has been for companies that are respected in the field
and which provide ongoing training programmes. The name of ABC Ltd keeps
coming up as a top company.

I am an experienced voice and data communications specialist with a substantial
background in IBM environments. If you have an opening for someone in this area,
you will see that my CV demonstrates a person of unusual dedication, efficiency and
drive. My experience and achievements include:

● The complete redesign of a data communications network, projected to increase
  efficiency company-wide some 12 per cent.
● The installation and troubleshooting of a Defender II call-back security system
  for a dial-up network.

I enclose a copy of my CV and look forward to examining any of the ways you feel
my background and skills would benefit ABC Ltd. While I prefer not to use my
employer's time taking personal calls at work, with discretion I can be reached on
020 8123 4567 to initiate contact. However, I would prefer to be contacted on 03176
471640 in the evening. Let's talk!

Yours sincerely,

James Swift

James Swift

Jane Swift
18 Park Street, London X1 0BB
020 8123 4567

David Doors, Director of Marketing   14 January, 20–
ABC Ltd
Industry Square
London X2 2EF

Dear David Doors,

I have always followed the performance of your fund in the *Financial Times.*

Recently your notice regarding a Market Analyst in INVESTORS DAILY caught my eye – and your company name caught my attention – because your record over the last three years shows exceptional portfolio management. Because of my experience with one of your competitors, I know I could make significant contributions.

I would like to talk to you about your personnel needs and how I am able to contribute to your department's goals.

An experienced market analyst, I have an economics background (MSc London) and a strong quantitative analysis approach to market fluctuations. This combination has enabled me to consistently pick the new technology flotations that are the backbone of the growth-oriented technical fund. For example:

I first recommended ABC Fund six years ago. More recently my clients have strongly invested in XYZ (in the high-risk category), and ABC Growth and Income (for the cautious investor). Those following my advice over the last six years have consistently outperformed the market.

I know that CVs help you sort out the probables from the possibles, but they are no way to judge the personal calibre of an individual. I would like to meet you and demonstrate that along with the credentials, I have the professional commitment that makes for a successful team player.

Yours sincerely,

Jane Swift

Jane Swift

The executive briefing

The executive briefing is a different and dramatically effective form of job search letter whenever you have some information about an opening from a job ad, an online job posting, or a prior conversation. This kind of letter gets right to the point and makes life easy for the reader.

Why send an executive briefing?

1. It quickly matches stated requirements against the skills you bring to the table, making analysis much easier for the reader.
2. The initial CV screener in Human Resources (HR) might not have an in-depth understanding of the job or its requirements, so the executive briefing helps match an open requirement directly to your abilities. This can be a real help to someone working on fifty or more different openings at a time.
3. Your general CV invariably needs customizing for any specific job. (Overly broad CVs are like 'one-size-fits-all' clothes – one size usually fits none.) The executive briefing allows you to fill in the gaps in a succinct and helpful manner.
4. Imagine for a moment that a great opportunity comes your way, but your CV is somewhat (or more than somewhat) out of date and you have to send something out immediately to take advantage of the opportunity of a lifetime. The executive briefing allows you to bring that work history right up to date.

An executive briefing can also help you through a screening and multiple interview cycle. Let me explain. You will be interviewed by a number of people, not all of whom can be expected to have a thorough understanding of the needs of the job – perhaps surprising but nevertheless true. When this happens, the problems begin.

A manager says, 'Spend a few minutes with this candidate and tell me what you think.' This means that sometimes other interviewers do not have any way to qualify you fairly and specifically for the needs of the job. While the manager will be looking for specific skills relating to projects at hand, the personnel department will be trying to match your skills to the vagaries of the job-description manual.

Also, by taking multiple copies of your CV and the briefing, carefully stapled together, you guarantee that everyone with whom you interview will have the job's specific requirements and your matching skills front and centre when they sit down with you.

The executive briefing, which introduces your CV, as well as customizing and supplementing it, solves the above problems with its layout. It looks like this:

From: top10acct@aol.com
Subject: Re: Accounting Manager
Date: February 18, 2005 10:05:44 PM BSTGMT
To: rlstein@McCoy.com

Dear Ms Stein,

I have nine years of accounting experience and am responding to your recent posting for an Accounting Manager on Careerbuilder. Please allow me to highlight my skills as they relate to your stated requirements.

Your Requirements	My Experience
Accounting degree, 4 years exp.	Obtained a C.A. degree in 2000 and have over four years' experience as an Accounting Manager.
Excellent people skills and leadership	Effectively managed a staff of 24; ability to motivate staff, including supervisors.
Strong administrative and analytical skills	Assisted in the development of a base reference skills-library with Microsoft Excel for 400 clients.
Good communication skills	Trained new supervisors and staff via daily coaching sessions, communication meetings, and technical skill sessions.

My CV, pasted below and attached in MSWord, will flesh out my general background. I hope this executive briefing helps you use your time effectively today. I am ready to make a move, hope we can talk soon.

Sincerely,

Joe Black

Joe Black

The executive briefing ensures that each CV you send out addresses the job's specific needs and that every interviewer at that company will be interviewing you for the same job. It provides a comprehensive picture of a thorough professional, plus a personalized, fast and easy-to-read synopsis that details exactly how you can help with an employer's needs.

The use of an executive briefing is naturally restricted to jobs you have discovered through your own efforts or seen advertised. It is obviously not appropriate when the requirements of a specific job are unavailable.

The broadcast letter

The broadcast letter is a simple but effective variation on the job search letter. You can use it when:

- you don't have a CV;
- your CV is inappropriate for the position;
- your CV is too dreadful to send out;
- your CV isn't getting the results you want, and you want to try something different while you are retooling it.

Much of the information will be culled from your CV, because the intent of the broadcast letter is to *replace* the CV, as a means of introduction and a tool to initiate conversation. You would be well advised to conduct an in-depth analysis of your background as it relates to a specific target job, in much the same way you would for a CV (see Chapter 4). Now, although a broadcast letter can get you into a telephone conversation with a potential employer, that employer may still ask to see a CV. If this happens always try to arrange the interview and bring the CV with you; this way you buy a little more time to customize your CV to the employer's specific needs.

You should also know that broadcast letters are most frequently used by mature, successfully established professionals.

Beware: if you don't have a CV, you might well have to fill in one of those dreadful application forms. This requires putting your background in the format the employer wants – not the package of your choice. Consequently, I do not advise using this kind of letter as the spearhead or sole thrust of your campaign. Rather, you should use it as an integral part of the campaign in one of these ways:

- For small, highly targeted mailings to specific high-interest companies, where it works as an effective customizing technique.

- For small, highly targeted mailings to specific high-interest jobs about which you have enough detailed knowledge that such a letter would supersede the effectiveness of your CV.

- As an initial thrust, but with the more traditional job search letter and CV already in place for a back-up second mailing. In practice, the cold-mailed broadcast letter often results in a request for a CV, and other times results in a telephone interview and subsequent invitation to a face-to-face interview – with the request that you bring a CV.

- As part of a multiple-contact approach where you are approaching a number of people within a company with personalized letters (see Chapter 6).

- As a back-up approach when your job search letter and CV don't generate the response you want from individual target companies.

- To headhunters, who, if you have the skills they are looking for, will help you package your professional background.

Here is an example of a typical broadcast letter; you can see a whole selection of them starting on p163.

Jane Swift
18 Park Street, London X1 0BB
020 8123 4567

2 October, 20–

Dear Employer,

For the past seven years I have pursued an increasingly successful career in the sales profession. Among my accomplishments I include:

SALES
As a regional representative, I contributed £1,500,000, or 16 per cent, of my company's annual sales. I am driven by achievement.

MARKETING
My marketing skills (based on a BSc in marketing) enabled me to increase sales 25 per cent in my economically stressed territory, at a time when colleagues were striving to maintain flat sales. Repeat business reached an all-time high.

PROJECT MANAGEMENT
Following the above successes, my regional model was adopted by the company. I trained and provided project supervision to the entire sales force. The following year, company sales showed a sales increase 12 per cent above projections. I am a committed team player, motivated by the team's overall success.

The above was based on my firmly held zero price discounting philosophy. I don't cut margins to make a sale. It is difficult to summarize my work in a letter. The only way I can imagine providing you with the opportunity to examine my credentials is for us to talk to each other. I look forward to hearing from you.

Yours faithfully,

Jane Swift

Jane Swift

Recruitment agencies and executive recruiters

Headhunters appreciate, and deserve, appropriate professional respect. They are, after all, the most sophisticated salespeople in the world – they and they alone sell products that talk back!

A headhunter will be only faintly amused by your exhortations 'to accept the challenge' or 'test your skills by finding me a job' in the moments before he or she practises their aim with the remains of your letter and the waste- paper basket. They don't have the time or inclination to indulge such whimsical ideas. So with headhunters – whether they are working for an employment agency or a retained search firm – bear in mind these two rules and you won't go far wrong:

1. Tell the truth. Answer questions truthfully and you will likely receive help. Get caught in a lie and you will have established a career-long distrust with someone who possesses a very diverse and influential list of contacts.

2. Cut immediately to the chase. For example:

   'I am forwarding my CV, because I understand you specialize in representing clients in the _____ field.'

   'Please find the enclosed CV. As a specialist in the _____ field, I felt you might be interested in the skills of a _____.'

   'Among your many clients there may be one or two who are seeking a person for a position as a _____.'

Remember that in a job search letter sent to executive search firms and employment agencies, you should mention your salary and, if appropriate, your willingness to relocate.

Here is an example of a job search letter you might send to a corporate headhunter:

James Swift
18 Park Street London X1 0BB
020 8123 4567

2 December, 20–

Dear Mr O'Flynn,

I am forwarding my CV, as I understand you specialize in the accounting profession. As you may be aware, the management structure at _____ will be reorganized in the near future. While I am enthusiastic about the future of the agency under its new leadership, I have elected to make this an opportunity for change and professional growth.

My many years of experience lend themselves to a finance management position in any medium-sized service firm, but I am open to other opportunities. Although I would prefer to remain in London, I would entertain other areas of the country, if the opportunity warrants it. I am currently earning £40,000 a year.

I have enclosed my CV for your review. Should you be conducting a search for someone with my background at the present time or in the near future, I would greatly appreciate your consideration. I would be happy to discuss my background more fully with you on the phone or in a personal interview.

Yours sincerely,

James Swift

James Swift

enclosures

So those are four basic types of letter that you can adapt to just about any job search situation. You can see how they can be assembled, in part, by harvesting suitable phrases from the samples later in the book. However, doing a simple cut and paste could lead to the wrong things going in and the right things being left out. That's what we are going to address next.

3

What goes in, what stays out

The rules of the game have changed; now more than ever, communication skills are a prerequisite for any job. Saying 'I'm a great engineer. Give me a chance and I'll prove it to you' just doesn't cut it any more. Today, your job skills and professionalism are under closer scrutiny than ever before. The evaluation process starts the moment you make contact – which means that the content and style of your cover letter set the tone for your entire application.

The one overriding objective for your initial cover letter is to grab the reader's attention. With subsequent follow-up letters, your goal is to hold your reader's attention by moving the conversation forward; your letters should work to keep your application foremost in the employer's mind. You achieve this in part by demonstrating your awareness and possession of the learned behaviours that all managers look for when they hire.

Desirable professional behaviours

There are a handful of universally admired behaviours that help you become successful in any profession. Each is something you can learn and apply in your career, and collectively their application will contribute a major ingredient to the success of your entire career; they are, in short, your passports to success.

Remember that first day at work on your first job? You got thirsty and went looking for the coffee machine, and there on the wall behind it was a big handwritten sign that read: 'Your mother doesn't work here. Clear up after yourself'.

And this was the moment you realized that working at a job meant that there was a whole new way of behaving that you had to learn, and so you set about watching the successful people in your profession and emulating their behaviours.

When reading your cover letter, interviewers will look for clues to determine what kind of professional you really are and what you will be like to work with. Your cover letter therefore becomes a prime opportunity to set yourself apart from the competition. As you read through the following pages explaining each of these universally admired behaviours, you will often recognize that you already possess and apply that particular behaviour in your professional life. When this happens, I want you to come up with examples of your using that particular behaviour in the execution of your duties. The examples you recall can be used in your letters, and later in your answers to interviewer's questions. Then, for example, when you get asked, 'So why are you different?' you will have a meaningful reply, replete with the real world illustrations that give a ring of truth to your answers. As you read the next few pages, you might also come across behaviours that you realize are not adequately developed. When that happens, don't worry – you have just identified an area for professional growth.

Here, then, are a dozen hallmarks of professional behaviour that every employer looks for and values (or should):

Communication & Listening Skills: This covers your ability to communicate effectively to people at all levels in a company, is a key to success, and refers to verbal and written skills along with technological adeptness, dress, and body language. This is an especially important consideration when it comes to your cover letter and CV, because these written documents are the first means an employer has of judging your communication skills. It means you have to take the time to craft and edit, and re-edit your cover letter until it communicates what you want it to, and at the same time demonstrates that you have adequate communication skills.

I recently counselled an executive in the 400K a year range; he was having problems getting in front of the right people. The first paragraph of his CV stated that he was an executive with 'superior communication skills'. Unfortunately, the other twelve words of the sentence boasting of his communication ability gave the lie to his claims: they contained two spelling errors! In an age of spelling checkers this sloppiness isn't acceptable at any level.

Communication embraces *Listening Skills:* Listening and understanding, as opposed to just waiting your turn to talk; there is a big difference between the two. Consciously develop your 'listening to understand' skills and the result will be improved persuasive communication abilities.

Goal-orientation: All employers are interested in goal-oriented professionals: those who achieve concrete results with their actions and who constantly strive to get the job done, rather than just filling the time allotted for a particular task. Whenever possible, you should try to use an example or reference to this behaviour in your letters and CV.

Willingness to be a team player: The highest achievers (always goal-oriented) are invariably team players: employers look for employees who work for the common good and always with the group's goals and responsibilities in mind. Team players take pride in group achievement over personal aggrandizement; they look for solutions rather than someone to blame.

Motivation and energy: Employers realize a motivated professional will do a better job on every assignment. Motivation expresses itself in a commitment to the job and the profession, an eagerness to learn and grow professionally and a willingness to take the rough with the smooth.

Motivation is invariably expressed by the energy someone demonstrates in their work, always giving that extra effort to get the job done and to get it done right.

Analytical skills: Valuable employees are able to weigh the short- and long-term benefits of a proposed course of action against all its possible negatives. We see these skills demonstrated in the way a person identifies potential problems and so is able to minimize their occurrence. Successful application of analytical skills at work requires understanding how your job and the role of your department fit into the company's overall goal of profitability. It also means thinking things through and not jumping at the first or easiest solution.

Dedication and reliability: We are speaking here of dedication to your profession, with an awareness of the role it plays in the larger issues of company success, and of the empowerment that comes from knowing how your part contributes to the greater good. Dedication to your professionalism is also a demonstration of enlightened self-interest. The more you are engaged in your career, the more likely you are to join the inner circles that exist in every department and company enhancing opportunities for advancement; this dedication will therefore repay you with better job security and improved professional horizons.

Your dedication will also express itself in your *Reliability:* Showing up is half the battle; the other half is your performance on the job. To demonstrate reliability requires following up on your actions, not relying on anyone else to ensure the job is done well, and keeping management informed every step of the way.

Determination: Someone with this attribute does not back off when a problem or situation gets tough; instead, he or she is the person who chooses to be part of a solution rather than standing idly by and being part of the problem. Determined professionals have decided to make a difference with their presence every day and are willing to do whatever it takes to get a job done, even if that includes duties that might not appear in a job description.

Confidence: As you develop desirable professional behaviours, your confidence grows in the skills you have and in your ability to develop new ones. With this comes confidence in taking on new challenges. You have the confidence to ask questions, the confidence to look at challenges calmly, the confidence to look at mistakes unflinchingly, and the confidence to make changes to eradicate them. In short, you develop a quiet confidence in your ability as a professional who can deliver the goods.

Pride and integrity: Pride in yourself as a professional means always making sure the job is done to the best of your ability; paying attention to the details and to the time and cost constraints. Integrity means taking responsibility for your actions, both good and bad; it means treating others, within and without the company, with respect at all times and in all situations. With pride in yourself as a professional with integrity, your actions will always be in the best interests of the company, and your decisions will never be based on whim or personal preference.

When it comes down to it, companies have very limited interests: making money, saving money (the same as making money), and saving time, which saves money and makes time to make more money. Actually, you wouldn't want it any other way, as it is this focus that makes your pay slip good come payday. Developing these professional behaviours and maintaining sensitivity to the profit interests of any business endeavour is the mark of a true professional. To this end, the following three behaviours demonstrate an aware-ness of the need for procedures, efficiency, and economy; they round out the profile of the consummate professional:

Efficiency: Working efficiently means always keeping an eye open for wasted time, effort, resources, and money.

Economy: Most problems have two solutions – and the expensive one usually isn't the best. Ideas of efficiency and economy engage the creative mind in ways other workers might not consider; they are an integral part of your analytical proficiency.

Ability to follow procedures: You know that procedures exist to keep the company profitable, so you don't work around them. Following the chain of command, you don't implement your own 'improved' procedures or organize others to do so.

Together, these twelve learnable behaviours spell long-term career success. As these behaviours are universally admired in all profes-sions and at all levels, it is important that you are able to communi-cate your awareness of their importance to prospective employers in your written communications and in your conversations. Conse-quently, your goal is to draw attention to your professional behav-ioural profile by direct statement, inference, and illustration. Integrate these behaviours into your answers to interview questions too.

    Writing a cover letter for a job is a bit like baking a cake. In most instances the ingredients are essentially the same – what determines the flavour is the quantity of each ingredient, and how and in what order they are blended and ultimately presented for consumption. There are certain ingredients that go into almost every letter, whether it is a cover, broadcast, networking, follow-up, acceptance, rejection, or resignation letter. There are others that rarely or never go in, and there are those special touches (a pinch of this, a smidgen of that) that may be included, depending on your unique situation and the need your letter will satisfy.

Brief is beautiful

Ads and job search letters have a great deal in common. The vast majority of ads in any media can be heard, watched, or read in under 30 seconds – the upper limit of the average consumer's attention span.

It is no coincidence that both job search letters and CVs adhere to the same rules, as they compete for attention from distracted consumers, and their initial purpose is simply to grab the reader's attention so that your CV will get read with serious attention – a seemingly easy goal that isn't necessarily so easy in its execution.

Before getting started, good copywriters imagine themselves in the position of their target audience. They understand their objective is to package and sell the product, so they consider what features their product possesses and what benefits it holds for the purchaser.

This is an approach you might find useful in creating effective job search letters. For the next 15 minutes, imagine yourself in one of your target companies, or in the personnel department on 'screening' detail. Fortunately, it is a slow morning and there are only 30 CVs and job search letters that need to be read. Go straight to the example sections of this book now and read 30 examples without a break, then return to this page. You will probably feel disoriented, as if your brain has turned to mush.

Can you imagine what it might be like to do this every day for a living? Of course, you had it easy. The letters you read were good, interesting ones – letters that got real people real jobs. Even so, you probably felt a little punch drunk at the end of the exercise. But you learnt a very valuable lesson: brevity is beautiful.

This is the environment in which your letters and CVs have to function, and now you have some idea what it feels like. It also helps to understand the essential criteria applied whenever managers are considering employing someone. When hiring decisions are made, they are based on five basic criteria, and an awareness of these can inform the structure of your letters and CV, as well as your performance at job interviews. Every decision to employ is made on a job applicant's ability to satisfy these five concerns of the employer:

1. ability and suitability;
2. willingness to go the extra yard, to take the rough with the smooth;
3. manageability and teamwork: taking direction and constructive input for the good of the team;
4. problem-solving attitude;
5. a comprehensive and supportive behavioural profile.

A question of money

Recruitment ads sometimes request salary information, either current salary or salary history. With the right letter and work history you will rarely be denied at least a telephone interview, even if you do omit your salary history. I have heard that some personnel people consider the word 'negotiable' annoying, though they completely understand why it is used, so it is rarely grounds for refusing to see an applicant. Nevertheless, there may be factors that make you feel obliged to include something.

If you choose to share information about salary, it should go on the job search letter or be attached to it, never on the CV itself. This is because your CV may be kept in a database for years, and there-fore typecast you as, say, an entry-level professional in the eyes of the company's computer. When you're asked to state the salary you're looking for, don't restrict yourself to one figure; instead, give yourself a range with a spread between the low and the high end. This dramatically increases your chances of 'clicking onto' the available salary range that is authorized for every position.

When salary history is requested, the prospective employer is usually looking for a consistent career progression. Gaps or signifi-cant cuts could raise red flags. If you have nothing to hide and have a steadily progressive earnings history, spell it out on a separate sheet. By the way, when background does get checked, salaries and dates of employment always get verified.

Many of us have imperfect salary histories for any number of perfectly valid reasons. Consequently, we don't want to release these figures unless we are there in person to explain away any anomalies. In these instances the matter is best skirted in the job search letter itself with either a range or the word 'negotiable'.

Here is one way to address the topic of money in your letters should you feel it is necessary to do so. You will find others later in the book.

*'Depending on the job and the professional development envi-
ronment, my salary requirements are in the £ _____ to
£ _____ range, with appropriate benefits. I would be willing
to relocate for the right opportunity.'*

Telephone and e-mail

Once you have determined a primary contact number you must
ensure that it will be answered at all times. There is no point in
mounting a job-hunting campaign if prospective employers can
never reach you. Invest in an answering machine or voice mail
system. Keep the message businesslike and, once recorded, replay it
and listen carefully to the message for clarity, tone of voice and
recording quality. Does it present you as a clearly-spoken, confident
professional?

In your letter, you should always list your e-mail address immediately beneath your telephone number, as initial contact is often by e-
mail. Under no circumstances should you ever use your company
telephone or e-mail for any job search, as that can only lead to
heartache and regret.

Ingredients: a basic checklist

When you examine the sample letters in Chapter 8, you will note
that they:

- address a person, not a title… and whenever possible, a person
  who is in a position to make the decision on whether to employ
  you;
- are tailored to the reader as far as is practical, to show that you
  have done your homework;
- show concern, interest and pride for your profession;
- demonstrate energy and enthusiasm;
- clearly establish why you are writing and the outcome you hope
  to achieve;
- maintain a balance between professionalism and friendliness;
- whenever possible, include information relevant to the job you
  are seeking;
- ask for the next step in the process clearly and without apology
  or arrogance.

Now take another few moments to browse through the sample section to examine the variety of letters you have to work with – there are enough examples to help you maximize both the volume of interviews you generate and the value of the offers you receive. With the wide range of examples you'll find later in the book, you can create unique letters for any situation. Use that highlighter as you go through the book to flag phrases that seem especially useful to you. It will be a breeze then to customize letters of your own for any circumstance.

4

Assembling your job search letter

You need solid content to put in your cover letters, and that can take a little thought. To make this job easier, complete the questionnaire on the next couple of pages. Do not skip this exercise; it will give you a greater sense of what you have to offer employers, and will provide insight and illustrations for your letters. The exercises will also be of real help later, when the time comes to sell yourself at the interview.

Answer every part of every question for every job you have held, starting with the most recent and working backwards.

Take some time over this exercise and go back carefully over your past jobs. If you do this it won't be necessary to craft sentences from scratch; you'll be able to cut and paste from the samples and then insert your questionnaire answers to personalize the content – the end result will be a unique and arresting letter.

The entirely original parts of your letter will be your awareness of the employer and the job, your contributions, and your achievements. That means you need to spend adequate time in this period of preparation. Do not worry about crafting proper sentences now, as whatever you jot down can be polished later on in the editing process. It is easier to do this when you have the whole letter in front of you rather than labouring over every sentence as you write it.

Gather information

If you are preparing a CV at the same time as a cover letter, the following steps will help you to work toward that end as well.

Step 1: identify your target job

Your job search – and the CV and letters that go with it – will be incalculably more productive if you begin by clearly defining a target job that you can land and in which you can be successful. Start by identifying this target job title. Then take out a lined sheet of paper (or open a blank computer document, if you prefer) and write it down.

Step 2: research the target job

Go and surf the web for an hour and collect as many job descriptions as you can with this target job title. Once you have a selection, deconstruct them into a series of bullets, and write them below your Target Job Title as your answer for Step 2.

Any evaluation of your background must begin with an understanding of what potential employers will be looking for when they come to your cover letter and CV.

Step 3: go through your recent work history

Once you understand the sort of information your readers are going to be looking for, it is time to start working through your work history. This process is helpful not only for gathering all the information necessary for a CV, but also for reminding yourself of all kinds of data that employers are likely to require at different stages of the selection cycle. Consider carefully the following three elements:

A. Current or last employer

Identify your current or last employer by name and location, and follow it with a brief description (5–6 words) of the company's business/products/services.

Note: This includes part-time or voluntary employment if you are a recent graduate or about to re-enter the work force after an absence. Try looking at your school as an employer and see what new information you reveal about yourself.

Write down the following information:

Starting date: _____

Starting title: _____

Starting salary: _____

Leaving date: _____

Leaving title: _____

Reason for leaving: _____

Potential references for this job: _____

Leaving salary: _____

B. Deliverables

Make a bulleted list of the duties/responsibilities/deliverables in this position. Then prioritize that list.

C. Skills and special knowledge

Now, for each of your identified deliverables, answer the following questions:

● What special skills or knowledge did you need to perform this task satisfactorily?

● What educational background and/or credentials helped prepare you for these responsibilities?

● What are your achievements in this area?

For each of your major areas of responsibility you should consider both the daily problems that arise and also those major projects/problems that stand out as major accomplishments. Think of each as a problem-solving challenge, and the analytical processes and subsequent actions you took to win the day. There is a four-step technique you will find useful here called **PSRV**:

P. Identify the *project* and the problem it represented, both from a corporate perspective and from the point of view of your execution of duties.

S. Identify your *solution* to the challenge and the process you implemented to deliver the solution.

R. What was the *result* of your approach and actions?

V. Finally, what was the *value* to you, the department, and the company? If you can, define this in terms of time saved, money saved, or money earned. This is not always possible, but it is very powerful whenever you can.

Step 4: Consider teamwork and your professional profile

Next, ask yourself the following questions:

- What verbal or written comments did peers or managers make about your contributions in each area of your job?
- What different levels of people did you have to interact with to achieve your job tasks? What skills and methods did you use to get the best out of superiors? Co-workers? Subordinates?
- What aspects of your personality were brought into play when executing this duty?

To help you address that last issue (it's a vitally important one), look over the list of professional behaviours discussed in Chapter 3; these are in demand by all employers for all jobs at all levels. Going through the list, you will probably recognize that you already apply some or many of these behaviours in your work. As you read, come up with examples of using each particular behaviour in the execution of each of your major duties at this job. The examples you generate can be used in your CV, in your cover letters, and as illustrative answers to questions in interviews.

Step 5: Add in your previous work history

The next step is to do the same things you did in Steps 3 and 4 for your current or most recent job with your previous positions. Do not skimp on this process; all you write may not go into the final version of your CV or cover letter, but all your effort will reward you at some point during the selection process and lead to more and better job offers.

It is not unusual to have held a number of different titles with a specific employer. Such professional progression speaks to your competency and promotability; you should repeat Steps 3 and 4 for each successive title, and make sure they are reflected on your CV.

Step 6: Compile endorsements

Looking at each of your major areas of responsibility throughout your work history, write down any positive verbal or written commentary others have made on your performance that you can find. As you will see in some of the sample letters in Chapter 8, words about you that come from someone else often have a much greater impact than any description you could come up with your-self.

Creating punchy sentences

A cover letter is a collection of sequenced sentences organized around a single goal: to get your CV read with serious attention. It is likely that you will need to create more than one type of cover letter, so my best advice is to concentrate on one first, perhaps the one going to postings and recruitment ads. You can then use this letter as a template to cut, paste, and otherwise adapt it to suit cover letters going to specific contacts, headhunters, etc.

Concise, punchy sentences grab attention.

Ultimately any letter is only as good as the individual sentences that carry the message; the most grammatically correct sentences in the world won't get you interviews because such prose can read as though every breath of life has been squeezed out of it. Your goal is to communicate an energizing message and entice the reader to action. The use of verbs always helps energize a sentence and give it that concise, cut-to-the-chase feel.

For example, one professional – with a number of years at the same law firm in a clerical position – had written:

> *'I learned to manage a computerized database.'*

Sounds pretty ordinary, right? Well, after discussion of the circum-stances that surrounded learning how to manage the computerized database, certain exciting facts emerged. By using verbs and an awareness of employer interests as they relate to a specific target job, this sentence was charged up and given more punch. Not only that, but for the first time the writer fully understood the value of her contributions, which greatly enhanced her self-confidence for inter-views:

> 'I analysed and determined the need for automation of an estab-lished law office. I was responsible for hardware and software selection, installation, and loading all the data. Within one year, I had achieved a fully automated office. This saved forty hours a week.'

Notice how the verbs show that things happened when she was around the office, and put flesh on the bones of that initial bare statement. Such action verbs and phrases add an air of direction, efficiency, and accomplishment to every cover letter. Succinctly, they tell the reader what you did and how well you did it.

As you look through the answers to the questionnaire for information that will affect your cover letter, rewrite the chosen phrases to see if you can give them more depth with the use of verbs. While a cover letter is typically one page, or one screen shot, don't worry about the length right now. The process you go through helps you think out exactly what it is you have to offer and also creates the language and ideas you will use to explain yourself during an interview. To help you in the process, here are over 175 action verbs you can use. This list is just a beginning. Just about every word processing program has a thesaurus; you can type any one of these words into one and get more choices for each entry.

accomplished	critiqued	indoctrinated	purchased
achieved	cut	influenced	recommended
acted	decreased	informed	reconciled
adapted	delegated	initiated	recorded
addressed	demonstrated	innovated	recruited
administered	designed	inspected	reduced
advanced	developed	installed	referred
advised	devised	instigated	regulated
allocated	diagnosed	instituted	rehabilitated
analysed	directed	instructed	remodelled
appraised	dispatched	integrated	repaired
approved	distinguished	interpreted	represented
arranged	diversified	interviewed	researched
assembled	drafted	introduced	restored
assigned	edited	invented	restructured
assisted	educated	launched	retrieved
attained	eliminated	lectured	revitalized
audited	enabled	led	saved
authored	encouraged	maintained	scheduled
automated	engineered	managed	schooled
balanced	enlisted	marketed	screened
budgeted	established	mediated	set
built	evaluated	moderated	shaped
calculated	examined	monitored	solidified
catalogued	executed	motivated	solved
chaired	expanded	negotiated	specified
clarified	expedited	operated	stimulated
classified	explained	organized	streamlined
coached	extracted	originated	strengthened
collected	fabricated	overhauled	summarized
compiled	facilitated	oversaw	supervised
completed	familiarized	performed	surveyed
composed	fashioned	persuaded	systemized
computed	focused	planned	tabulated
conceptualized	forecast	prepared	taught
conducted	formulated	presented	trained
consolidated	founded	prioritized	translated
contained	generated	processed	travelled
contracted	guided	produced	trimmed
contributed	headed up	programmed	upgraded
controlled	identified	projected	validated
coordinated	illustrated	promoted	worked
corresponded	implemented	provided	wrote
counselled	improved	publicized	
created	increased	published	

As noted above, your letters will be most effective when they are constructed with short punchy sentences. As a rule, try keeping your sentences under about 25 words; a good average is around 15. If your sentence is longer than the 25-word mark, change it. Either shorten it by restructuring or make two sentences out of one. At the same time, you will want to avoid choppiness, so vary the length of sentences when you can.

You can also start with a short phrase ending in a colon:

- followed by bullets of information;
- each one supporting the original phrase.

These techniques are designed to enliven the reading process, for readers who always have too much to read and too little time. Here's how we can edit and rewrite the last example.

- *analysed and determined need for automation of an established law office;*
- *responsible for hardware and software selection;*
- *coordinated installation of six workstations;*
- *trained users;*
- *full automation achieved in one year;*
- savings to company: £25,000.

K.I.S.S. (keep it simple, stupid)

Persuading your readers to take action is challenging, because many people in different companies will see your letters and make judgements based on them. This means you must keep industry 'jargon' to a reasonable level (especially in the initial contact letters); the rule of thumb is only to use the jargon and acronyms necessary to communicate your abilities. There will be those who understand the intricacies and technicalities of your profession – and those who do not.

Within your short paragraphs and short sentences, beware of name-dropping and acronyms, such as 'I worked for Dr. A. Witherspoon in Sys. Gen. SNA 2.31.' Statements like these can be too restricted to have validity outside the small circle of specialists to whom they speak. Unless you work in a highly technical field, and are sending the letter and CV to someone by name and title whom you know will understand the importance of your technical language, you should be sure to use technical phrases with discretion.

Your letters demand the widest possible appeal, yet they need to remain personal in tone. You are not writing a novel, but rather trying to capture the essence of the professional you in just a few brief paragraphs, so short words for short sentences help make short, gripping paragraphs: good for short attention spans!

Voice and tense

The voice you use for different letters depends on a few important factors:

- getting a lot said in a small space;
- packaging your skills and credentials for the target job;
- being factual;
- capturing the essence and personality of the professional you.

There is considerable disagreement among the 'experts' about the best voice, and each of the following options has both champions and detractors, but whichever voice you use in your letters should be consistent throughout.

Sentences in all types of cover letters can be truncated (up to a point), by omitting pronouns and articles such as *I, you, he, she, they*:

> "Automated office."

In fact, many authorities recommend the dropping of pronouns as a technique that both saves space and allows you to brag about yourself without seeming boastful. It gives the impression of another party writing about you. Others feel that to use the personal pronoun – '*I automated the office . . .*' – is naive, unprofessional, and smacks of boasting.

At the same time, some recommend that you write in the first person because it makes you sound more human.

> "I automated the office."

In short, there are no hard and fast rules – they can all work given the many unique circumstances you will face in any given job search.

Use whatever style works best for you. If you do use the personal pronoun, try not to use it in every sentence; it gets a little monotonous, and it can make you sound like an egomaniac. The mental focus should not be on 'I' but on 'you', the person with whom you are communicating.

A nice variation is to use a first-person voice throughout the letter and then a final few words in the third person. Make sure these final words appear in the form of an attributed quote, as an insight to your value:

> *"She managed the automation procedure, and we didn't experience a moment of downtime."*
>
> *– Jane Ross, Department Manager*

Don't mistake the need for professionalism in your job search letters with stiff-necked formality. The most effective tone is one that mixes the conversational and the formal, just the way we do in our offices and on our jobs. The only overriding rule is to make the letter readable, so that the reader can see a human being and a professional shining through the page.

Length

The standard length for a cover letter is usually one page, or the equivalent length for e-mails: typically this is as much as you can see on your screen without scrolling. Subsequent letters stemming from verbal communications – whether over the telephone or face-to-face – should also adhere to the one-page rule, but can run to two pages if the complexity of content demands it.

Generally speaking, job-search letters should be held to one page, and no job-hunting letter should exceed two pages. With conscientious editing over a couple of days, that two-page letter can usually be reduced to one page without losing any of the content, and at the same time it will probably pack more punch; as my editor always says, 'If in doubt, cut it out."

Having said this, I should acknowledge that all rules are made to be broken. Occasionally a three-page letter might be required, but only in one of the following instances:

1. You are at a level, or your job is of such technical complexity that you cannot edit down to one page without using a font size that is all but unreadable.

2. You have been contacted directly by an employer about a specific position and have been asked to present data for a specific opportunity.

3. An executive recruiter who is representing you determines that the exigencies of a particular situation warrant a dossier of such length. (Often such a letter and CV will be prepared exclusively – or with considerable input – by the recruiter.)

You'll find that thinking too much about length considerations will hamper the writing process. Think instead of the story you have to tell, and then layer fact upon fact until your tale is told. Use your words and the key phrases from this book to craft the message of your choice. When *that* is done you can go back and ruthlessly cut it to the bone.

Ask yourself these questions:

● Can I cut out any paragraphs?
● Can I cut out any sentences?
● How can I reduce the word count of the longer sentences?
● Where have I repeated myself?

Whenever you can, cut something out – leave nothing but facts and action words! If at the end you find too much has been cut, you'll have the additional pleasure of reinstating your deathless prose.

Your checklist

There are really two proofing steps in the creation of a polished cover letter. The first happens now. You want to make sure that all the things that should be included are – and that all the things that shouldn't, aren't. The final proofing is done before printing. *Warning:* It is easy, in the heat of the creative moment, to miss crucial components or mistakenly include facts that give the wrong emphasis. Check all your letters against these considerations:

Contact information

● You need contact information – name, address, postcode, personal telephone number, and e-mail address – at the top of the page; if in rare instances you have to run to second page (and avoid this at all costs), remember to include your name, telephone number and e-mail address.

- Your current business number is omitted unless it is absolutely necessary and safe to include it. This will only be the case if your employer understands that you are leaving and you have permission to use company time and equipment for your search.
- If your letter is more than one page long, and is going by traditional mail, each page should be numbered 'page 1 of 2', etc., and the pages stapled together. Remember the accepted way of stapling business communications: one staple in the top left-hand corner.

Objectives

- Does your letter state why you are writing?
- Is the letter tied to the target company?
- Is it focused on a target job, such as skills that apply from the ad or agenda items addressed during a conversation?
- Does it include reference to desirable professional behaviours?
- Is your most relevant and qualifying experience prioritized to lend strength to your letter?
- Have you avoided wasting more space than required with employer names and addresses?
- Have you omitted any reference to reasons for leaving a particular job? Reasons for making a change might be important at the interview, but they are not relevant at this point. Use this precious space to sell, not to justify.
- Unless they have been specifically requested, have you removed all references to past, current, or desired salaries?
- Have you removed any references to your date of availability? If you aren't available at their convenience, why are you wasting their time?
- Do you mention your highest educational attainment if it is relevant, and if it adds credence to the message?
- Have you avoided listing irrelevant responsibilities or job titles?
- Have you given examples of your contributions, your achievements, and the problems you have successfully solved during your career?
- Have you avoided poor focus by eliminating all extraneous information?

● Is the letter long enough to whet the reader's appetite for more details, yet short enough not to satisfy that hunger?

● Have you let the obvious slip in, like heading your letter 'Letter of Application' in big bold letters? If so, cut it out.

Style

● When possible, substitute short words for long words, and one word where previously there were two.

● Keep your average sentence to less than twenty-five words. Break longer sentences into two, if they cannot be shortened.

● At the same time, try to vary the length of sentences.

● Keep every paragraph under five lines, with most paragraphs shorter; this leads to more white space on the page and makes your message more accessible to the reader.

● Make sure your sentences begin with or contain, wherever possible, powerful action verbs and phrases.

5

The final product

Layout

Your job search letter typically arrives on a desk along with many others, all of which require screening. You can expect your letter to get a maximum of 30 seconds attention, and that's only if it's accessible to the reader's eye and speaks to their needs.

The complaints about job search letters that see them nosediving into the waste-paper basket in record time are:

- They have too much information crammed into the space and are difficult to read.
- The layout is disorganized, illogical and uneven. (In other words, it looks shoddy and slapdash – and who wants an employee like that?)
- In the age of spellcheckers, there are no excuses for misspellings; they are not acceptable.

Fonts

The font you choose has a big impact on the readability of your work, so choose business-like fonts; stay away from script-like fonts or those that have serifs. They may look more visually exciting, but the goal is readability for the reader who is ploughing through stacks of CVs when he or she gets your message. At the same time, recognize that capitalized copy is also harder to read.

How to brighten the page

Once you decide on a font, stick with it. More than one font on a page can look confusing. You can do plenty to liven up the visual impact of the page within the variations of the font you have chosen. For letters going through traditional mail you can, of course, use a different font for the contact information as you create the letterhead.

Most fonts come in a selection of regular, bold, italic and bold italic, so you can vary the impact of key words with italics, under-lined phrases, and boldface for additional emphasis.

Another no-no is the use of 'clip art' to brighten the page. Those little quill pens and scrolls may look nifty to you, but they look amateurish to the rest of the business world.

Proofing and printing

It simply isn't possible for even the most accomplished professional writer to go from draft to print, so don't try it. Your pride of author-ship will hide blemishes you can't afford to miss.

You need some distance from your creative efforts to give yourself detachment and objectivity. There is no hard and fast rule about how long it should take to come up with the finished product. If you think you have finished, leave it alone at least overnight. Then come back to it fresh. You'll read it almost as if you were seeing it for the first time.

Before you e-mail or print your letters make sure that what you've written is as clear as possible. Three things guaranteed to annoy readers are incorrect spelling, poor grammar and improper syntax. Go back and check all these areas. If you think syntax has something to do with the HM Revenue and Customs, you'd better get a third party involved. Here's a practical solution that one job seeker found: she went to the library, waited for a quiet moment, and got into a conversation with the librarian, who subsequently agreed to give her letter the old once-over. (Everyone loves to show off special knowl-edge!) Another effective technique is to read your letter aloud. If it reads smoothly you did your job well, but if something sounds stilted it needs another round of polishing.

With mailed letters the quality of paper always makes an impres-sion on the person holding the page. The people receiving your letter see dozens of others every day, and you need every trick avail-able to make your point. Compared to printer paper, good quality paper sends an almost subliminal message about attention to detail.

By the way, if an emergency demands you send a letter by fax, remember to follow it up with a copy on regular paper. This is because everything you send is likely to end up in your 'candidate dossier', and a fax can have print-out problems.

Although you should not skimp on paper costs, neither should you buy or be talked into using the most expensive available. Indeed, in some fields (health care and education come to mind), too ostentatious a paper can give a negative impression. The idea is to create a feeling of understated quality.

As for colour, white is considered the prime choice. Cream is also acceptable, but I reject the opinion that some of the pale pastel shades can be both attractive and effective. These pastel shades were originally used to make letters and CVs stand out. But now everyone is so busy standing out of the crowd in magenta and passionate puce that you just might find it more original to stand out in white or cream. White and cream are straightforward, no-nonsense colours. They say BUSINESS, as should your letters.

It is a given that letter stationery should always match the colour and weight of your envelopes and CV. Most office supply shops have packs of matching paper and envelopes for coordinating your letter, CV and envelope. To send a white letter – even if it is your personal stationery – with a cream CV is gauche and detracts from the powerful statement you are trying to make. In fact, when you print the finished letter, you should print some letterhead sheets at the same time and in the same quantity. You don't need to get too fancy; base your design on other stationery you've been impressed with.

All subsequent letters (a follow-up letter after an interview, for example) should be on the same paper. Your written communication will be filed. Then, prior to the decision on whom to employ, the manager responsible will review all the data on all the short-listed candidates. Your coordinated written campaign will paint the picture of a thorough professional, with the sum of your letters becoming powerful because they exist as a coordinated package.

For example, when you are sending your letter and CV in response to an internet job posting or recruitment advertisement, you can bold or italicize those words used by the employer in the recruitment copy, emphasizing your match to their needs.

Another letter writer who wants to emphasize professional behaviours might italicize those words or phrases that describe such behaviours. This is relevant to all professions, and it can be especially useful for people in sales and customer service when dealing with others is a critical skill. That way, the message gets a double fixing in the reader's mind. You will also notice powerful letters that employ no typographic pyrotechnics and still knock 'em dead! In the end, it's your judgement call.

Beware if you're crafting a letter for mass distribution using the mail-merge feature of a word processing program. What this does is fill in the blanks: 'Dear _____' becomes 'Dear Fred Jones'. Make sure the printed letter does not look like this:

> *Dear* **Fred Jones***:*
>
> *Your* **11 January, 2001** *ad in the* Daily Telegraph *described a need for an accountant.*

By italicizing the person's name or putting it in bold, all you achieve is to state loud and clear that this is a form letter sent, in all likelihood, to hundreds. Why needlessly detract from your chances of being taken seriously?

Envelopes send messages too

Throughout this advice I have been differentiating, where necessary, between the considerations of e-mails and traditional letters, but I'd like to note that approaching employers through both mediums certainly doesn't diminish your chances of getting noticed. With this in mind, what goes on the envelope affects the power of the message inside. Over the last six months, I've asked a number of line managers and human resources professionals about the envelope's appearance. Did it affect the likelihood of the letter being read and if so, with what kind of anticipation? Here's what I heard:

> *'I never open letters with printed pressure-sensitive labels; I regard them as junk mail, and I simply don't have the time in my life for ill-targeted marketing attempts.'*
>
> *'I never open anything addressed to me by title but not by name.'*
>
> *'I will open envelopes addressed to me by misspelt name, but I am looking with a jaundiced eye already; and that eye is keen for other examples of sloppiness.'*
>
> *'I always open correctly typed envelopes that say personal and/or confidential, but if they're not, I feel conned. I don't hire con artists.'*

'I always open neatly handwritten envelopes. What's more, I open them first, unless there's another letter that is obviously a cheque.'

This last comment is especially interesting in an age when just about all correspondence is printed. In fact, over a two-week period every letter I sent out had a hand-addressed envelope, and do you know about 50 per cent of the recipients actually commented on not having seen a hand-written envelope in ages.

There are those who recommend enclosing a stamped self-addressed envelope to increase the chances of response. You can do this, but don't expect many people in the corporate world to take advantage of your munificence. I have never known this tactic to yield much in the way of results. On the whole, I think you are better advised to save the stamp money and spend it on a follow-up telephone call. Only conversations lead to interviews. I have never heard of a single interview being set up exclusively through the mail.

Neat trick department: I recently received an intriguing CV and job search letter; both had attached to the top right-hand corner a circular red sticker. It worked as a major exclamation point; I was impressed. I was even more impressed when I realized that once this left my hands, no other reader would know exactly who attached the sticker, but they *would* pay special attention to the content because of it. Nice technique; don't let the whole world in on it, though.

Appearance

Remember that the first glance and feel of your letter can make a powerful impression. Go through this checklist before you seal the envelope:

- Is the paper A4-sized and is it of good quality, 100 grams per square metre (gsm) in weight?
- Have you used white, off-white, or cream-coloured paper?
- Did you make sure to use only one side of the page?
- Are your name, address and telephone number on every page?

- If more than one page, have you numbered your letter: '1 of 2' and so on at the bottom of the page?
- Are the pages stapled together? Remember, one staple in the top left-hand corner is the accepted protocol.

With e-mail:

- Ditto for spelling checks and so on.
- Do you have an informative and/or intriguing subject line?
- Have you correctly used bold and italic?

6

The plan of attack

Even a company that isn't officially hiring can still be expected based on national averages to experience a 14 per cent turnover in staff in the course of a year. In other words, every company has openings sometimes, and any one of those openings could have your name on it.

The problem is you won't have the chance to pick the very best opportunity unless you check them all out. Every intelligent job hunter will use a multi-channel approach to their job search, including:

- Internet job postings
- Newspaper advertisements
- Personal and professional networking
- Direct-researched opportunities
- Recruitment agencies and head hunters
- Business and trade publications

Online job postings

Here is where the internet can play an especially useful role. There are thousands of job sites that advertise vacancies or job postings; almost every one of these sites has a CV bank.

Here's how to use them to greatest effect.

Visit the job sites and search for appropriate job openings. Most of these job sites have a powerful feature called an 'e-mail alert.' The alert allows you to identify the type of work you are seeking and receive an e-mail from the site every time a suitable job is advertised by one of their clients. You don't want these e-mails to come to you indiscriminately at work, so be sure to use your personal e-mail address in any job search.

The onsite CV banks will work well for you too. From an employer's or headhunter's point of view, these CV banks are like big fish tanks. The fishing analogy works for you too: your CV in CV banks is like having a baited hook in the water while you go about your business. CV banks often delete your CV after 90 days, so if you are looking longer than this you will need to go back and reload. Actually, it is not a bad idea to keep a CV posted online as a career management tool; it will keep you aware of who is looking for what and how much they are paying, and it will keep your finger on the pulse of the job market. At the very least, you will always know what skills are in demand; beyond that, you don't have to be interviewed for those jobs, and if you do decide to interview, you don't have to accept the offers. Overall, you will be in far greater control of your professional destiny.

If you are writing as a result of an online job posting, you should mention both the website and the date you found it:

> 'I read your job posting on your company's website on 5 January and felt I had to respond...'

> 'Your online job posting regarding a _____ on CareerCity.com caught my eye, and your company name caught my attention.'

> 'This e-mail, and my attached CV, are in response to your job posting on _____.'

Job advertisements

A first step for many is to go to the job ads and do a mass mailing. Bear in mind, there should be a method to your madness when you do this. Remember, if it is the first idea that comes to your mind, hitting the job ads will be at the front of everyone else's thoughts, too.

A single job advertisement can draw hundreds of responses. The following ideas might be helpful:

● Most newspapers have an employment section every week, when, in addition to their regular advertising, they have a major drive for recruitment ads. Make sure you always read this edition of your local paper.

- So-called authorities on the topic will tell you not to rely on the job ads – that they don't work. Rockinghorse droppings! Job ads and online job postings don't work only if you are too dumb to know how to use them. Look for back issues, and when online check for job posting archives. Just because a company is no longer advertising does not necessarily mean that the vacancy has been filled. The employer may well have become disillusioned, and is now using a professional recruiter to work on the position. They may have filled the position, but perhaps the person never started work or simply did not work out in the first few months. Maybe they took on someone who did work out well and now they want another person for a similar position. When you go back into the job ads you'll find untold opportunities awaiting you, and instead of competition from 150 other job hunters responding to this week's job ad you'll be tapping into the hidden job market of unadvertised positions. In fact, I had a letter from a reader recently who told me he had landed a £60,000 job from a seven-month-old job ad he came across in a pile of newspapers in his father-in-law's garage! (You see? There is a use for in-laws, after all.)

- As mentioned above jobs are available but just aren't being advertised in what is referred to as the 'hidden job market'. Likewise, in some high-demand occupations where job ads aren't famous for drawing the right calibre of professional, the employer may only run one or two major 'institutional' ads a year for that type of position.

- Be sure to cross-check the categories. Don't rely solely on those ads seeking your specific job title. For example, let's say you are a graphic artist looking for a job in advertising. You should flag all advertising or public relations agencies with any kind of need. If they are actively taking on staff at the moment, logic will tell you that their employment needs are not restricted to that particular title. It's arrogant to assume that all jobs are being advertised where you happen to be looking today.

- If you are writing as the result of a newspaper advertisement, you should mention both the publication and the date. Do not abbreviate 'advertisement' to 'ad' unless space demands, and remember to underline or italicize the publication's title:

'I read your advertisement in the Daily News *on 6 October for a* _____ *and, after researching your company, felt I had to write ...'*

'Ref: Your advertisement in the Daily News *on Sunday the 8th of November ....'*

'As you compare your requirements for the above-mentioned position with my attached CV, you will see that my entire background matches your requirements.'

'Your notice regarding a _____ in _____ caught my eye, and your company name caught my attention.'

'This letter and attached CV are in response to your advertisement in _____.'

Networking

Networking is one of those dreadful words from the 1970s that unfortunately is so entrenched we might as well learn to live with it. I'd prefer, however, that you think of it as *professional connectedness*, because becoming properly connected to your profession is simply the best approach for ongoing professional growth; it is also the activity that will generate the widest range of relevant contacts for this and future job hunts.

The danger with the traditional concept of networks is that once you are comfortably networking among friends and acquaintances, you might unconsciously derail your job search by ignoring other and possibly more fruitful avenues of exploration for job opportunities. An effective job search requires more than writing to and chatting to old cronies on the telephone. Besides, you will often discover that your network is not as comprehensive as you might have wished.

The important thing for any professional to grasp is that to have a friend you must be a friend. Just because you worked with someone five years ago, and haven't spoken to them since doesn't mean they still regard you as a friend. From personal experience and surveys through my own professional networks, and through your own observations, I think you'll find we both share the following conclusions on connectivity.

To those requests from people I didn't know, I asked for a CV. (Of course, if they'd had an introduction or were fellow members of an association things would be different.) If I received it in good time with a thoughtfully prepared accompanying letter, I would give that person help if I could.

To those requests from people with an introduction from someone

I liked and respected, I gave time and consideration and, wherever possible, assistance.

To those requests from friends, people I had worked with at one time and *who had kept in touch* since we had worked together, I stopped everything and went through my address book. I provided leads, made calls on their behalf, and insisted they keep in touch. I also initiated follow-up calls myself on behalf of these people.

To those requests from people who regarded themselves as friends but who had not maintained contact, or who had only re-established contact when they wanted something, I looked through my address book once but for some reason was unable to find anything. I wished them the best of luck. 'Sorry I couldn't help you. If something comes to mind, I'll be sure to call.'

Nothing works like a personal recommendation from a fellow professional – and you get that best by *being* a fellow professional, by being connected to your profession and professionals within it. It is no accident that successful people in all fields know each other – they helped each other get that way.

If you are going to use business colleagues and personal friends in your job search, don't mess up and do it half-heartedly. We live in a very mobile society, so you shouldn't restrict yourself to family, friends and colleagues just where you are looking. Everyone can help – even Aunt Matilda in Manila. Maybe she just happens to have had her cousin's wife's brother, who is a senior scientist at IBM, as her house guest for a month last summer and he is now forever in her debt for the holiday of a lifetime. Maybe not, but still, people know people, and they know people not just here but all over. Sit and think for a few minutes; you will be amazed at the people *you* know all over the country. Every one of them has a similar network.

Here are some tips for writing letters asking for assistance; you can also use these guidelines as a structure for networking conversations.

1. Establish connectivity. Recall the last memorable contact you had or someone in common that you have both spoken to recently.

2. Use your common membership in professional associations as a bridge builder to other members. If you're not currently a member of any associations and organizations, try using internet search engines to research some likely ones.

3. Let contacts know what you are looking for. They will invariably want to help, but you have to give them a framework within

which to target their efforts. At the same time do not get too specific, or allow your ego to get in the way of leads for jobs you could really do. You want to be non-specific: 'I'm looking for something in operations within telecom' gives the listener the widest possible opportunity for coming up with leads.

4. Tell them why you are writing: 'It's time for me to make a move; I just got laid off with a thousand others and I'm taking a couple of days to catch up with old friends.'

5. Ask for advice and guidance: 'Who do you think are the happening _____ companies today?', or 'Could you take a look at my CV for me? I really need an objective opinion and I've always respected your viewpoint.' Don't ask specifically, 'Can you employ me?' or 'Can your company take me on?'

6. By all means ask for leads within specific target companies, but don't rely on a contact with a particular company to get you into that company. Mount and execute your own plan of attack. No one has the same interest as you in putting bread on your table.

7. When you do get help, say thank you. And if you get it verbally, follow it up in writing. The impression is indelible, and just might get you another lead.

8. You never know who your friends are. You will be surprised at how someone you always regarded as a real pal won't give you the time of day and how someone you never thought of as a friend will go beyond the call of duty for you.

9. Whether they help you or not, let them know when you get a job, and maintain contact in one form or another at least once a year. A career is for a long time. It might be next week or a decade from now when a group of managers (including one of your personal network) are talking about filling a new position and the first thing they will do is say 'Who do we know?' That could be you ... if you establish 'top of the mind awareness' now and maintain it.

When you write networking letters and make the follow-up calls you might be surprised to find who your friends are: people you thought of as friends will give you the cold shoulder while people you hardly know will go out of their way to help you.

Whether they help you or not, let all your contacts know when you get situated and offer to be a resource for them, and maintain contact in one form or another at least once a year. A career is for life and, who knows, one day maybe years from now one of your personal network could be talking to a manager who asks, 'Do you know of anyone who could possibly fill this new position we have in mind?' If you've maintained your connection with your contact, it might be your name that's going to come to mind.

If you are writing as the result of a referral, say so and quote the person's name if appropriate:

> 'Our mutual colleague John Stanovich felt my skills and abilities would be valuable to your company ...'

> 'The manager of your Ipswich branch, Pamela Bronson, has suggested I contact you regarding the opening for a _____.'

> 'I received your name from Henry Charles last week. I spoke to Mr Charles regarding career opportunities with _____, and he suggested I contact you. In case the CV he forwarded is caught up in the mail, I enclose another.'

> 'Arthur Gold, your office manager and my neighbour, thought I should contact you about the upcoming opening in your accounts department.'

Direct-research contacts

The internet is now the most comprehensive job hunting resource. There are many websites that provide company profiles, and often you can e-mail the companies you're interested in right from their website. In addition to researching contacts, you can look up information on the status of the company you're interested in, do salary surveys, get advice on finding a job, and post your CV on online CV banks.

Most companies are also listed in one of the reference sources in your library. Take the time to do library research and you will discover job opportunities that 90 per cent of your professional competitors never dreamed existed.

Again, the reference librarian will be pleased to help you. Search each of the appropriate reference works for every company within the scope of your search that also falls within your geographic boundaries.

Your goal is to identify and build personalized dossiers on the companies in your chosen geographic area, so do not be judgemental about what and who they might appear to be: you are fishing for possible job openings, so cast your net wide and list them all. To this end you should also check out your local Yellow Pages, which lists smaller local companies. Don't turn your nose up at this option, because the majority of all job growth is in companies with 100 employees or fewer. Only if you present yourself as a candidate for all available opportunities in your geographic area of search is there any realistic chance of landing the best possible opportunity.

> Tip: if you are over 50 and experiencing age discrimination, smaller companies (where most of the job growth is anyway) are far more likely to feel the need for an experienced hand.

Develop electronic documents or paper files containing all the relevant information for each company. You'll want to include the names of the company's CEO and chairman of the board, a description of the company's services and/or products, the size of the company, and the locations of its various branches. Of course, if you find other interesting information, copy it down, by all means. For instance, you might come across information on growth or shrinkage in a particular area of a company; or you might read about recent acquisitions the company has made. You can use Google or other search engines to track industry news.

All this information will help you target potential employers and stand out in different ways. Your knowledge will create a favourable impression when you first contact the company; that you made an effort is noticed and sets you apart from other applicants who don't bother. The combination says that you respect the company, the opportunity and the interviewer; combined, these perceptions help say that you are a different quality of job candidate.

All your efforts have an obvious short-term value in helping you guarantee job interviews and offers. Who would *you* interview and subsequently employ? The person who knows nothing about your company, or the person who knows everything and shows enthusiasm with that knowledge?

Your efforts also have value in the long term, because you are building a personalized reference work of your industry/speciality/ profession that will get you off to a running start the next time you wish to make a job change.

E-mail blasts and mailing lists

Posting your CV online is a sensible passive job search technique, although the blasting of your CV across the internet with one of the CV blasting services doesn't always live up to its apparent promise. In fact, until recently I was pretty much against the approach as I just wasn't seeing the results; however, I've just been working with an executive in international port security who got twenty responses resulting from an e-mail blast to some four hundred executive recruiters. Of course, he is in an in-demand occupation and had an arresting message expressed in his cover letter. And nowadays when everyone is delivering everything by e-mail it might just be the time to think about a serious traditional mail campaign to support (but not as the sole or main thrust of your job search campaign) your other job-hunting activities. You can put together your own lists of people to pitch your CV to or use the services of an online or print broker.

Associations

You're a member of an appropriate professional body, aren't you? If not, you'll want to invest in membership just as soon as humanly possible. You don't know of an appropriate association? Your local librarian should be able to point you to directories of associations, or you could look on the internet.

The professional connectedness you achieve through membership, the skills you will learn, and the contacts you will make will pay dividends throughout your career. Not to mention the networking database and directory you will get to use immediately.

Alumni/ae associations

Many schools and colleges have an active alumni/ae association. The mailing list you can obtain from this source can vary from just names to names and occupations and (sometimes) names of employers. Being a fellow alumni/ae probably gives you a claim to 60 seconds of attention. Nearly every working alumni/ae could be worthy of a networking letter (just check through the examples) and a follow-up call. Never ever underestimate the power of 'the old school tie'.

Recruitment agencies

(This section is taken from *Your Job Search Made Easy*, 3rd edn, by Mark Parkinson, published by Kogan Page.)

In most situations indirect applications involve approaching a recruitment agency that deals with your job area. You'll find plenty advertised in the Yellow Pages and newspapers. Professional agencies will invite you to call and discuss the sort of job you would like, and your circumstances, skills and abilities. They may give you some tests or exercises to complete. These are designed to find out more about the sorts of job that would suit you and what you are like as a person. If you're dealing with a professional agency, they will then describe the sorts of company they work with, and the vacancies they have on their books. After the first meeting they will send your details to the most likely companies and arrange interviews on your behalf. This means that you don't have to contact potential employers directly.

The problem is that agencies are not impartial since they make their money out of their commercial clients. This means that they are unlikely ever to say anything bad about them. In view of this you need to consider a little quality control. Try these checks:

- How is the first meeting conducted?
- Is it thorough and professional?
- Do they appear to care about you as an individual?
- Do you feel comfortable asking questions?
- Can they answer your questions?
- Do they assess your needs accurately?
- Do they use plain English or is it all jargon?
- How hard do they try?
- Do they approach just one company or lots of them?
- Do they approach the companies you suggest?
- If you have an unsuccessful interview, do they find out why?
- Do they keep you up to date with progress?

If the agency doesn't measure up, try another one: after all, it's your career that is at stake. Also remember to visit your local Jobcentre, which can help you to find local jobs and arrange interviews. Since Jobcentres are non-profit making the advice given will be independent and unbiased.

Business magazines

There are a number of Online and Print uses here. The articles about interesting companies can alert you to growth opportunities, and the articles themselves can be mentioned in your job search letter. Many professional association and trade magazines rely more or less on the contributions of industry professionals. So articles bylined by John Brown, CEO of Openings at ABC Furnaces, could go into a dossier for targeted contacts. It's also a good idea to enclose the article with your letter. These mailings to sometime authors can be tremendously rewarding. Writing is hard, and writers have egos of mythical proportions (just ask my editor), so a little flattery can go a long way.

By the same token, you can write to people who are quoted in articles, again with an article or a link. It's great to see your name in print; in fact there is only one thing better, and that is hearing that someone *else* saw your name in print and now thinks you're a genius. Bear in mind that most of these magazines also carry a recruitment section.

These ideas are just some of the many unusual and effective ways to introduce yourself to companies. Browse through all of the sample letters in Chapter 8 to uncover other effective ideas.

Sending out your job search letter

Letters are more effective when you can find an individual to whom you can address it. As noted earlier, 'Sir/Madam,' or 'To whom it may concern' says you don't care enough about the company to find out a name – they will pay more attention to a letter addressed by name, and if nothing else it guarantees that the letter will be opened and read. Additionally, your research pays off because you have someone to ask for by name when you make your follow-up telephone call.

Must you send out hundreds or even thousands of letters in the coming weeks? I took a call from a woman on a phone-in TV show recently who had 'done everything and still not got a job'. She explained how she had sent out almost 300 letters and still wasn't employed. After I asked her several questions, it turned out that she had been job hunting for almost two years (that equals two or three letters a week), and there were, conservatively, 3,000 companies she could work for. (This equals a single approach with no follow-up to only one in 10 potential employers.) Two employer contacts a week will not get you back to work – or even on track with the kind of job that can help you advance towards your chosen life goals. Only if you approach and establish communication with every possible employer and follow up properly will you create the maximum opportunity for yourself.

In the world of headhunters the statistical average is 700 contacts (that's letters, e-mails, making and receiving calls) between offers and acceptances. These are averages of professionals representing only the most desirable jobs and job candidates to each other. When I hear that it takes a white collar worker about eight months to get a job nowadays, I have a feeling those 700 or so contacts are being spread out needlessly. If you approach the job search in a professional manner, the way executive search professionals and recruitment agencies approach their work, you can be happily installed on the next rung of your career ladder much sooner than the national average.

I am not recommending that you immediately make up a list of 700 companies and mail letters to them today. That isn't the answer. Your campaign needs strategy. While every job-hunting campaign is unique, you will want to maintain a balance between the *number* of e-mails and letters you send out on a daily and weekly basis and the *kinds* of letters you send out. This needs to be integrated into an intelligent overall campaign that includes other job-search activities; just sending CVs with none of the other productive job-search approaches is a sad excuse for a job campaign.

The key is to send out a balanced mailing representing all the different types of leads, and to send them out regularly and in a volume that will allow you to make follow-up calls. There are many headhunters who manage their time so well that they average over 50 calls a day, year in and year out. While you may aim at building your call volume up to this number, I recommend that you start out with more modest goals.

To start the campaign:

Source	Number of Letters Per Day
Internet job postings	10
Newspaper ads	10
Networking (associations, alumni/ae, colleagues)	10 (5 to friends, 5 to professional colleagues)
Direct-research contacts (online searches, reference works, magazines, etc)	10
Headhunters	10

Do you need to compose more than one letter?

Almost certainly. There is a case for all of us having letters and CVs targeted for different specific needs. The key is to do each variation once and do it right. Your computer makes this job many times easier than it used to be, and you can use these letters again and again as your circumstances demand.

Sometimes you may find it valuable to send upwards of half a dozen contact letters to a desirable target company, to ensure that they know you are available. To illustrate, let's say you are a young engineer crazy for a job with Last Chance Electronics. It is well within the bounds of reason that you would submit a job search and CV letter to any or all of the following people, with each letter addressed by name to minimize its chances of going straight into the waste-paper basket:

- Company Chairman
- CEO of Engineering
- Chief Engineer
- Engineering Design Manager
- Head of Human Resources
- Technical Engineering Recruitment Manager
- Technical Recruiter

Each of these letters might require a slightly different introductory paragraph, while the body of the letter could remain the same.

The plan

A professionally organized and conducted campaign should include both an e-mail and traditional dimension. So when I talk about 'mail' and 'mail campaign', understand that the terms embrace both communication mediums.

Approach 1

A carefully targeted approach to a select group of companies. You will have first identified these 'super-desirable' places to work as you researched your long list of potential employers. You will continue to add to this primary target list as you unearth fresh opportunities in your day-to-day research efforts. In this instance you have two choices:

1. Mail to everyone at once, remembering that the letters have to be personalized and followed up appropriately.

2. Start your mailings off with one to a line manager and one to a contact in human resources. Follow up in a few days and repeat the process to other names on your hit list.

With the e-mail dimension of your campaign, you can bookmark target companies and check in on their openings on an ongoing basis. As employers cannot be relied upon to keep your CV in front of them, you should submit it to your target companies on a regular basis, say every six weeks. The worst that can happen is that someone finally pays attention!

Approach 2

A carpet-bombing strategy designed to reach every possible employer on the basis that you won't know what opportunities there are unless you find out. (Here, too, you must personalize and follow up appropriately.)

Begin with a mailing to one or two contacts within the company and then repeat the mailings to other contacts when your initial follow-up calls result in referrals or dead ends. Remember, just because Harry in engineering says there are no openings in the company, that's not necessarily the case; always find out for yourself. Even if he doesn't have a need himself, another contact in the same company could know the person who is just dying to meet you.

Once you have received some responses to your mailings/follow-up calls and scheduled interviews, your emphasis will change. Those contacts and interviews will require follow-up letters and conversations. You will be preparing for interviews.

This is exactly the point where most job hunts stall. We get so excited about the interview activity we convince ourselves that 'This will be the offer.' The headhunters have a saying, 'The offer that can't fail always will.' What happens is that the offer doesn't materialize, and you are left with absolutely no interview activity.

The more letters you send out, the more follow-up calls you can make to schedule interviews. The more interviews you get, the better your interview skills become and the better you feel.

So no matter how good things look with a particular company, continue the campaign – maintain activity with those companies with whom you are in negotiation. You must also maintain your marketing schedule. The daily plan now looks like this:

Source	Number of Letters Per Day
Internet job postings	5
Newspaper ads	5
Networking (associations, alumni/ae, colleagues)	5
Direct-research contacts (online searches, reference works, magazines, etc)	5
Headhunters	5
Follow-up letters and calls	15–20

Small but consistent mailings have many benefits. The balance you maintain is important, because most job hunters are tempted simply to send the easy letters and make the easy calls (ie, network with old friends). Doing this will knock your job search off balance.

Even when an offer is pending, keep plugging, and by 'pending' I include all variations on 'Harry, you've got the job and you can start Monday; the offer letter is in the mail'. Yeah, just like the cheque in the proverb. Never accept the 'yes' until you have it in writing, have started work, and the first pay cheque has cleared at the bank! Until then, keep your momentum building.

Following up: a cautionary tale

In theory, your perfect letter will generate a 100 per cent response, but this is not reality. Although you will get calls from your mailing, if you sit there like Buddha waiting for the world to beat a path to your door, you may wait a long time.

A pal of mine put a two-line ad in the local paper for an analyst. The ad also appeared on the paper's website. By Wednesday of the following week he had received over a hundred responses. Ten days later he was still ploughing through them when he received a follow-up call (the only one he did receive) from one of the ad respondents. The job hunter was in the office within two hours, returned the following morning, and was employed by lunchtime.

The candidate's paperwork was simply languishing there in the pile waiting to be discovered. The follow-up phone call got it discovered. The call made the interviewer sort through the enormous pile of paper, pull out the letter and CV, and act on it.

Follow-up calls work

You'll notice that many letters in Chapter 8 mention that they will follow up with a phone call. This allows the writer to explain to any inquisitive receptionist that Joe Bloggs is 'expecting my call' or that it is 'personal', or 'It's accounting/engineering/customer service business'.

I find it surprising that so many people are nervous about calling a fellow professional on the phone and talking about what they do for a living. To help reduce any nervousness, understand that there is an unwritten professional credo shared by the vast majority of successful professional people: you should always help another if it isn't going to hurt you in the process. Because of this, almost everyone you speak to will recognize and be sympathetic to your cause.

If you are not already successful in management, you need to know the principle outlined in my management books *Hiring the Best* and *Keeping the Best*: 'The first tenet of management is getting work done through others'. A manager's success is truly based on this single idea. Managers are always on the lookout for competent professionals in their field for today and tomorrow. In fact, the best managers maintain a private file of great professionals they can't use today but want to keep available. I know of someone who got a job as a result of a letter retained in these files. She got the interview (and the job) from the letter and CV she'd sent months earlier.

No manager will take offence at a call from a competent fellow professional.

Using a contact tracker

To ensure that you keep track of the contacts you have made and the results of the follow-up phone calls, I recommend that you create a contact tracker on a spreadsheet program like Microsoft Excel. Create columns for the company name, telephone number, e-mail address and contact name. A mailing today will allow you to have a follow-up plan set and ready to go a few days later. As a rule of thumb, a mailing sent today is ripe for follow-up four to eight days from now. Any sooner and you can't be sure it has arrived; much later and it may already have been lost or been passed on. With e-mail you will probably want to follow up within two or three days. In addition to your contact tracker, it may be helpful to use your computer address book to keep track of who you contact.

You will know that your job search is on track when you are filling in more contacts every day as a result of a mailing, and creating a second contact tracker as a result of your follow-up calls.

If you follow the advice in this book, you will get interviews. If you follow the advice in *Ultimate CV*, you will get multiple job offers.

Recently I spoke to a man on a radio phone-in show who had been out of work for some months. He had bought the books and followed my advice to the letter and had generated four job offers in only five weeks. I have lost count of the number of similar encounters I've had over the years. Follow my advice in letter and spirit and the same good fortune can be yours. After all, good fortune is really only the intersection of opportunity, preparation and effort.

7

How the internet can help in your job search

The internet offers you an array of opportunities to get your CV on the desks of thousands of companies and recruiters. This communication medium makes research and contact easier than it has ever been, but you shouldn't rely on the obvious online approaches exclusively.

The internet is especially effective in identifying all the target employers in a specific geographical area, whether it is where you live today or where you plan to live as soon as possible. Its usefulness diminishes when you are only looking for jobs in your immediate area, and that area is a small town, although there are still many useful ways you can use the medium.

From the corporate perspective, internet recruitment serves a dual purpose: their personnel openings are advertised cost-effectively to attract candidates, and the technologically challenged screen themselves out.

How can the internet benefit your job search? It allows you to:

- research your industry and identify companies;
- create customized electronic documents and communicate with potential employers and recruiters pretty much instantly;
- find job openings through job banks and employers' job sites;
- have potential employers find you, whether you are currently looking for a position or just maintaining your visibility for career growth opportunities;
- use database and networking sites to identify names and titles;
- pick up useful job search and career management advice.

You can post your CV on the internet so that companies and recruiters can find you; you can surf for job openings and you'll have access to more information about prospective employers, making you a better-informed candidate. The internet offers you access to millions of job openings, and tens of thousands of companies and recruiters. Of course, they are not all going to be in your town, so the wider your geographical parameters, the more useful the tool will become.

What you need to start an online job search

You need computer access from outside the workplace. Using your office computer for writing your CV, sending out e-mails, or surfing the net for job listings is regarded by the corporate world as theft of time and services; it can cost you your job and the reason for termination will make the next one more difficult to find. Studies show that 50 per cent of all companies read their employees' e-mail and/or track their internet usage. Some companies have even assigned IT staff members whose job it is to track inappropriate internet use, and they have software packages to help with that tracking. Originating primarily in the high-tech industries, this practice seems to be on the rise in industries across the board. Don't ignore this warning because you feel your boss is computer illiterate, too stupid to catch you, or too trusting to snoop.

Online privacy and organization

Personal privacy and confidentiality become serious issues when you use the internet for job-hunting and CV distribution. It's a good news/bad news situation: with the ease of electronic document distribution comes the fear of prying eyes. So take precautions to protect your privacy. Almost all companies are using the internet for recruitment purposes; someone in Human Resources could easily stumble across your online CV, which lists the company for which you're currently working.

If you have internet access at home, it is probably through a local ISP (internet service provider). These accounts typically come with more than one e-mail address, so you can use one of the additional addresses for career management activities. If you are currently employed and executing a confidential search, it is a good idea to set up a separate online identity and maintain it exclusively for your job search.

As your experience broadens, your education and professional experience will allow you to pursue a number of different jobs. Therefore, you have the option of creating multiple professional identities online to separate these activities. Setting up separate e-mail accounts for each of these career-specific identities will allow you to keep things organized by job classification, giving more focus to your search and allowing you to effectively manage your job-hunting activities.

Privacy is a concern for everyone

Don't be afraid to use the internet in your job search, but be aware that the information that you post is readily available to other users. Be careful about the type of information and the amount of personal data you make electronically available.

Anyone who has an e-mail account is familiar with junk e-mail, commonly referred to as 'spam'. Reverse spamming is when an electronic 'spider' grabs your personal information, e-mail address, or CV, then redistributes it to other sites or a third party. An electronic spider is a programmed tool that searches the internet for certain types of information the 'spider owner' specifies, so you must be circumspect about the personal information you make available in electronic documents.

You put your professional identity at risk when listing professional licences or certificate numbers on your CV. Similarly, other personal information such as dates of birth, driver's licence numbers and National Insurance numbers should never be included on electronic CVs or any other publicly-available document. With that information alone, someone could steal your identity and ruin your personal or professional credibility.

Don't include too much personal information in an online CV. It could allow unscrupulous people to use your personal or professional identity for their own purposes; at the same time, posting your home phone number or address on the internet can attract junk mail and telemarketing calls.

Rules to protect your online privacy

Here are some general guidelines for making online job sites and CV banks work *for* you rather than *against* you:

- Look at the site's privacy statement. Read it carefully to understand the extent of protection afforded to personal information. Even without guarantees, this is a security starting point.

- Only post your CV to sites that protect their CV bank with a password (this is the best prevention against those spiders). Password protection means that the site electronically screens all visitors. This helps to ensure that only credible employers and recruiters have access to your CV.

- Know who owns and operates the site. The owner's contact information should be available. If they are unwilling to share their identity with you, don't share yours with them.

- You must be able to update, edit and remove your posted CV, along with any other personal information whenever you choose.

- Blocked CV bank services are services that supposedly allow you to block access to your information from specifically unwanted viewers, such as a current employer. Do not trust these services to actually do so. Technology is not foolproof, so only post items that you don't need blocked, or create a secure online identity.

- If you decide to build and create your own website to post your CV and work samples, you might wish to password-protect it at certain times.

- Never put your National Insurance number, driver's licence number or professional licence number on your CV in any format.

- Do not use your company e-mail address, computer, or internet connection to search for jobs or to access your private e-mail account.

Free e-mail accounts

There are dozens of sites that offer free e-mail accounts that take only minutes to set up. While many personal interest sites offering free accounts exist, remember that your career e-mail address shouldn't contain any personal information. For example, *Martin@match.com* (from a dating site) reveals too much personal information, and isn't appropriate for professional use. You want to create a professional, eye-catching image right from the start; take time in selecting your professional e-mail service and user names.

As an example of the process, let's create a secure identity for a fictional job search candidate, Susan O'Malley, using Hotmail. Go to *www.hotmail.com*, and then select the 'New Account Sign Up' icon on the front page of the site. That will link you to a page requesting a user profile. When you complete the profile, you will be directed to the site user agreement. This explains user rules and the site's privacy policy. Read this information carefully; you have to accept the terms of the agreement before your address becomes active. Stick with the larger, more public firms, because they tend to be more reliable and honourable about such terms. Typically, public sites offer paid upgrades to your new account that allow you more control over your e-mail address. Upgrades are unnecessary if you limit the number of messages stored in your mailbox at any given time, or don't care to pay to limit spam.

Choose a professional user name for Susan: SOMALLEYHRPRO – this gives her the e-mail address *somalleyhrpro@hotmail.com*. Remember: this account is set up strictly for job search purposes. An appropriately named professional e-mail like this will grab the attention of prospective employers.

Should you run into a situation where the user name you want is not available, choose your alternatives wisely. Most sites will make suggestions, usually by adding numbers to the end of the user name. This is not always the best idea for job-hunting and career management needs. You do not want to be confused with *jsmith118@hotmail.com* when you are assigned the name *jsmith119@hotmail.com*, nor do you want to choose a number that could easily be mistaken for your year of birth. Instead, make it a career-related screen name as we did for Susan.

How to organize your job-hunting e-mail account

If you use public or shared computers, free accounts such as this one offer a nice security feature at the front door. Susan activated the highest level of security by clicking on the 'Public/shared computer' button. At this increased level of security, Susan will be asked for her user name and password whenever she attempts to enter her account from any computer. If Susan always uses her home or private computer, the 'Neither' or the 'Keep me signed in' option assumes that every time her web browser links to Hotmail, she is identified as the user and is automatically logged in. This also allows her to keep her job search secure on her family computer, so those darling rugrats don't destroy all her work. For your own safety, emulate Susan and set up your account at the highest security level possible.

Whether you use Hotmail, Yahoo!, Outlook, or some other major e-mail program, all of them allow you to create and manage folders. (The buttons are usually labelled something like 'Create Folder' and 'Manage Folder') Think of these as the electronic equivalent of paper folders and filing cabinets. What folders do you need? Let's start with the two major sites where Susan will be posting her CV and searching for jobs: Monster.co.uk and SHRM.org (the Society for Human Resource Management website). Like most job sites, both of these sites offer job delivery services, automatically linking her to relevant new jobs whenever they are posted on the site.

Susan will also create a folder for leads. As the leads mature into communication and contact with specific companies and recruiters, she can create specific folders for them. Susan can add new folders as she needs them.

You could have folders for different geographic areas, or professional areas of expertise, for headhunters and the like; then as communications develop with specific companies, said companies might warrant separate folders of their own. Now traditionally we dump much of this info once it has been processed: for example when that recruiter tells us that she has nothing, or when we come in second at that company, or when we realize that none of those X number of companies are going to interview us. But times have changed and some of the old traditions don't make much sense any more.

It's pretty much a given that you are somewhere in the middle of a half-century work life, and that in that time you are likely to change jobs about every four years and have three or more distinct careers in that time. Given this likely scenario your current job search is not likely to be your last, so why not save all this data and information? A few years down the road, you'll be able to update the CV and retool the cover letters. And you know those companies who were hiring accountants back in 2007? Well, they are still hiring accountants! Even if your contact Jim Smith has since left that one company, the fact that you knew him will ensure that you are given his replacement's name. Organize and save today's work and next time you come to a job search you won't be starting from scratch!

Locate the tab labelled 'Address Book'. This tab sends you to another screen, where you are given additional options. These options allow you to send e-mail, view and edit messages, delete e-mail, and, most importantly for your organizational efforts: create a new address book.

In creating new address books, you want to organize groups of addresses, not just add individual ones. Each 'group' will contain a separate set or group of addresses, tailored to specific audiences for current or future job searches. Typically, these groups fall into three categories: companies, recruiters and networking prospects/professional colleagues. By creating an address book group for each of these categories, you create a database for your working life.

Additions to these groups needn't be based on direct contact, interviews, or job offers. If you see a recruiter within an industry of interest, put that address in the recruiter book. If you find a company in your geographic area or professional field, put that address in the company book. By doing this regularly, you create a vehicle for launching a massive career blitz whenever the need arises. Organize yourself now, and the information you collect along the way can be used throughout your entire working life. You'll have an enormous database loaded and ready to go!

Job search letters and online job-hunting

A productive CV plays a significant role in job search success, but it will remain unread without a dynamite letter to pave the way. In the online world, your job search letter is the e-mail message preceding your CV.

The internet and the subsequent growth of the electronic recruitment process have been both a blessing and a curse for corporate recruiters. Although electronic recruitment can be much more efficient for them in many ways, it tends to yield more responses from a wider range of candidates. This creates a time-management challenge for corporations and recruiters who must review the avalanche of CVs the medium generates. Consequently, there has been a dramatic growth in CV software capable of scanning CV databases by keywords.

These programs allow companies to store digitally encoded documents such as CVs and letters, saving them for later access using keywords and other criteria to rank their usefulness. Initially, only large companies could afford these services, but with competition and the growth of the internet, CV scanning and searching capabilities are now available to virtually all companies and recruiters.

With traditionally mailed CVs, a powerful cover letter separates you from the crowd. The same is true with emailed CVs; a well-crafted cover letter can save your CV from cursory review and relegation to the company's CV's bin.

An e-mailed cover letter must adhere to all the same criteria that we have already set out. The message is the same, but at the same time it is smart to be sensitive to the medium through which it is delivered. Think of your e-mail cover letter as an electronic talent agent, the opening act for your CV. The two must complement each other because working together they both play crucial roles in a successful online job search. No matter how well written your cover letters are, inappropriately presented documents will result in wasted effort.

Differences between electronic and paper job search letters

Today's workplaces tend to demand 50+ hours weekly from busy, multitasking employees. I've spoken to corporate executives who base their decision on whether to listen to voice mail messages on the first 10 words recorded. Your e-mailed job search letter competes for the attention of this same audience.

The amount of e-mail traffic grows exponentially, so hit your main points quickly, or you will lose the reader's attention. A good subject line grabs attention, but if the first two sentences don't succinctly state your purpose, they'll have little reason for wasting any more precious time on the rest of your message.

Cover letters typically consist of three to five carefully constructed paragraphs. Very rarely should they exceed one full page; in most cases, as we have discussed, a second page simply won't get read. Just as you would limit a paper job search letter to one page, you should try to keep an electronic job search letter to one screen view where possible. This can sometimes be less than the length of our original script, so edit as strongly as you can. If you cannot get your entire letter in one screen view, at least make an effort to get the meat of your pitch onto that first full screen.

Before discussing formatting, let's take a minute to focus on job search letter content issues. We've established the fact that e-mail job search letters need to be concise, giving the reasons why the message is being sent and why the reader should move on to your CV. Review the samples below. Look for the ways in which these letters build bridges between writers and readers, use keywords, make points about the writers' suitability for the positions, and then request next step information.

Sample 1

I was excited to see your opening for a Financial Analyst (job 1854) on the ABCJob.com website. As my attached CV demonstrates, the position is a perfect match for my payroll, general ledger and accounts receivable experience. I welcome the opportunity to discuss my skills and your job requirements in greater detail. Please respond with a time of day I might call you.

Sample 2

While browsing the jobs database on the MedZilla.com website, I was intrigued by your Regional Sales Manager job posting (MZ - wj25508). Although I am currently employed by one of your competitors, I have kept my eyes open for an opportunity to join your organization. Over the past year I have: ● Built a sales force of 7 reps ● Exceeded my quota-growing revenue to £2.3 million ● Implemented a customer service plan that successfully retains clients.

Please review my attached CV and contact me confidentially to schedule a time for us to meet.

Sample 3

It was great meeting you on Monday for lunch. I enjoyed sharing ideas with a fellow association member and, as you suggested, I have attached a copy of my current CV. Since our meeting I have given more thought to your company goals and believe they are closely related to my skill set and career objectives. I will call you next week to schedule a time when we can continue our conversation.

Sample 4

Your colleague Bill Jacobson suggested that I send you my CV. He mentioned that your department is looking for a Database Administrator with experience in Intranet implementation and management. As my attached CV demonstrates, I have done that type of work for six years with a regional organization on a platform of 15,000 users. I welcome the opportunity to discuss your specific projects and explore the possibility of joining your team.

Sample 5

Although I am currently employed by one of your major competitors, I must admit that I was captivated by your company's mission statement when I visited your website. Your dedication of resources within assisted care facilities not only piqued my interest but are also, as my attached CV indicates, precisely my area of expertise. With significant experience in an area of such importance to your firm, I look forward to the opportunity to discuss available positions.

Sample 6

A colleague of mine, Diane Johnson, recommended your recruiting firm to me as you recently assisted her in a career transition. I understand that your firm specializes in the consumer products industry. As a Marketing Director with 12 years of experience in consumer products, I have:

- *doubled revenues in just 18 months;*
- *introduced a new product which captured a 38% market share;*
- *successfully managed a £5 million ad budget.*

I have pasted and attached my CV for your review and will call you in the next couple of days to discuss any openings for which your firm is currently conducting searches.

The content of each of these electronic job search letter samples follows a similar format. They all accomplish four goals:

- They identify why you are sending your CV.
- They identify why the reader should read the CV.
- They ask for the interview or next contact.
- They do so succinctly.

Let's examine each of these points more closely:

Identify why you made contact: You probably initiated contact because of a job posting, a colleague, or because your research identified them as a potential employer or suitable recruiting firm. Just state the reason and tell the reader you see a match. When submitting because of a job posting, always indicate the job title or job number if there is one. Likewise, if a friend, associate, or colleague initiated the contact, clearly state their name and your connection. If you found the opening through internet research, state that as well.

Give them a reason to read your CV: Quickly and concisely identify why you believe you are a match. Read the job posting again and then repeat the keywords that you share with it. If appropriate, explain the reason why your mutual acquaintance or colleague referred you as a segue into stating your credentials. This is your chance to whet the reader's appetite. If you are currently employed by, or have worked for a competitor, say it here – many companies seek the expertise of their competitors, and love to lure employees away from them.

Ask for the next step: Wrap up this brief but powerful communication by suggesting a meeting, phone call, or interview. Go ahead and state that you will follow up, especially if you are currently employed and confidentiality could be an issue. But if you say you are going to follow up, you must make time to do it.

The need for multiple electronic job search letters

You will be sending your CV and job search letter in response to many different situations (as well as in many different delivery mediums). To maximize effectiveness, you will have to tailor your job search letters to specific audiences. Addressees may include:

1. Companies and recruiters in response to online job postings.
2. Companies you've found from research, newspapers, trade publications and the internet.
3. Recruiters and the all-important headhunters.
4. Friends and professional colleagues as a means of networking.

When sending CVs to each of these types of contacts, slightly different job search letters will be required. You'll find lots of examples to emulate and customize later in this book. It's best to compose job search letters using a word processing program, not in your e-mail folder.

Even though you are most likely to send the letter via e-mail, it is best to compose and edit it in a word processing program and move it into e-mail when you're satisfied with the content. Within the e-mail you can do the final polish that customizes the document for a specific employer. Creating and saving letters in a word processing document allows you to use each letter you create as a template that can be pasted into an e-mail and customized to the unique needs of that particular situation.

In the long run, templates make you more time-efficient in your job hunting campaign because you will always have a base from which to start.

Go to your 'My Documents' or 'My Briefcase' folder, then create a series of new folders for the various documents and relationships you will be building.

Create a separate section in the 'My Documents' folder, then create a series of subfolders for 'CVs', 'Job Search Letters', 'Job Descriptions', 'Follow-up Letters' and 'Interview Research'. Reserve space for 'Job Offers' and 'Employment Contracts' folders to handle such responses when your job search gains momentum.

Remember, in each of these folders, you need to name documents appropriately; create additional subfolders like 'Text Job Search Letters', which is embedded in the 'Job Search Letters' folder. Keep your electronic job search letters separate from paper versions. Get organized now and never worry about it again.

Make sure your job search letter templates are electronic transmission compatible

Let's visit Susan O'Malley in the process of editing her job search letter template and converting it to a text-based document for e-mail distribution.

Susan's job search letter is nicely formatted, matching the layout of her CV. At this point, the letter is one full page in length, listing a dozen bullet points regarding her skill set. It can certainly be shortened and/or customized for a specific opening where she has some idea of the requirements.

Unlike regular business letters, e-mail letters do not follow typical letter-writing protocols. For example, you would not include your address, because your contact information is entered automatically, along with the date and time of your communication.

Begin your business e-mail messages with a simple salutation: 'Dear Tiffany Carstairs', for example. Basic professional courtesies still apply, so don't address the recipient on a first-name basis unless you are already familiar with them; use the same courtesy and respect you would in a hard copy version. Always end your business e-mails stating your name and a brief summary of your contact information (confidential phone or fax number).

Remove the traditional 'CV enclosed' statement, and state that the CV is *attached* (the correct term), or that it's pasted into the body of the e-mail. You would obviously prefer to have your nicely formatted CV viewed as an attachment, but you should always paste it into the body of your e-mail because many people simply don't open attachments from people they don't know personally.

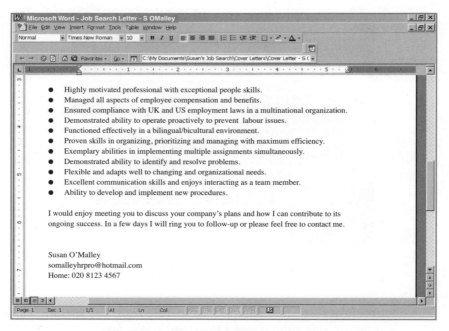

The first edit of the job search letter

Although this letter is still too long, it allows flexibility for specific tailoring. She can edit the bulleted list according to the requirements of any individual position she seeks. At this point Susan's letter can be altered as needed, so let's ignore the length issue to focus on format. If placed into the body of an e-mail message, this text would develop character and spacing problems. To avoid such problems, convert your job search letters to ASCII or a text-based document before pasting it into your e-mail. This is accomplished by following these simple steps.

Copy the entire document by choosing 'select all' from the 'edit' pull-down menu. Then, choose 'copy' from the 'edit' pull-down menu or Ctrl+C for Windows. With a Macintosh you simply choose 'save' from the pull-down file menu, click 'save' and then, when the dialogue box opens, click on 'format' and scroll to 'text'.

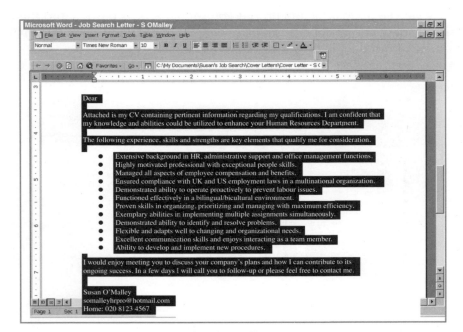

Selecting all text

The document will still lose many of its features and the spacing can change dramatically, so you need to spend some time proofreading this new document before sending. Any tabs, tables or columns can wreak havoc in new text-based versions. In order to prevent wrapping or flowing issues, you may need to delete empty spaces and tabs to make the document flush left.

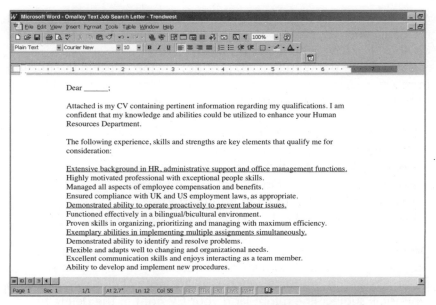

A job search letter with formatting removed

Since the bullets have disappeared in the translation, either adjust the spacing to create a new type of emphasis, or use characters on your keyboard such as * to replace the bullets. In addition, the bullet statements need to be shorter and more concise. If you allow statements to wrap to the next line, your electronic job search letters will be unappealing, less effective and too long. Save your document to protect all these changes. Keep in mind, this is a template. Once an actual contact or job opening has been identified, customization will be the next step.

E-mail subject lines

The use of a powerful subject line can mean the difference between getting your CV read by human eyes and being relegated to the HR CV database. When sending e-mail – not just job related e-mails, but all e-mails – it is only professional to provide a clear, concise and professional subject line. It should allow the receiver to immediately know who you are and what you want.

The subject line of an e-mail containing your CV needs to be factual, professional and intriguing. The subject line you use is like the headline for a newspaper article; its intent is to attract the reader or turn them off. The intent of your e-mail subject line must be to grab the reader and draw him or her into the body of the e-mail message and your CV. Do not use the subject line to state the obvious, like 'CV' or 'Jim Smith's CV'.

If you are responding to a job posting, the job title and job posting number are necessary, but just a start. Combine this factual information with a little intrigue such as:

Job 6745 – Top Sales Professional Here
IT Manager – 7 yrs IT Consulting
Financial Analyst MB450 – CPA / MBA / 8 yrs exp
Benefits Consultant – Non-Profit Exp in London
Posting 2314 – Oxford Grad is interested
Referral from Tony Banks – Product Management Job

Do not go overboard and use an overly aggressive subject line. Do not think you can trick someone into reading your CV by claiming to be an Oxbridge graduate when you are not. At the same time, a whimsical subject line might land your CV right in the delete bin.

How to customize and send your electronic job search letter and CV

Let's pull it all together and watch Susan, an HR professional, customize her electronic job search letter, pick an effective subject line, and send her CV to a potential employer.

Susan is looking for a job in the USA and has been using the Society for Human Resource Management career site (www.shrm.org) and has found an appealing position in sunny California. A vacation resort company is seeking a Regional HR Manager.

The job posting has requested that correspondence be sent in the following manner:

Qualified candidates send resume, salary history and cover letter to: jadariav@gourmetaward.com *or fax 555-555-1234.*

Susan is going to e-mail and post her customized job search letter and electronic CV (resume) to this employer. Since the employer did not provide any additional direction, it is best if Susan attaches the CV to her e-mail message as well as pasting it into the body of the e-mail. Let's start by customizing her electronic job search letter template and then choose a strong subject line.

Since Susan was smart enough to get herself organized, she can

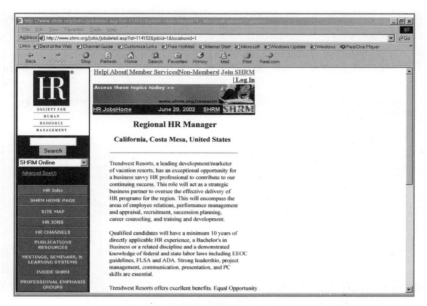

Job posting

quickly find her electronic letter template. By comparing this longer template to the actual job description, she can easily spot the 'hot points'. This position requires 10 years of experience and the job description indicates that knowledge of employment laws such as EEOC, FLSA and ADA are important. As Susan has studied and worked with both US and UK employment law in her job with a major multinational, and since she is interested in moving to California, this is a good match.

Susan has customized her letter template well: she stated why she is sending the e-mail, hit her 'hot points' to get the reader's attention, and asked for the follow up. In fact, she even renamed the document to reflect the company she will be sending it to and saved it in her job search letter folder.

The next step is to create the e-mail, paste and attach the CV. Susan will go back to her newly established Hotmail account, enter her user name and password, and create a new message by choosing 'Compose' from the tabs along the top of the page. By placing her cursor within the message of the newly created e-mail, Susan can then paste the contents of her custom electronic letter in the message box. Simply choose 'Paste' from the 'edit' pull-down menu or Ctrl + V for Windows, with a Mac you'll choose copy and paste.

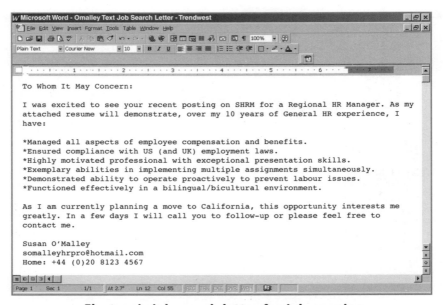

Electronic job search letter for job opening

Sending an e-mail to employers

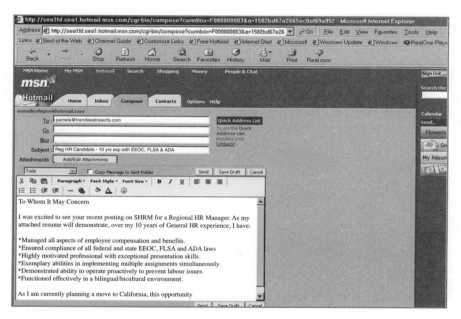

Adding the e-mail address and subject line

With the letter safely pasted in the body of the e-mail, turn your attention to addressing the e-mail to the proper recipient and drafting your subject line. The subject line needs to be factual, professional, yet intriguing: for example 'Your next Reg HR Manager – EEOC, FLSA & ADA exp' or 'EEOC, FLSA & ADA candidate'?

Many people do not realize that the subject line can hold many characters. While a message in your inbox will reveal 60+ characters, an opened or maximized message will show over 150 characters. To be safe, you should get your headline in the first 30 characters, but do feel free to use this extra headline space for a subhead; for example 'Your next Reg HR Manager – EEOC, FLSA and ADA. 10 years experience in all facets of HR including arbitration, campus and executive recruitment selection, compensation, training and development".

This will only be seen when someone opens the document, but it will be seen and noticed. This technique is most effective when you have detailed knowledge of the job and your skills are a good match.

It's a smart strategy to keep a copy of all correspondence. In some e-mail programs it's automatic, in others you can do this by selecting that option from virtually any e-mail program. With Hotmail, there is a small box that can be clicked directly above the message box that

Attaching your CV

reads 'Copy Message to Sent Folder'. This means that a copy of each e-mail you send will be saved in the 'sent' folder. This way, you can always refer back to see what was sent, to whom, and when. In addition, you can always move messages from one folder to another once you have started a communication stream with a particular company and need to isolate and follow the flow of ongoing communication.

Finally, we need to talk a little about the CV. Under the subject of the new e-mail Susan created, there is a button for 'Add/Edit Attachments.' In other programs, such as Microsoft Outlook, there is a button that looks like a paper clip handling the same function; regardless of the program all the attachment devices work pretty much the same way. Once selected, you will then need to find the document you want to attach. Follow the instructions on the screen. Once you have 'browsed' to locate the file, select 'open'. In Hotmail, once you've browsed and found the file you must then select 'attach'. The name of your file will appear in the attachment box. Continue to follow the instructions and select 'OK'.

Before you send this message, recall two points we addressed earlier when Susan initially found this job posting. First, the employer did not suggest a format in which to send the CV. The most popular is what we have done, but it is not 100 per cent effective if the employer does not have Microsoft Word or cannot, for some reason, open the attachment.

Here's a quick solution. Just as you copy and paste your ASCII letter into the e-mail message box, do the same with your CV. You already have it created – simply go to your 'Text CVs' folder, select the text, copy it, and then return to the e-mail message you just created.

Scroll down through your electronic job search letter. Below your name and contact information insert a few asterisks and then paste in your 'Text' saved CV. If the employer has trouble with the attachment, you have sensibly provided a backup solution, which speaks well of your general professional skill sets. Now all that is left to do is to hit the 'send' button.

Reaching the right person

One challenge with the electronic part of your job search is to reach human eyes. When the job posting does not list a person's name to contact, you may need to do a little sleuthing to find it. From the contact information, we have an e-mail address and a physical address. Often with company e-mail addresses, the website of the company is part of the address that comes after the person's username and the '@' symbol.

Surf the company site and look for a job board, the bios and contacts of company executives and press releases. Your mission is to find another doorway into this company, perhaps another name to whom you can also send your submission with a slightly different job search letter. With a little extra effort, you could establish a direct connection to your next boss and avoid the corporate CV database altogether. You might also gather other useful information about the company that will help you stand out at the interview.

Electronic signatures and 'fake' real stationery

While most of the free e-mail programs will not support these features, they are available in both Microsoft Outlook and Outlook Express, and in the other deluxe programs. By going to your e-mail program and choosing the 'Tools' menu button and then selecting 'Options', you will find a box full of many options to customize your e-mail. Under 'Options', if you select 'Mail Format', you will find both the stationery and signature capabilities.

Although I advise against the use of e-mail stationery or any unusual fonts, I will propose a middle ground on the signature – use the many fonts available in your word processing program. When you receive an e-mail that contains what appears to be a real signature, it makes an impression. However, you should never use your real signature – with a minimum of technical expertise, anyone could copy it and electronic signatures can have the same legal validity as a written signature. Don't risk your online security.

Accuracy is essential

Maybe your family doesn't mind the jokes with misspelt words, and perhaps your colleagues forgive typos, understanding that you are busy. But this is your career, and you need to put your best professional foot forward. Under 'Options' choose 'Spelling'.

Now this is a truly useful little tool. Here you can set your e-mail to check spelling before each and every message is sent. Set this feature to always check before sending, but never forget that automatic spellchecking is not perfect.

Before you send any online communication, take a deep breath and remember to proof your CVs, job search letters and any other career communications. Practise using your e-mail and send electronic letters and CV attachments to yourself, friends, family members and colleagues – make sure that what you think you are sending is received in the way you intended.

You know what it takes to put together the Ultimate Cover Letter; now it is time to work through all the examples with your highlighter to get a feel for the many different styles that can work for your campaign. Flag the phrases you like and then go to work creating your own job search letter templates.

8

Sample letters

Now we come to the letters. Apart from the sender's name and address (the personal stationery aspect), all letters adhere to Houghton Mifflin's *Best Writer's Guide* specifications. To those who might notice these things, it is important that we present an impeccable attention to detail.

E-mail response to online job posting
(technical sales representative)

From: Jane Swift [jswiftsalespro@hotmail.com]
To: mbroome@abxworksecurity.com
CC:
Subject: Tech sales/key acct/new territory dev/negotiator/customer services

Dear Ms Broome,

Please accept this letter as application for the Technical Sales Representative position currently available with your company, as listed on Monster.com. My confidential CV is attached for your review and consideration, and I believe you will find me well qualified.

Detailed on my CV you will find a solid background in Sales and Marketing, with over two years in technical sales. In this capacity, I have developed an expertise in new and key account acquisition, new territory development and management, contract negotiation, and customer service. I am confident that my experience in these areas will prove to be an asset to ABC Ltd.

In addition, I am familiar with blueprints, part number breakdowns, and the bidding process of our major accounts, which include _____, _____, _____ and _____ plc. I have doubled my sales from £30,000/month to £60,000/month in just two years, and I am known for effectively identifying and resolving problems before they affect related areas, personnel or customers.

I would welcome the opportunity to discuss with you how I might make similar contributions to the success of ABC Ltd. I look forward to hearing from you to schedule a personal interview at a time convenient to you.

Sincere regards,

Jane Swift
020 8123 4567
jane@anyaddress.co.uk

E-mail response to online job posting
(investment banker)

From: Jane Swift [jsinvestment@aol.com]
To: lwilliam@taweles.com
CC:
Subject: 'can do' administrator

Dear Mr William,

In response to your job posting for a _____ on your company's Web site, I have attached my CV for your consideration.

My experience as an administrative investment banker and assistant to a Director is, I believe, readily adaptable to your needs. I have spent five years in a position best described as 'doing whatever needs to be done' and have capitalized on my ability to undertake a large and widely varied array of projects, learn quickly, find effective solutions to problems, and maintain a sense of humour throughout.

My years as a line and administrative professional have also provided me with an unusual sensitivity to the needs of senior professionals. I have substantial computer experience and am fully computer literate. I have been told my verbal and written communication skills are exceptional.

I believe your firm would provide a working atmosphere to which I would be well suited, as well as one where my diverse experience would be valuable.

My salary requirements are reasonable and negotiable based on the responsibilities and opportunities presented.

Sincerely,

Jane Swift
020 8123 4567
jane@anyaddress.co.uk

E-mail response to online job posting
(legal administrator)

From	Jane Swift [swiftlegalpro@earthlink.net]
To:	ggoodfellow@budownoble.com
Cc:	
Subject:	Administrator/mgmnt/cmptr/acctg/planning/personnel

Dear Ms Goodfellow,

I am responding to your job posting on Hotjobs.com for a legal administrator of a law firm. I wrote to you on [date] about law administrator positions in the _____ area. I have attached another CV of my educational background and employment history. I am very interested in this position.

I have been a legal administrator for two law firms during the past six years. In addition, I have been a law firm consultant for over a year. Besides my law firm experience, I have been a medical administrator for over 10 years. I believe that all of this experience will enable me to manage the law firm for this position very successfully. I possess the management, marketing, computer, accounting/budgeting, financial planning, personnel, and people-oriented skills that would have a very positive impact on this law firm.

I will be in the _____ area later in the month, so I hope we can meet at that time to discuss this position. I look forward to hearing from you, Ms Goodfellow, concerning this position. Thank you for your time and consideration.

Very truly yours,

Jane Swift
020 8123 4567
jane@anyaddress.co.uk

E-mail response to online job posting
(manufacturing)

From: James Swift [manufacturerjs@mindspring.com]
To: CVs@NextPress.com
Cc:
Subject: Warehouse pro committed to productivity

Dear Sir/Madam,

Please accept the attached CV in application for a position with your company that will make use of my extensive background in material handling, shipping, receiving and warehousing. Throughout my career I have demonstrated my loyalty, commitment to excellence and solid work ethic. I am confident that I will make an immediate and long-term contribution to your company.

For the past 26 years, I have been successfully working in manufacturing and warehouse settings. I am a hard working employee who always looks for ways to improve productivity, efficiency and accuracy. In past positions, I have identified ways to reduce down time and waste, as well as methods to increase production.

I am dedicated to the principles of quality, continuous improvement and customer satisfaction. My supervisor has noted my record of 'excellent attendance and dependability' and praised me as 'reliable and highly motivated'.

I would like to meet you to discuss my qualifications. Please call me at the following phone number, or leave a message, to arrange an interview. Thank you for your consideration.

Sincerely,

James Swift
020 8123 4567
james@anyaddress.co.uk

E-mail response to online job posting
(production supervisor)

From: James Swift [productionpro@yahoo.com]
To: hr@TimesXYZ.com
CC:
Subject: Production Super matches your exact requirements

Dear Sir/Madam,

In response to the job posting on your company's Web site, please consider my CV in your search for a Production Supervisor.

With a hi-tech background in Blue Chip companies, I feel well qualified for the position you described. I am presently responsible for the coordination of production in three assembly and test areas which employ 35 personnel. Maintaining control of work of this magnitude and complexity requires my ability to function independently, and a willingness to make decisions quickly and effectively.

I am accustomed to a fast-paced environment where deadlines are a priority and handling multiple jobs simultaneously is the norm. I enjoy a challenge and work hard to attain my goals. Constant negotiations with all levels of management and employees have strengthened my interpersonal skills. I would like very much to discuss with you how I could contribute to your organization.

I am seeking an opportunity to excel in a more dynamic company and am looking forward to relocating to the _____ area.

Please contact me at your earliest convenience so that I may share with you my background and enthusiasm for the job. Thank you for your time and consideration.

Sincerely,

James Swift
020 8123 4567
james@anyaddress.co.uk

Response to newspaper advertisement (health care management)

This applicant wants to move to an administrative position in the field of health care; thus we highlighted her leadership and administrative skills.

Jane Swift   18 Park Street, London X1 0BB
                                                          020 8123 4567
                                                          jswift586@hotmail.com

February 15, 20–

Human Resources Coordinator
Sunny Home Nursing Service   *We make a living by what we get,*
Industry Square   *but we make a life by what we give.*
London X2 2EF   *—Winston Churchill*

Re: ADMINISTRATOR OF HEALTH CARE SERVICES

Dear Human Resource Coordinator,

Your recent classified ad in the *Healthcare Journal* caught my eye. As an experienced registered nurse, I am currently investigating career opportunities in the field of management in the health care industry where my highly developed skills will nicely transcend. The enclosed CV reflects an exceptionally viable candidate for the above-named position.

I am a well-established native of this area with a background as programme director, school nurse, operating room circulator, and charge nurse in clinic, ED, OR, and hospital floor environments. The following skills and characteristics are reason to take a closer look at my credentials. I am:

- **strong in handling multiple tasks and multifaceted situations while maintaining satisfactory interpersonal relationships with staff, physicians, patients, students, and families.**
- **an expert at ensuring compliance with regulations while keeping costs within budget.**
- **talented in prioritizing issues and tasks and visualizing the 'big' picture when considering the long-term effects of my decisions.**
- **an outcome-oriented self-starter with superior organizational and administrative skills.**

After reviewing my CV, you will discover that my qualifications are a good match for this position. The opportunity for a personal interview to further discuss employment possibilities would be mutually beneficial. You may reach me at 020 8123 4567 to schedule an appointment at a time convenient to you. In the meantime, thank you for your time and consideration.

Sincerely,

Jane Swift

Jane Swift

Enclosure: CV

Response to newspaper advertisement
(speech therapist)

A speech therapist in a local school district, this candidate is looking for an adjunct faculty position with a community college.

Jane Swift

020 8123 4567   18 Park Street, London X1 0BB   janeswift@aol.com

January 12, 20–

Ms Alexandra Kinkead
Director of Human Resources
City Community College
Industry Square
London X2 2EF

Dear Ms Kinkead,

Your recent advertisement for a speech therapist has captured my serious interest. I am confident that my 25 years' experience as a speech therapist in the Central School provides me with the capabilities to fulfil the **Voice and Articulation** position mentioned in the ad. Accordingly, I have enclosed a CV that briefly outlines my professional history.

Some key points you may find relevant to this opportunity include:

✔ *Experience assessing needs of and providing instruction to disabled people. In my current position, I work one-to-one with students having hearing loss, emotional disorders, ADHD, autism, and other physical disabilities impacting their ability to acquire speech. I also develop IEPs and participate in the CSE process to define students' needs and implement instruction plans.*
✔ *Excellent leadership skills, with experience mentoring co-workers. Currently, I mentor speech therapists and teachers working with hearing-impaired students, as well as direct the activities of two other speech therapists.*
✔ *A master's degree in Speech Pathology, plus Certification as a Speech and Hearing Disabled Teacher. In addition, I have attended workshops in Phonemic Awareness, Autism, and Pervasive Developmental Disorders.*

In my current role, I am accountable for addressing the needs of approximately 300 primary and secondary school students with various speech deficiencies. I believe that my knowledge and expertise would allow me to effectively serve your students in this Voice and Articulation instructional role. I would enjoy speaking with you in person to discuss in fuller detail how my qualifications can fulfil your needs. Please contact me via phone or e-mail to arrange a mutually convenient date and time for us to meet.

Thank you for your time and consideration. I look forward to talking with you soon.

Sincerely,

Jane Swift

Jane Swift

Enclosure

Response to newspaper advertisement
(hydrogeologist)

Applying for positions in a newly emerging scientific discipline; her CV requires a heavy emphasis on educational background information.

Jane Swift
18 Park Street, London X1 0BB
020 8123 4567 • janeswift@msw.com

June 30, 20–

Human Resources Department
ABC
Industry Square
London X2 2EF

RE: Position of Hydrogeologist/Groundwater Modeller, Company Job ID: ACHZ4121-234059, AJB Reference Number: 4950495, Job ID #0000BZ/BBBB

Dear Human Resources Representative,

I learned about your position description for a Hydrogeologist/Groundwater Modeller with great interest, as my qualifications match your requirements for this position. Therefore, please accept my CV for your review and allow me to explain briefly how I can contribute to the future success of ABC.

With an MSc in Hydrologic Sciences and over 7 years of research experience, I have developed a strong background in advanced theories of solute transport modelling; consequently, I have developed effective quantitative skills and a practical understanding of the fundamental principles and concepts associated with hydrogeology.

My CV will provide additional details regarding my educational background and professional experience. Beyond these qualifications, it may be helpful for you to know that I have worked successfully in both independent and team project environments, adapt readily to rapidly changing work conditions, and enjoy the prospect of contributing to ABC's '80-year reputation as a water industry leader' in the advancement of hydrogeologic and groundwater projects.

I would welcome the opportunity to interview for this position and discuss the results you can expect from me as a member of your team. Thank you for your time and consideration.

Sincerely,

Jane Swift

Jane Swift

Enclosure

Response to newspaper advertisement
(customer service representative)

An ad response with requested salary history.

James Swift
18 Park Street, London X1 0BB • 020 8123 4567 • swift123@custsrv.net

----

February 4, 20–

Mr Josh Williams
Personnel Director
ABC Ltd
Industry Square
London X2 2EF

Dear Mr Williams,

In response to your open position announcement in *Newsday* for a customer service representative, I am forwarding my CV for your review and consideration. Ideally, this position will make optimal use of my experience working in capacities that require strong interpersonal communication and customer needs assessment skills, an ability to interface effectively with internal/external contacts, and a skill for ensuring the accurate, timely processing of electronic, verbal, and written information.

Since 1994, I have held longstanding positions of increased responsibility for leading financial services organizations, in charge of tracking, monitoring, reviewing, and processing of account and market-related data. In these positions, I have proved and continue to prove myself as a capable, take-charge team player with an ability to coordinate diversified departmental and customer support functions. Combined with my ability to proficiently manage and train others on the complexities of comprehensive databases and improve workflow efficiencies, I am confident that I would be an asset to your customer service organization.

I would welcome the opportunity to meet you for an in-depth interview. Thank you for your review and consideration. I look forward to hearing from you soon.

Sincerely

James Swift

James Swift

Salary Requirement:
£36,000–£44,000

Salary History:
XYZ Financial Group: Starting £29,000; Ending £40,000
Credit Checkers: Starting £20,000; Ending £26,000

Response to newspaper advertisement
(sales associate)

An entry-level cover letter to convince the employer that he can tackle a full-time job even though he is still at university.

JAMES SWIFT

September 3, 20–

Mr John Relka
Sales Manager
ABC Sports Outfitters
Industry Square
London X2 2EF

Re: Sales Associate Position

Dear Mr Relka,

If you are searching for a success-driven Sales Associate who is a hard worker and an innovator, look no further. Highlights of my achievements include the following:

● Awarded with three plaques and nominated for Sales Award for exemplary sales performance.
● Started a business from scratch and grew customer base using multiple marketing methods.
● Earned most of my own university expenses for the last four years.

Although I will not graduate until December, I am eager to start work as soon as possible – either full- or part-time. I am certain that I can balance the responsibilities of a Sales Associate position with my studies, because I have successfully handled employment with a full course load in the past.

My CV is enclosed for your consideration. I believe that I can make a positive contribution to ABC Sports Outfitters and look forward to discussing my qualifications in detail.

I will call you next week to arrange for a meeting at a mutually convenient time. Thank you for your consideration.

Sincerely,

James Swift

James Swift

Enclosure

18 Park Street   •   London X1 0BB   •   020 8123 4567   •   jswift@dotresume.com

Response to newspaper advertisement
(skilled labourer)

This cover letter had to overcome an obvious 'overqualification' barrier.

James Swift

18 Park Street   •   London X1 0BB   •   jswift555@yahoo.com   •   020 8123 4567

Tuesday, 11 November, 20–

Mr Drake Norris
ABC Ltd
Industry Square
London X2 2EF

Dear Mr Norris,

When I saw your announcement for a skilled labourer at ABC Ltd, I made writing this letter my first priority. Of course, I've already applied online. But, the more I thought about this opportunity, the more it seemed a perfect match for both of us. And so I wanted you to have a good deal more than the usual, impersonal, application.

I think you deserve to see the contributions I can make to the ABC team at once. That's why you'll find my CV different from others you may have run across. In place of the usual 'objective statement,' you'll read about four productivity-building capabilities I can bring to the job. And, right below them, are seven examples of the kinds of contributions I've made to my employers.

But I am concerned that you may think I am 'overqualified'. To put that in plain language, you may feel I will be bored by the job. In fact, your position fits in nicely with my goal of getting my degree in Aerospace Engineering. I can't think of a better opportunity to see the OT&E process at work than being 'in the trenches' on a project like yours.

I do best when I can learn about my employer's special needs. May I call in a few days to explore how I might fit best onto your team?

Sincerely,

James Swift

James Swift

Encl.: CV

Response to newspaper advertisement
(assessment coordinator)

18 Park Street, London X1 0BB   **JANE SWIFT**
020 8123 4567
jane@anyaddress.co.uk

2 PAGES VIA FAX   [Date]
DEPT HD 020 7123 4567

Your advertisement in *The Times*, on 9 June, 2000, for an **Assessment Coordinator**
seems to perfectly match my background and experience. As the International Brand
Coordinator for ABC, I coordinated meetings, prepared presentations and materials,
organized a major off-site conference, and supervised an assistant. I believe that I am an
excellent candidate for this position as I have illustrated below:

YOUR REQUIREMENTS

A highly motivated, diplomatic,
flexible, quality-driven professional

MY QUALIFICATIONS

Successfully managed project teams involving
different business units. The defined end results
were achieved on every project.

Exceptional organizational skills
and attention to detail

Planned the development and launch of the
ABC Heritage Edition bottle series. My
former manager enjoyed leaving the 'details'
and follow-through to me. Undertook project
management training.

Degree and minimum 3 years
relevant business experience

BA from London University (1994). 5+ years
business experience in productive,
professional environments.

Computer literacy

Extensive knowledge of Windows &
Macintosh applications.

I'm interested in this position because it fits well with my new career focus in the human
resources field. Currently, I am enrolled on an adult career planning and development
certificate programme and working at XYZ.

I have enclosed my CV to provide more information on my strengths and career
achievements. If after reviewing my material you believe that there is a match, please
ring me. Thank you for your consideration.

Yours faithfully,

Jane Swift

Jane Swift

enclosure

Response to newspaper advertisement
(office administrator)

JANE SWIFT
18 Park Street, London X1 0BB
020 8123 4567   jane@anyaddress.co.uk

[Date]

Philip _____
[title]
ABC Ltd
Industry Square
London X2 2EF

Dear Mr _____,

Your notice for an **Office Administrator** caught my attention because my background appears to parallel your needs. Please refer to the enclosed CV for a summary of my qualifications. I am sure you have been flooded with hundreds of qualified applicants; please allow me to explain why you would want to call me first.

   I am very **self-sufficient** and able to **work independently with little supervision**. With little formal training, I have taken the initiative to learn about and remain current with my company's products, processes and expectations. I am looked at as **an information resource** and enjoy sharing my knowledge with others. I also enjoy **managing projects** and **planning meetings, trips and special events**.

   I am always looking for ways to **streamline processes** and become more efficient. I have **developed systems and processes** using available software to automate production reporting, notify customers of changes, and inform the field staff of corporate changes or initiatives. When supervising clerical staff, I always try to **plan ahead** to make the best use of their time.

   I work well with executives, sales representatives, customers, vendors and co-workers, and demonstrate strong interpersonal communication skills and good judgement. I always try to listen closely and understand what others need. Then, I look for ways to help solve the problem. I have particularly found that listening, without interrupting, can diffuse a tense situation and allow the issue to be resolved more quickly with a positive outcome.

   I am confident that I can deliver similar results for ABC Ltd. I would appreciate the opportunity to speak to you to schedule an appointment and provide you with more information. Thank you for your time and consideration; I look forward to speaking to you soon.

Sincerely,

Jane Swift

Jane Swift

enclosure

Response to newspaper advertisement
(legal secretary)

JANE SWIFT
18 Park Street, London X1 0BB
020 8123 4567   jane@address.co.uk

[Date]

Emily _____
[Title]
General Council of the Bar
Industry Square
London X2 2EF

RE: GENERAL COUNCIL OF THE BAR, LEGAL SECRETARY

Dear Mrs _____,

   It is with continued interest and enthusiasm that I respond to your advertisement for Legal Secretary to the General Council of the Bar. I believe that my education and experience combine to create a perfect match for the position, and would appreciate careful consideration of my credentials as presented below and within my CV, enclosed.

   It has long been my dream to pursue a career in the legal arena, and my goal to associate with the top professionals in the field. Where better to continue my professional development than within the heart of the organization as a provider of administrative support to members of the Bar itself!

   Although a relative newcomer to the field, I have earned my HNC in Legal Studies and Paralegal Certificate. With more than two years of experience after qualifying, providing administrative and clerical support in private practice, I am confident that I possess the expertise and dedication that will make an immediate and significant contribution to the efficiency and organization of the Council.

   If you are looking for a legal support professional who is committed to the highest standards of performance, relates well to others, is self-directing and highly motivated, and is looking for a long-term employment relationship, please contact me to arrange an interview. I will make myself available at your earliest convenience.

   Thank you for your consideration; I look forward to the opportunity to speak to you soon.

Sincerely yours,

Jane Swift

Jane Swift

enclosure (CV and Professional References)

Response to newspaper advertisement
(accounting manager)

James Swift
18 Park Street, London X1 0BB
020 8123 4567   james@anyaddress.co.uk

[Date]

Phillip _____
[Title]
ABC Ltd
Industry Square
London X2 2EF

Dear Mr _____,

Re: File No. 213

I have nine years of accounting experience and am responding to your recent advertisement for an Accounting Manager. Please allow me to highlight my skills as they relate to your stated requirements:

Your Requirements	**My Experience**
A recognized accounting qualification plus several years of practical accounting experience.	Obtained CIMA membership and have over four years' practical experience as an Accounting Manager.
Excellent people skills and demonstrated ability to motivate staff.	Effectively managed a staff of 24 including two supervisors.
Strong administrative and analytical skills.	Assisted in the development of a base reference library with Microsoft Excel for 400 clients.
Good oral and written communication skills.	Trained four new supervisors via daily coaching sessions, communication meetings and technical skill sessions.

I believe this background provides the management skills you require for this position. I would welcome the opportunity for a personal interview to discuss my qualifications further.

Yours truly,

James Swift

James Swift

enclosure

Response to newspaper advertisement
(international sales manager)

Jane Swift
18 Park Street, London X1 0BB
020 8123 4567   jane@anyaddress.co.uk

[Date]

Phillip _____
[Title]
ABC Ltd
Industry Square
London X2 2EF

Dear Mr _____,

Re: International Sales Manager, *Globe & Mail*, — September, 20 —

I was recently speaking with Mr _____ from your firm and he strongly
recommended that I send you a copy of my CV. Knowing the requirements for the
position, he felt that I would be an ideal candidate. For more than eleven years I have
been involved in international sales management, with seven years directly in the
aerospace industry. My qualifications for the position include:

- establishing sales offices in France, Germany and Italy;
- recruiting and managing a group of 24 international sales representatives;
- providing training programmes for all of the international staff, which included full briefing
  on our own products as well as competitor lines;
- obtaining 42%, 33% and 31% of the French, German and Italian markets, respectively,
  dealing with all local engine and airframe manufacturers; and
- generating more than £32 million in sales with excellent margins.

My Bachelor of Science degree in Electrical Engineering was obtained from the
University of _____ and my languages include French, German and Italian.

I feel confident that an interview would demonstrate that my expertise in setting up
representative organizations and training and managing an international sales
department would be an excellent addition to your growing aerospace corporation.

I look forward to meeting with you, Mr _____, and will ring you to follow up on
this letter the week of [date] _____.

Yours truly,

Jane Swift

Jane Swift

enclosure

Response to newspaper advertisement
(executive assistant)

JAMES SWIFT
18 Park Street • London X1 0BB
020 8123 4567   james@anyaddress.co.uk

[Date]

Box 9412
London X2 2EF

Dear _____,

I was very pleased to learn of the need for an Executive Assistant in your company from your recent advertisement in _____. I believe the qualities you seek are well matched by my track record:

Your Needs
Independent Self-Starter

My Qualifications
- Served as company liaison between sales representatives, controlling commissions and products.
- Controlled cash flow, budget planning and bank reconciliation for three companies.
- Assisted in the promotion of a restaurant within a private placement sales effort, creating sales materials and communicating with investors.

Computer Experience

- Used Lotus in preparing financial spreadsheet for private placement memoranda and Macintosh to design brochures and flyers.
- Have vast experience with both computer programming and the current software packages.

Compatible Background

- Spent 5 years overseas and speak French.
- Served as an executive assistant to four corporate heads.

A CV is enclosed that covers my experience and qualifications in greater detail. I would appreciate the opportunity to discuss my credentials in a personal interview.

Sincerely,

James Swift

James Swift

enclosure

Power phrases

Consider using adaptations of these key phrases in your responses to newspaper advertisements.

I believe that I am particularly well qualified for your position and would like to have the opportunity to meet you to explore how I may be of value to your organization.

Your advertisement 5188 in the 25th March edition of The _____ has piqued my interest. This position has strong appeal to me.

I am confident that with my abilities I can make an immediate and valuable contribution to _____.

I would be pleased if you contacted me for an interview.

I was recently speaking with Mr _____ from your firm and he strongly recommended that I send you a copy of my CV. Knowing the requirements for the position, he felt that I would be an ideal candidate.

I've had both large and small company experience and it is my preference to work in a smaller operation where goals are measurable, results are noticeable and contributions really make a difference!

I feel confident that an interview would demonstrate that my expertise in setting up representative organizations, and training and managing an international sales department, would be an excellent addition to your growing _____ company.

I look forward to meeting you, Mr _____, and will give you a ring to follow up on this letter the week of —th September.

The opportunity to work with your client is appealing to me, and I would appreciate an opportunity to discuss the position further. I look forward to hearing from you soon.

I believe this background provides the management skills you require for this position. I would welcome the opportunity for a personal interview to discuss my qualifications further.

In response to your advertisement, please consider my CV in your search for a Sales Service Coordinator.

I look forward to hearing from you in the near future to schedule an interview at a time convenient to you, during which I hope to learn more about your company's plans and goals and how I might contribute to the success of its service team.

I am accustomed to a fast-paced environment where deadlines are a priority and handling multiple jobs simultaneously is the norm. I enjoy a challenge and work hard to attain my goals. Constant negotiations with all levels of management and employees have strengthened my interpersonal skills. I would like very much to discuss with you how I could contribute to your organization.

I am seeking an opportunity to excel in a dynamic company and am looking forward to relocating to _____.

Please contact me at your earliest convenience so that I may share with you my background and enthusiasm for the job.

Your advertisement captured my attention.

My personal goal is simple: I wish to be a part of an organization that wants to excel in both _____ and _____. I believe that if I had the opportunity of an interview with you it would be apparent that my skills are far-reaching.

Although I'm far more interested in a fine company and an intriguing challenge than merely in money, you should know that in recent years my compensation has been in the range of £30,000 to £40,000.

May we set up a time to talk?

What you need and what I can do sound like a match!

Please find enclosed a copy of my CV for your review. I believe the combination of my _____ education and my business experience offers me the unique opportunity to make a positive contribution to your firm.

As you will note in my CV, I have not only 'grown up' in and with the Operations and Warehousing area of a major (clothing) (consumer products) company, I have also established my expertise and my value to a discriminating and brilliant employer who depended upon me – on a daily basis – to represent and protect his interests and contribute significantly to his profitability.... I am seeking an opportunity to replicate this situation and again use my considerable abilities to dedicate myself to the profitability of my employer.

I am available to meet you to discuss my qualifications at a time convenient to you. I can be reached at _____. I would like to thank you in advance for your time and any consideration you may give me. I look forward to hearing from you.

Having been born and raised in the _____ area and wishing to return to this area to work as a _____, I have been researching _____ firms that offer the type of experience for which my education and work experience would be of mutual benefit. Highlights of my attached CV include: _____.

Please consider my qualifications for the position of _____ which you advertised.

As you will note on the enclosed CV, the breadth of my expertise covers a wide area of responsibilities, thereby providing me with insights into the total operation.

Recently, I saw an advertisement in the _____ for a position as a Technical Trainer. My candidacy for this position is advanced by my experience in three areas: training, support and a technological background.

I thrive on challenge and feel that my skills and experience are easily transferable.

I would appreciate an opportunity to discuss my abilities in more depth, and am available for an interview at your earliest convenience.

Is the ideal candidate for the position of _____ highly motivated, professional and knowledgeable in all functions concerning _____? Well, you may be interested to know that a person possessing these qualities, and much more, is responding to your advertisement in the _____ for this position.

I very much enjoy working in a team environment and the rewards associated with group contribution.

The skills you require seem to match my professional strengths.

I have a strong background in telemarketing small and medium-size businesses in the _____ district and outlying areas.

I look forward to hearing from you soon to set up an appointment at a time convenient to you. Please feel free to ring me at my office on _____ or leave a message at my home number, _____.

As a recent MBA graduate, my professional job experience is necessarily limited. However, I believe that you will find, and previous employers will verify, that I exhibit intelligence, common sense, initiative, maturity and stability, and I am eager to make a positive contribution to your organization.

I read with a great deal of interest your advertisement in the 20 October _____, issue of _____.

Please allow me to highlight some of my achievements which relate to your requirements: _____.

I would greatly appreciate the opportunity to discuss this position in a personal interview. I may be contacted at _____ to arrange a meeting.

I would appreciate an opportunity to meet you. At present I am working as a temp but am available to meet you whenever would be convenient for you. I look forward to meeting you.

Thank you for taking the time recently to respond to my questions concerning a _____ position with _____.

I will be in your area on Friday —th December, and will call you early next week to see if we might schedule a meeting at that time.

This experience has provided me with a keen appreciation of the general practice of _____.

A salary of £30,000 would be acceptable; however, my main concern is to find employment where there is potential for growth.

'Cold' cover letter to a potential employer (entry-level network administrator)

Network administrator seeking entry-level opportunity; highlights his certifications to emphasize recent professional development. Good idea when attempting ground-floor position.

JAMES SWIFT

18 Park Street • London X1 0BB • 020 8123 4567 • js@hotmail.com

Dear Sir or Madam,

I have received my **MCP Certification**, and I am currently working on my **A++ Network Certification**. I am seeking an opportunity that will enable me to use my training and hands-on technical exposure within an **entry-level Network Administrator** position. A brief highlight of the skills and values I would bring to your organization include:

● Knowledge of installation, configuration, troubleshooting and repair of sophisticated, state-of-the-art software and hardware developed through recent computer operations training.
● Analytical, research, troubleshooting, interpersonal and organizational skills developed through on-the-job training within an IT environment.
● Proven success in prioritizing time, completing projects and meeting deadlines under time-sensitive circumstances, achieving stellar results.
● An energetic, enthusiastic, and 'people-driven' communication style.

Since a CV can neither fully detail all my skills and accomplishments, nor predict my potential to your organization, I would welcome a personal interview to further explore the merging of my training and knowledge with your **IT** needs.

Very truly yours,

James Swift

James Swift

Enclosure

'Cold' cover letter to a potential employer (entry-level librarian)

Jane, who emigrated from Poland, has completed her master's in library science and is looking for her first full-time position in her career field.

Jane Swift

020 8123 4567   18 Park Street • London X1 0BB   janeswift@nsn.com

November 15, 20–

Mr Jeffery Devine, Library Division Director
Anytown Public Library
Industry Square
London X2 2EF

Dear Mr Devine,

Does your library anticipate the need for an **Entry-Level Research or Reference Librarian or Cataloguer?** With my recent MSc in Information and Library Management from a CILIP accredited programme, as well as internship experience in the reference department of academic and business libraries, perhaps I can be of service.

My CV is enclosed for your review. You will find evidence of my librarianship training, library database and computer skills, and work history. What you will not immediately see on my CV are my character traits and achievements – allow me to list some of them for you that I believe are relevant:

✔ *Hard-working, determined achiever* – *I set my sights high, whether attaining a degree at the University of London in a demanding* **MSc Degree** *programme, or responding to reference requests with a high-level of customer service and promptness (within 1–3 hours).*
✔ *Information technology savvy and fast learner* – *My references will attest to how quickly I assimilated knowledge of library databases, computer software, and integrated library automation systems. With hands-on experience using* **Voyager Module, AACR2r, LC classification scheme, MARC format, and OCLC,** *as well as* **Lexis-Nexis, Dow-Jones, Dialog Web and Classic,** *I have worked with diverse reference materials such as legal, business, genealogy documents, as well as periodicals.*
✔ *Proactive problem-solver and team player* – *using my broad foreign language skills (Polish, Russian, Slovak, German, Latin) allowed me to problem-solve with confidence and correctly catalogue foreign language materials while serving a* **reference library internship** *with* **The Anytown County Library.** *As an* **intern cataloguer,** *I worked cooperatively with others in serial publication cataloguing and serial control, achieving high rates of daily production.*

Providing high-level customer service and efficiency is my goal in library services and support. My knowledge and practical use of Internet resources and navigational tools, combined with my experience with library databases, affords you the opportunity to hire an entry-level professional with proven librarianship success. May we meet soon to discuss your needs? I will call your office next week to schedule a mutually convenient appointment, if that is agreeable with you. Thank you for your time and consideration.

Sincerely,

Jane Swift

Jane Swift

Enclosure

'Cold' cover letter to a potential employer (manager)

Concerned that his company is not doing well financially, James had decided to 'test the waters' for another position similar to those he has held in the past.

James Swift
18 Park Street
London X1 0BB

020 8123 4567
jswift@hotmail.com

December 12, 20–

Mr Jacob Abernathy
ABC Services
Industry Square
London X2 2EF

Dear Mr Abernathy,

More than ever, good companies need proven performers who can get results in competitive industries and a tough economy, whether working independently or leading teams. If you are in need of a Warehouse Manager, Inventory Control Specialist, Production Manager, or Assembly Order Fulfilment Supervisor, consider my track record:

✔ Efficiently scheduled assembly, material handlers, and warehouse personnel, and closely monitored interplant transfers of raw materials from 20 warehouses. Assembly production and distribution procedures yielded high levels of productivity: 90% on-time delivery, including emergency orders, of up to £1 million in SKUs per week. (Expediter/Production Dept. Scheduler, XYZ Ltd.)

✔ Developed cooperative relationships with field sales reps of major corporations, such as DEF Ltd, GH Healthcare, and IJK Ltd, and served as liaison with in-house account executives and customer service reps at The LMN Group, to streamline receiving and shipping operations and upgrade quality control. (Warehouse Manager, The OPQ Group)

✔ As final assembly and inspection member of 4-person team, met heavy production schedule (35 to 60 complex, fabricated units per day) with 6% or less error rate. (Order Fulfilment Clerk, XYZ Ltd.)

✔ Working as part of a team, created, tested, packaged, and directed to shipping custom ship sets of complex hose assemblies, meeting deadlines 99-plus per cent of the time. Utilized quality assurance testing methods, including pressure testing of assembled units, to ensure highest level of customer satisfaction. (Hose Fabrication Technician, XYZ Ltd.)

I am confident I can deliver similar results for your company.

With well-rounded experience in assembly, expediting and scheduling, shipping and receiving, order fulfilment, customer service, sales, supervision and training, and a 15-year track record of meeting deadlines in demanding (even emergency) situations, I believe I have the proven skills that can benefit your company.

James Swift
Page 2 of 2

In addition, I realize it is hard-working and cooperative people who deliver results. My focus on teamwork and productivity has proven successful in my past assignments. I am confident I can convince you that I have the technical experience and knowledge that you need, as well as the intangible qualities – enthusiasm, strong work ethic, dedication and dependability – to get the job done right.

May we meet soon to discuss your needs? I will contact your office next week to schedule a mutually convenient appointment, if that is agreeable with you. Thank you for your consideration.

Sincerely,

James Swift

James Swift

Enclosure

'Cold' cover letter to a potential employer (mental health)

An applicant with a MSW seeking to advance his career.

James Swift

Dear Sir or Madam,

Throughout my career, I have held increasingly complex positions within the Mental Health Service, gaining extensive experience in working both with patients and in administrative functions. My particular areas of expertise are:

- Physical Medicine and Rehabilitation
- Adult Intervention
- Family Counselling
- Legal Issues
- Government Regulations
- Child Evaluation

My greatest strength lies in my ability to communicate with all types of people and different levels of professionals. Being able to work with patients, physicians, legal officers, and family members has enabled me to be a highly effective therapist and an advocate for the patient and the patient's family. As an Administration official, I have been inducted into the intricacies of the government and have been able to gain a thorough understanding of the workings of various government agencies as they relate to mental health, including the Benefits Agency, Department of Health, and other entities.

I feel my knowledge and strengths would be best applied as a consultant or private Mental Rehabilitation Therapist. Further, I desire to return to a more focused health care organization such as yours and would welcome an opportunity to interview with you in person.

I look forward to speaking with you at your earliest convenience and appreciate your time in reviewing my credentials and qualifications. I am confident that my professional knowledge and strengths, combined with my dedication, work ethic, and energy, will add measurable value to your organization. Thank you for your consideration.

Sincerely,

James Swift

James Swift

Enclosure

---

40 Land Avenue • London X1 2EP • 020 8123 4567 • jswift@msn.com

'Cold' cover letter to a potential employer (senior customer service specialist)

This candidate's most impressive qualifications are summarized in an eye-catching bulleted list.

Jane Swift
18 Park Road
London X1 0BB
Home: 020 8123 4567
Mobile: 07850 515536
swift@dotresume.com

March 3, 20–

Ms Jayne Longnecker
Customer Service Manager
ABC Insurance Company
Industry Square
London X2 2EF

Re: Senior Customer Service Specialist

Dear Ms Longnecker,

Are you looking for a Senior Customer Service Specialist who is:

- A consistent top performer with a strong desire to get the job done?
- A team player, able to achieve results through coordination with employees in all functional areas?
- An effective communicator with excellent writing, training, and telephone skills?
- Able to learn quickly, analyse complex information, and find solutions to problems?
- Organized, thorough, and precise?

If so, you will be interested in my qualifications. I have a degree in business administration and seven years of experience in the insurance/financial industry, serving in diverse roles as customer relations adviser and calculations processor. For more than a year and a half, I have consistently received the highest ratings in my unit despite the fact that the difficult cases frequently find their way to my desk. I have also contributed to my team by putting in extra time to clear backlogs and analysing existing procedures to devise more efficient methods of operation.

My CV is enclosed for your review. I believe that I can make a positive contribution to ABC Insurance Company and look forward to meeting you to discuss my qualifications in detail. Thank you for your time and consideration.

Sincerely,

Jane Swift

Jane Swift

Enclosure

'Cold' cover letter to a potential employer
(research professional)

James is a data specialist working for the government, compiling birth/death and census statistics.
He wants to enter the private sector to do more consumer/product research projects.

James Swift

MARKET RESEARCH ANALYST

Dear Sir/Madam,

As a research professional, I understand that success depends on a strong commitment to **customer satisfaction**. Executing the basics and using logic and reasoning to identify the strengths and weaknesses of alternative solutions, conclusions or approaches to problems are key to increasing performance and market share. I believe that my background and education reflect a commitment and ability to find solutions to these challenges. I developed excellent skills in **project coordination and the design and development of research projects** that increased the effectiveness of my organization.

I am considered an energetic, aggressive, and innovative leader who is extremely client-oriented.

My position encompasses multiple tasks and responsibilities that include:

- Examining and analysing statistical data to forecast future trends and to identify potential markets.

- Designing and implementing new formats for logging and transferring information while working as part of a team researching data and statistics.

Thank you for your consideration. I approach my work with a strong sense of urgency, working well under pressure and change. I look forward to meeting with you personally so that we may discuss how I may make a positive contribution to your organization.

Sincerely yours,

James Swift

James Swift

Enclosure

124 Liberty Street • London X2 2EF • 020 8123 4567 • jswift53@excite.com

'Cold' cover letter to a potential employer (personal trainer)

Moving into fitness training after a long and successful career in general management, sales, and customer relationship management.

JAMES SWIFT
18 Park Street • London X1 0BB
020 8123 4567 • jswift@hotmail.com

Dear Sir or Madam,

Reflecting on my professional sales and management experience within the marine industry, it is at this point in my career I am seeking to pursue a long-term personal and professional goal of a challenging opportunity as a Personal Trainer/Strength Coach within a health club, physical therapy and/or fitness facility. Let me briefly highlight the skills, values and contributions I will bring to your organization:

- **Certified Personal Trainer/Health Fitness Instructor at leading training facility.**

- Possess over 25 years' health club experience with most types of cardiovascular, plate and free-weight systems.

- Proven ability to plan and implement training programmes through experience as a Personal Trainer for a health club.

- Strong general management, sales, marketing and customer relationship management expertise developed through 16 years as an Owner/Operator of a marine business.

- Comprehensive experience in human relations, within the retail/service arena, has characterized me as considerate, dependable, honest, straightforward, hard-working, and personable.

Since a CV can neither fully detail all my skills and accomplishments, nor predict my potential in your organization, I would welcome the opportunity to meet and discuss the possible merging of my talent and experience with your **personal trainer** needs.

Very truly yours,

James Swift

James Swift

Enclosure

'Cold' cover letter to a potential employer (registered nurse)

An applicant moving out of the Navy, where he gained a great deal of experience with trauma treatment and crisis management.

JAMES SWIFT
18 Park Street • London X1 0BB • 020 8723 4567 • james@cs.com

January 12, 20–

Ms Florence Blackwell, RN
Director of Nursing
ABC Medical Centre
Industry Square
London X2 2EF

Dear Ms Blackwell,

In anticipation of completing my Navy service in April, 20–, I am seeking a civilian position that will capitalize on my experience and training as a Registered Nurse. I believe that my clinical background and specialized training in emergency response and crisis management would make me an asset to your nursing staff. With this in mind, I have enclosed a CV for your review that outlines my credentials.

Some key points you may find relevant to a nursing position with your facility include:

- **Caring for a broad array of patients, ranging from infants to senior citizens, and including post-operative, medical, infectious disease, oncology, and end-of-life scenarios.**
- **Developing rapport with diverse cultural groups, both in clinical and social settings. The patients I have dealt with cut across the full spectrum of ethnic and socioeconomic strata, from enlisted personnel to flag officers and their dependants. In my current assignment in Tokyo, I have had the opportunity to experience the local culture and interact with the local population.**
- **Completing training and engaging in field exercises that have prepared me for deployment to combat zones. This is relevant to a civilian setting because it encompasses mass casualty treatment, nuclear and biohazard treatment, and field hospital training, all of which relate to disaster response in a civilian community.**

I am confident that my dedication to caring for patients and capacity to function as an integral part of a treatment team would allow me to make a significant contribution to the health and well being of your patients. I would enjoy discussing with you how I can fulfil your needs in a clinical nursing role. Please contact me via phone or e-mail to arrange a mutually convenient date and time for an initial interview.

Thank you for your time and consideration. I look forward to speaking with you soon.

Sincerely,

James Swift

James Swift

Enclosure

'Cold' cover letter to a potential employer (entertainment industry)

This letter begins with an attention-grabbing opening followed by statements indicating that she understands the high-energy demands and realities of the entertainment industry. She ends the letter with a call to action.

Jane Swift

18 Park Street/London X1 0BB
Home 020 8123 4567/Mobile 07850 515536
js@email.com

[Date]

[Name]
[Address]
[City, Post Code]

Dear [Salutation],

Perhaps your company is in search of a highly motivated recent graduate who is passionate about the Entertainment Industry and has the energy and drive to 'pay her dues,' acquire knowledge and advance professionally. If so, then we should talk!!

I offer a combination of creative talents and a strong work ethic as well as the following qualifications:

- BA in Communications from the University of London
- Hands-on experience directing, acting in and producing short independent and student films
- Realistic understanding of the demands of the entertainment industry, gained through work experience for TV production company
- Operating knowledge of a variety of audio and video equipment

While my enclosed CV provides a brief overview of my background, I look forward to a personal meeting at which time we can discuss your needs and my qualifications in detail. I will call you next week to arrange a meeting; in the meantime, you can contact me at the above numbers. Thank you in advance for your time and consideration.

Sincerely,

Jane Swift

Jane Swift

Enclosure

'Cold' cover letter to a potential employer (management)

James's recent experience with his last employer focused on IT implementation and project management. He seeks to gain a project management position with an IT consulting firm where he can make use of both his technical expertise and his management skills.

JAMES SWIFT

18 Park Street • London X1 0BB
020 8123 4567 • js@earthlink.com

January 12, 20–

Mr Addison Elgar
Director of Client Engagement
ABC Computer Consultants
Industry Square
London X2 2EF

Dear Mr Elgar,

Capitalizing on a career that encompasses substantial IT project management experience and extensive sales/marketing experience, I am seeking a new professional challenge that will combine these skills in a senior account management, project management, or technical leadership role. With this goal in mind, I have enclosed for your review a CV that outlines my qualifications.

Some key points that you may find relevant to a position with your firm include:

- *Managing the technical deployment of six different releases of XYZ's SalesTeamXpert sales force automation tool over the past three years. This has involved ensuring that hardware platforms in the field are prepared to receive the latest release and resolving technical issues impacting end-user training for 6,000 users at 34 sites across the UK.*
- *Building relationships with key decision-makes at FTSE 100 companies while serving as a Marketing Manager for two different firms providing end-to-end transportation solutions for firms importing and exporting materials and products.*
- *Hands-on experience providing desk-side support to end-users; configuring hardware and installing software in the field; and delivering training to end-users and IT specialists.*

I am confident that my knowledge and expertise would allow me to make a meaningful contribution to the success of your firm and its clients. I would enjoy discussing with you in person how my capabilities can match your needs, and will contact you soon to arrange an appropriate time for an initial meeting.

Thank you for your time and consideration. I look forward to speaking with you soon.

Sincerely,

James Swift

James Swift

Enclosure

'Cold' cover letter to a potential employer (radiation safety officer)

This highly skilled and highly educated physicist is applying for the post of Radiation Safety Officer, which is his boss's job, as the boss leaves for another opportunity. He is competing with highly qualified external candidates, and his best asset is his familiarity with the institution, based on existing experience.

James Swift
18 Park Street / London X1 0BB / 020 8123 4567
james@earthlink.com

January 12, 20–

Mr Zachary P. Emerson
University of London
Industry Square
London SX 2EFF

Dear Mr Emerson,

Please accept this letter and the enclosed CV as an expression of my interest in the Radiation Safety Officer position you are currently seeking to fill. I am confident that my education, experience, and familiarity with the University of London Research Centre facilities provide me with the necessary skills to meet or exceed your expectations in this role.

For the past year, I have been a Health Physicist with UL, with responsibility for a variety of functions, including:

- Testing & Monitoring Equipment
- Training Medical Staff
- Ensuring Compliance with Regulations
- Monitoring Staff Exposure
- Achieving CRESO Certification
- Supervising Four Technicians
- Serving on Various Committees
- Consulting with Physicians
- Maintaining Updated Technical Knowledge

Earlier, I held a similar position at University of Scotland's School of Medicine. There I trained and supervised the work of a six-person technical team. I ensured that all equipment, materials, and supplies were in compliance with regulations. Government inspection results were always outstanding. Throughout my career, I have built a reputation for quality, flexibility, and professionalism in all areas. My commitment to health and safety has resulted in a perfect safety record.

I hold two master's degrees, one in Nuclear Engineering from City University, the other in Nuclear Physics from XYZ University in Brazil. I have taught Biophysics at university level. In addition, I speak three languages (English, Portuguese, and Russian). Having lived and worked in other countries I have a sensitivity and understanding of diverse cultures and customs.

I have thoroughly enjoyed working at UL, and would welcome this opportunity to make an even more significant contribution to the success of its mission. I would enjoy discussing my qualifications with you in person and invite you to contact me to arrange an initial interview.

Thank you for your time and consideration. I look forward to speaking with you soon.

Sincerely,

James Swift

James Swift

Enclosure

'Cold' cover letter to a potential employer
(veterinary surgeon)

This veterinary surgeon practices in an elite niche, treating only competitive horses at racetracks. His goal is to split his time between a track in the Southeast during winter months and one in the Northeast during the summer, allowing him to follow the horses throughout the racing year.

JAMES SWIFT
18 Park Street • London X1 0BB • 020 8123 4567

January 12, 20–

Dr Amber Morgenstern
ABC Equine Hospital
Industry Square
London X2 2EF

FAX: 020 8123 4567
E-mail: jswift@juno.com

Dear Dr Morgenstern,

My extensive experience addressing the health and performance needs of elite race horses at major tracks makes me a strong candidate for the opening you recently advertised on the XYZ website. Accordingly, I have attached my CV for your consideration and review.

Some key points you may find relevant include:

- **Strong capacity to function independently and make critical decisions without direct supervision. My knowledge of horses and experience at several major tracks means that I will need minimal orientation to 'hit the ground running'.**
- **An excellent track record of maintaining the health of the elite thoroughbreds and quarter horses, as well as assisting trainers in enhancing the performance of horses by improving their respiratory and general health and dealing with lameness issues (references can be provided).**
- **The ability to effectively evaluate young horses prior to purchase, through observation and diagnostic testing. I routinely produce quality repository radiographs and review radiographs in a repository setting. I also accompany buyers to auctions to assess horses being considered.**
- **Experience assisting trainers setting up effective farm-based training programmes, as well as helping breeders address reproductive health issues.**

I believe that I can be an asset to your organization and would enjoy discussing further how my knowledge, expertise, and professional dedication can address your needs. Please feel free to contact me to arrange either a phone or in-person interview at a mutually convenient date and time.

Thank you for your time and consideration. I look forward to speaking to you soon.

Sincerely,

James Swift

James Swift

Enclosure

'Cold' cover letter to a potential employer (work placement)

A cover letter to apply for a competitive college placement in the financial services industry.

James Swift

Current Address
City University
Park Road
London X1 0BB

Telephone: 020 8123 4567
E-mail: swift@bu.edu

Permanent Address
18 Park St.
London X2 0BB

Telephone: 020 8123 4567

January 13, 20–

Karen Carmichael
ABC Finance Ltd
Industry Square
London X2 2EF
Re: Finance Placement

Dear Ms Carmichael,

Are you looking for a driven overachiever committed to excelling in business and finance?

As a student at City University, I am pursuing a BA in Business Administration with an emphasis on Finance. My passion for financial markets and economics has steadily increased over the last five years and I am committed to developing my career path as a business leader within a major corporation.

I approach all of my work with discipline and focus; as an intern with your organization, I would look forward to effectively contributing to your programme goals. City University, XYZ Academy, and The ABC Club of London have acknowledged my academic and leadership achievements for excellence in academic studies, volunteerism, and peer mentoring.

Please feel free to contact me at my number in London, 020 8123 4567. Thank you for your consideration. I am enthusiastic about working at ABC. My background, professionalism, and enthusiasm will make me an effective member of your team.

Sincerely,

James Swift

James Swift

Enclosure

'Cold' cover letter to a potential employer (teacher)

A letter sent with the CV hard copy as a follow-up to the CV submission via e-mail.

JAMES SWIFT

November 14, 20–

Ms Jennifer Jones
Personnel Coordinator
ABC Language Corporation
Industry Square
London X2 2EF

Dear Ms Jones,

   Although I recently submitted my CV to your office via e-mail, I am submitting the enclosed hard copy as a follow-up. I welcome any questions you might have.

   With this letter, I would like to reiterate my sincere motivation to teach in Japan. My experience as a substitute secondary school teacher has helped me to understand methods of student interaction and reach a level of comfort in the classroom. I strive to build relationships with students – as much as a substitute teacher can – to facilitate classroom activities and inspire the learners. It is something I really enjoy.

   The ABC web site encourages 'all outgoing, dynamic, and flexible people to apply'. In my current position as a flight attendant for XYZ Airlines, I am required to demonstrate these characteristics daily. Communication and quick-thinking skills are a must on board an aircraft full of passengers. Flexibility is essential in the areas of customer service, in interaction with colleagues, and in work scheduling.

   My motivation is indeed genuine, and I look forward to the possibility of discussing the opportunity with you. I will gladly make myself available for a telephone or videoconference interview.

Respectfully,

James Swift

James Swift

Enclosure: One-page CV

18 Park Street • London X1 0BB • 020 8123 4567 • james@jameswift.com

'Cold' cover letter to a potential employer (production supervisor)

Two problems to overcome: moving from automotive service manager to production supervisor and a break in employment of more than a year.

JAMES SWIFT
18 Park Street
London X1 0BB

020 8123 4567
JS5505@bellsouth.net

October 28, 20–

Mr Charles W Worth
Director for Operations
ABC Ltd
Industry Square
London X2 2EF

Dear Mr Worth,

How big is that gap between what the ABC leadership wants from its skilled, semi-skilled and unskilled employees and what the ABC bottom line gets? If you'd like to shrink that costly mismatch, we should explore adding me to your team as your transportation manager.

On the next pages, you'll see more than a half-dozen contributions I have made in this area. They illustrate the five profit-building capabilities I've listed right at the top of the next page. I'd like to put those advantages to work for you right away.

Over the last year, the health of a family member made the most demands upon me and guided my relocation from Bristol to London. Now that problem is resolved and I am ready to return to my first love: helping teams wanting to do well.

If my approach and philosophy appeal to you, please let me suggest a next step. I would like to hear about your special needs in your own words. May I call in a few days to arrange a time to do that?

Sincerely,

James Swift

James Swift

Encl.: CV

'Cold' cover letter to a potential employer (sales professional)

James has two special needs: to show the sales aspect of his previous career as an accountant, and to convince a new employer that his desire to leave his current company was based solely upon having to work in an oversold market.

James Swift   18 Park Street – London X1 0BB
                          020 8123 4567 – 07850 515536 [mobile] – jswift102@charter.net

July 20, 20–

Ms Laura Worth
Sales Manager
ABC Ltd
Industry Square
London X2 2EF

Dear Ms Worth:

I want you to get the credit for adding ROI to the ABC sales team. Specifically, I'd like to become your newest sales professional. And, perhaps the best way to link those two ideas is with this graph that shows how I'm performing right now.

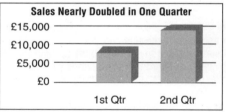

What I do isn't magic. I just work harder and smarter than my competition by finding some profitable way to say 'yes' to every customer and potential customer.

My focus on your sales needs starts on the next pages. I wanted you to see a CV that offers more than the usual recitations of job titles and responsibilities. That's why you'll find six capabilities I want to put at ABC's disposal at once. Backing them up are a dozen examples of sales that show those capabilities in action.

My company values what I do. And, if I thought our market was growing as fast as yours, I would stay with them. While I cannot control market conditions, I am interested in making even greater contributions to my employer. That's why I'm 'testing the waters' with this confidential application.

I do best using the consultative approach to sales. So, as a first step, I'd like to hear about ABC's sales needs in your own words. May I call in a few days to arrange a time to do that?

Sincerely,

James Swift

James Swift

Encl.: CV

'Cold' cover letter to a potential employer (credit account specialist)

Jane wants to affiliate herself with a larger company that offers a more challenging role in analysing and managing financial accounts; she also seeks to take on more responsibility to allow her to grow professionally.

JANE SWIFT
18 Park Street • London X1 0BB • 020 8123 4567

December 8, 20–

Marcy Johnson
ABC Accounting Company
Industry Square
London X2 2EF

Dear Ms Johnson,

As a well-qualified credit account specialist, I demonstrate my ability to effectively communicate with clients, resolve payment issues, and collect on past due payments. I bring over 18 years of accounts receivable experience in addition to being involved in all processing stages of collections. The scope of my experience includes, but is not limited to, commercial, automotive, and manufacturing environments.

My focus is to deliver results and provide superior service by quickly identifying problem areas in accounts receivable and developing a solution strategy to ensure issues are resolved. My expertise lies in my strong ability to build rapport with clients, analyse accounts, and manage all aspects related to my appointed position and areas of responsibilities. I find these qualities to be my greatest assets to offer employers.

Due to an unforeseen circumstance, I was unable to continue my employment as a cash applications analyst with a well-known automotive industry leader. Since my employment with XYZ Ltd, I have accepted a temporary position as an invoice assistant with a local company. My objective is to secure a position in accounts receivable and credit collections with an established company. As you will note, my CV exhibits a brief review of contributions I have made to my employers and I enjoy challenges.

A complete picture of my expertise and experience is very important. Therefore, I will follow up with you next week. I look forward to speaking to you soon to answer any questions you may have regarding my background.

Regards,

Jane Swift

Jane Swift

Enclosure

'Cold' cover letter to a potential employer (sales)

After 'playing around' with part-time and seasonal positions for six years after college, James was ready to combine his variety of sales and customer service achievements into a bid for a serious, high-paying sales career.

JAMES SWIFT

18 Park Street • London X1 0BB
020 8123 4567 (Home) • 07850 515536 (Mobile) • gatehouse@aol.com

---

Dear Hiring Professional,

My competitors were like flies – they kept popping up everywhere, opening with lots of glitz, taking all the customers, and then crashing and burning after six months. But during those six months they were trying to take all my customers! As a newly graduated student in his first real management position, these were serious challenges to which I responded with all the advertising ideas and new gimmicks I could muster – free pool playing, fruity drinks for girls; I even gave away free beer one night using three kegs we couldn't get rid of.

Today I am the same aggressive, ambitious sales professional I was then. OK … these days I wouldn't give away free beer (it might even have been illegal), but I do respond to sales challenges with all the competitiveness, creativity, and customer concern in my heart. In my last sales position, I was quite successful selling holiday packages by telephone for several reasons:

- I qualified my targets well.
- I was very knowledgeable about the products and painted a good picture of the product in the customer's mind.
- I think well and profitably on my feet.
- I'm honest and a natural rapport-builder.

The point of my enclosed CV is that I would like to talk with you about bringing all the sales, problem-solving, and customer service skills to which it refers to work for your organization. When can we meet?

Sincerely,

James Swift

James Swift

enc.

'Cold' cover letter to a potential employer (media)

Letting her professors speak for her and then confirming their words with her own words of commitment is a very effective strategy. The strength of the text is enhanced by the brevity of the letter.

JANE SWIFT   janeswift@aol.com

18 Park Street   ◆   London X1 0BB   ◆   020 8123 4567

'I would rank Ms Swift's work in the top 10% of students I have taught; she is not afraid to tackle tough projects; I believe she has the ability to quickly make positive contributions …'

– John Smith, Ph.D., Chairperson, Department of Communications, ABC College

'Jane was an exemplary Journalism student. She took charge of the tasks given to her and performed them in a superior manner. I admire her strong enthusiasm and her attention to detail…'

– Stephen Brown, Assistant Director of Television Technical Operations, ABC College

Dear Selection Committee,

Tenacious and driven are terms my colleagues have used to describe my work habits. It is with a strong sense of career commitment that I submit my CV for your review.

Having completed classes in August, I will be granted a BA in Journalism from ABC College in December 20–. Sometimes holding two jobs while attending college, I will have completed my degree in three years. It is with the same passion, integrity and energy that I intend to pursue my career.

Like so many, I possess the talent and understanding of how demanding a career in media can be. But unlike most, I am willing to 'pay the price' of hard work, rough work schedules and total availability that the industry requires.

Thanks so much for your consideration. I am eager to learn more about the challenges facing your organization and to discuss how I can make a difference.

Best Regards,

Jane Swift

Jane Swift

'Cold' cover letter to a potential employer (director)

James Swift
18 Park Street ● London X1 0BB
020 8123 4567   james@anyaddress.co.uk

[Date]

Emily_____
[Title]
ABC Ltd
Industry Square
London X2 2EF

Dear Ms _____,

As a Chief Financial Officer, I have built a reputation for my strong ability to provide decisive leadership. For the past few years, my career as a senior-level executive has provided me with opportunities to promote high-level strategic business and financial planning goals for worldwide multi-million pound corporations. My ability to identify challenges and capitalize upon opportunities to expand revenue growth, reduce operating costs and improve overall productivity has been one of my strongest assets to my employers.

My strengths in financial and accounting management as well as my thorough understanding of finance operations have vastly contributed to my career and success as a leader. I maintain self-confidence, credibility and stature to make things happen with colleagues inside and outside the company. Just as significant are my abilities to develop rapport among co-workers and management, build effective teams and promote team effort.

My objective is to secure a position as a CFO or Director and to pursue new opportunities with an organization providing new and exciting challenges. Having a complete picture of my expertise and experience is very important. As you will note in my CV, I have made significant contributions to my employers and take my job very seriously.

I appreciate your time and consideration and will be in contact next week to see if we are able to arrange a meeting date for an interview. I look forward to speaking to you soon.

Yours sincerely,

James Swift

James Swift

enclosure

'Cold' cover letter to a potential employer (pharmaceutical sales)

JAMES SWIFT
18 Park Street, London X1 0BB
020 8123 4567   james@anyaddress.co.uk

Emily _____
[Date]
[Title]
ABC Ltd
Industry Square
London X2 2EF

Dear Ms _____,

I currently hold a sales management position for a very successful retail company. My talents to achieve high sales volume, work cooperatively with diverse personalities, and focus on providing exceptional customer service have allowed me to excel in customer relations and succeed in sales and marketing.

I have always enjoyed a challenge and have made the decision to extend my experience to the pharmaceutical sales field. Pharmaceutical sales has been an interest of mine for some time and I am confident that my background and skills in customer service, human relations and product distribution would transfer well into pursuing this change. What I may lack in specific experience in your business, I more than make up for with my dedication, energy and determination.

I thoroughly understand the importance of developing customer relations, generating revenue from sales potential within a designated territory, and maintaining accurate customer information. I have the aptitude and willingness to learn the necessary technical medical materials to promote your products. I am fully capable of projecting a positive and professional image of an organization and its products, and I strongly believe I possess the necessary skills and qualifications your organization seeks to be successful in this field of work.

Your time in reviewing my confidential CV is greatly appreciated. I will follow up next week to answer any questions you may have regarding my qualifications. At that time, I would like to discuss the possibility of setting up a personal interview at a time to suit you. Please contact me if you would like to speak sooner.

Very truly yours,

James Swift

James Swift

enclosure

'Cold' cover letter to a potential employer (recruiter)

James Swift
18 Park Street, London X1 0BB
020 8123 4567   james@anyaddress.co.uk

[Date]

Alice _____
[Title]
ABC Executive Search Consultants
Industry Square
London X2 2EF

Dear Ms _____,

Having spent several years as an executive recruiter, I realize the number of CVs you receive on a daily basis. However, I remember how valuable a few always turned out to be.

The purpose of this communication is to introduce myself and then to meet you with a view to joining your organization.

When asked which business situations have been the most challenging and rewarding, my answer is the time spent in the search profession.

My background, skills and talents are in all aspects of sales and sales management. My research indicates that your expertise is in this area.

I have enclosed a CV which will highlight and support my objectives. I would appreciate the opportunity to meet and exchange ideas. I will ring you over the next few days to make an appointment. If you prefer, you may reach me in the evening or leave a message on 020 8123 4567.

Thank you and I look forward to our meeting.

Sincerely,

James Swift

James Swift

enclosure

'Cold' cover letter to a potential employer (project management)

JAMES SWIFT
18 Park Street, London X1 0BB
020 8123 4567   james@anyaddress.co.uk

[Date]

Mr _____
ABC Ltd
Industry Square
London X2 2EF

Dear Mr _____,

Information technology expertise, combined with visionary leadership and the ability to motivate cross-functional teams and develop cost-effective solutions are key to creating long-term customer satisfaction and loyalty.

As a seasoned **Project Manager** experienced in providing strategic direction in the design and deployment of technology solutions, I have:

- Successfully managed customer accounts from defining project requirements through to implementation.
- Engineered e-commerce business solutions for myriad organizations from start-up ventures to Blue Chip companies.
- Completed all of the coursework, including specialized electives, to obtain the Microsoft Certified Systems Engineer designation.
- Developed comprehensive RFIs and RFPs; selected the most qualified, cost-effective vendor; and directed cross-functional teams to ensure on-time, on-budget implementation.
- Efficiently prioritized projects, developed realistic timelines, and consistently met deadlines.
- Compiled and drove ratification of product requirements.
- Provided technical expertise to sales teams to assist them in closing the sale.

Could your company use a high achiever with a thirst for growth and new challenges? If so, I would like to discuss how my skills and experience could benefit your organization.

I look forward to speaking to you.

Sincerely,

James Swift

James Swift

enclosure

XYZ Newsletter

Whereas he worked as a Network Technician and Hardware Technician prior to his service as Deputy Director of IT for XYZ … he **served with distinction** as IT director from 1997 to 2000; and … **managed the correction** of the organization's complex year 2000 compliance-related issues **long before they became 'issues'** in 1996; and … established long- and short-term **technological strategic 'vision'** and goals for the organization and conducted negotiations with outside vendors/contractors that **saved taxpayers hundreds of thousands** of pounds; and … is **client-oriented** and **self-directed**, tireless and dedicated in the pursuit of a goal, has demonstrated the ability to **efficiently prioritize** projects and set schedules and deadlines, and can **assess potential problem areas and implement solutions** …

Charley Henson

Drew Smith

'Cold' cover letter to a potential employer (publishing)

JAMES SWIFT
18 Park Street ● London X1 0BB
020 8123 4567   james@anyaddress.co.uk

[Date]

Phillip _____
[Title]
ABC Ltd
Industry Square
London X2 2EF

Dear Mr _____,

In the interest of exploring opportunities in the publishing industry, I have enclosed my CV for your review.

Over the last two years, I have gained valuable knowledge and experience in many aspects of personnel assistance, office procedures and administrative operations. Recently I volunteered my time to edit a cookbook and have been responsible for editing the newsletter for my college. I consider myself a good writer and an avid reader and have always wanted to get into publishing. With my considerable energy, drive and ability to work long hours, I believe I could make a positive contribution to your organization, and I would appreciate the opportunity to discuss my qualifications with you.

Should any questions arise regarding the information on my CV, or if you need personal references, please do not hesitate to contact me at the address or telephone number shown above.

Thank you for your time and consideration. I look forward to meeting you.

Yours sincerely,

James Swift

James Swift

enclosure

'Cold' cover letter to a potential employer
(international sales)

JANE SWIFT
18 Park Street, London X1 0BB
020 8123 4567   jane@anyaddress.co.uk

[Date]

Phillip _____
[Title]
ABC Ltd
Industry Square
London X2 2EF

Dear Mr _____,

I received your name from Mr _____ last week. I spoke to him regarding career opportunities with _____ and he suggested contacting you. He assured me that he would pass my CV along to you; however, in the event that he did not, I am enclosing another.

As an avid cosmetics consumer, I understand and appreciate the high standards of quality that your firm honours. As you can see from my enclosed CV, I have had quite a lot of experience in the international arena. My past experience working overseas has brought me a greater understanding of international cultures and traditions, as well as a better understanding and appreciation of our own culture. These insights would certainly benefit a corporation with worldwide locations, such as your own. In addition, I have gained first-hand experience in the consumer marketplace through my various sales positions. I have noticed your recent expansion into the television media and am sure that an energetic individual would be an asset to ABC in this as well as other projects.

I would very much like to discuss career opportunities with ABC. I will be ringing you within the next few days to set up an interview. In the meantime, if you have any questions I may be reached at the number above. Thank you for your consideration.

Sincerely,

Jane Swift

Jane Swift

enclosure

'Cold' e-mail to a potential employer (banking)

From: James Swift [bankpro@hotmail.com]
To: hr@abccareers.com
Cc:
Subject: Financial management/sales orientation

Dear Human Resources,

Please include my name in your job search database. As requested, I have attached a copy of my current CV.

Banking today is definitely a sales environment. While my marketing skills will always be useful, my interests lead me now to seek a more distinct financial management position such as Controller, Treasurer or Head of Finance.

Since my CIMA Part III will be completed in January 20—, my search may be somewhat premature, but my transcript and results, combined with my practical experience, should offset my temporary lack of an accounting qualification. I would therefore like you to consider me immediately. As an Account Manager, I saw many different industries, and so would not feel constrained to any one sector.

Including a mortgage loan benefit, I am currently earning £3,000 per month plus a car allowance. This should provide you with an indication of my present job level. Your suggestions or comments would be appreciated. I am available for interviews, and can be reached at 020 8123 4567. Thank you.

Yours truly,

James Swift

james@anyaddress.co.uk

'Cold' e-mail to a potential employer (software development)

From: Jane Swift [softwarespecialist@aol.com]
To: hr@developers.net
Cc:
Subject: Developer with quality, productivity and commitment

Dear Sir or Madam,

ABC Ltd caught my attention recently as I began a search for a new employer in the London area. ABC Ltd is well known in the software industry for quality products and excellent customer service; it also maintains a strong reputation as a great employer. Your organization has created an environment in which people can excel, which is why I am writing to you today.

I am very interested in joining your software development team. I am confident that my background and experience will meet your future needs. My current position is Application Developer for XYZ. I enjoy it very much as it has provided me with extensive hands-on training in Visual Basic and other languages. However, I am ready to get more into the actual software writing, as well as return to the London area. I possess a Bachelor's degree in Computer Science as well as training in a variety of programming languages. I am also a fast learner, as demonstrated by my learning Visual Basic quickly after joining XYZ. In addition, I plan to pursue my Master's degree and have begun the application process.

I would appreciate the opportunity to meet you to discuss your goals and how I can help you meet them. I will ring you soon to arrange a meeting that is convenient for you. In the meantime, please feel free to ring me for further information on my background and experience.

Thank you for your consideration and reply. I look forward to meeting you in the near future.

Yours truly,

Jane Swift
020 8123 4567

'Cold' e-mail to a potential employer (work experience)

From: Jane Swift [internationalrelationspro@aol.com
To: hr@internationaljobs.com
Cc:
Subject: Motivated International Relations experience wanted

Dear Human Resources,

I am interested in being considered for a work experience position. I am currently in my second year at the University of London reading International Studies and Political Science with a concentration on Latin America.

My work experience has increased my knowledge of International Relations and enabled me to make use of my education in a professional environment. I am very serious about my International Relations education and future career and am eager to learn as much as possible. I am interested in working for your organization to gain practical experience and additional knowledge pertaining to my field of study.

My professional and academic background, along with my sincere interest in helping others, has enhanced my sensitivity to a diverse range of cultures. As a highly motivated professional, I enjoy the challenge of complex, demanding assignments. My well-developed writing and communication skills are assets to an office environment.

I welcome the opportunity to elaborate on how I could make a substantial contribution to your organization. I look forward to talking to you soon. Thank you.

Sincerely,

Jane Swift
020 8123 4567
jane@anyaddress.co.uk

Power phrases

Consider using adaptations of these key phrases in your 'cold' letters to potential employers.

My twenty-two-year operations management career with a multi-billion-pound _____ company has been at increasing degrees of responsibility. While I have spent the last five years in top management, I am especially proud of my record – I started as a driver many years ago and, like cream, have risen to the top. I have consistently accomplished all goals assigned to me, particularly overall cost reductions, improved productivity, and customer service. Some of my achievements are: ...

Your recent acquisition of the _____ chain would indicate an intent to pursue Southeastern market opportunities more vigorously than you have in the past few years. I believe that my retail management background would complement your long-term strategy for _____ very effectively.

With the scarcity of qualified technical personnel that exists today, it is my thought that you would be interested in my qualifications as set forth in the attached CV.

In approximately three months, I am moving to _____ with my family, and am bringing with me fifteen solid years of banking experience – the last eight in branch operations management. I would like particularly to make use of this experience with your firm.

I have noticed that you conduct laser exposure testing at your facility. If there is a need for laser technicians in this enterprise, I would like to be considered for a position.

As you can see from my CV, I am a psychology graduate and was president of our debating society in my final year. I feel both would indicate a talent for sales. I did some selling in my summer job in 20 – (ABC Books), and found not only that I was successful, but that I thoroughly enjoyed it.

The position you described sounds challenging and interesting. After receiving your comments about the job requirements, I am convinced that I can make an immediate contribution towards the growth of _____ and would certainly hope that we may explore things further.

The opportunity to put to use my medical knowledge as well as my English degree would bring me great pleasure, and it would please me to know that I was bringing quality to your company.

I feel that the combination of _____'s educational environment and my desire to learn as much as possible about the data processing field could only bring about positive results.

If you think after talking to me and reading my CV that there might be an opportunity with your client company, I would be very interested. I have been put in many situations where I had to learn quickly, and have always enjoyed the challenge.

My accomplishments include: …

As my CV indicates, I have demonstrated commitment to clients and to my employer's goals. That track record is consistent in my career endeavours as well as in my life as a whole. I dedicate myself to whatever task is at hand, marshal my resources and stay with the project until it is completed – to my satisfaction. Since my goals and demands are even more stringent than my employers' expectations, I consistently exceed quotas and objectives.

You will notice one common thread throughout my career – I am an administrator and a problem solver.

Currently I am considering opportunities in the £40-£50K range.

My confidential CV is enclosed for your review and consideration.

My current salary requirement would be in the mid-to-high £30Ks, with specifics flexible, negotiable, and dependent upon such factors as benefit structure and advancement opportunity.

Having spent several years as a _____, I realize the number of CVs you receive on a daily basis. However, I remember how valuable a few always turned out to be.

I would like the opportunity to discuss with you how we could mutually benefit one another. You may leave a message on my answering machine at my home and I will return the call. I look forward to hearing from you very soon.

I'm a clear communicator equally at ease with senior management, government officials and control agencies, vendors and contractors, and the construction/labour force. I'm a hard-driving manager who is project driven and is accustomed to inspiring the best job performance possible from associates and employees. I'm also creative enough to be in compliance with agency requirements without sacrificing profit or deadlines.

This job does seem to be the right challenge for me; I know that with my strong Java skills and manufacturing background experience I would be an asset to your company.

Hoping to meet you in person, I thank you for your time.

I will be ringing you on Friday, – August 20– to be sure you received my CV and to answer any questions you might have.

I have enclosed a CV that will highlight and support my objectives. I would appreciate the opportunity to meet and exchange ideas. I will ring you over the next few days to make an appointment. If you prefer, you may reach me in the evening or leave a message on 020 8123 4567.

'Cold' cover letter to employment industry professional (health care)

Adam has developed strong relationships with clinics, hospitals, and physicians throughout his career. He seeks to leverage this experience into a position with a clinic, capitalizing on his expertise in preventive health and chronic illness management programmes.

JAMES SWIFT

18 Park Street
London X1 0BB
020 8123 4567
E-mail: jswift@cs.com

January 12, 20–

Ms Greta Pederson, President
ABC Executive Search Ltd
Industry Square
London X2 2EF

Dear Ms Pederson,

As an accomplished professional with a 20-plus year track record in the pharmaceutical industry, I believe that I have unique talents that could benefit a clinic or a health care management organization. With this in mind, I have enclosed for your review a CV that briefly outlines my professional history.

Some of the key capabilities that I can bring to a new opportunity include:

- *Design and implementation of health management programmes. I have first-hand experience developing programmes for asthma management, and direct the implementation of programmes that have delivered substantial savings to client firms.*
- *Managing the development and implementation of Web-based services that are new revenue centres for my firm and value-added services to its physician customer base.*
- *Exceptional account relations skills. I currently call on and maintain business relationships with key client contacts at the highest levels.*
- *Certifications from the University of London in Quality Management and from the National Heart, Lung and Blood Institute.*

I am confident that my knowledge and expertise would allow me to deliver successful results for one of your clients in the health care industry. I would enjoy speaking to you in person to explore potential opportunities and how I can best serve someone's needs. Please call or e-mail me to arrange a convenient time for us to meet.

Thank you for your time and consideration. I look forward to talking to you soon.

As my employer is unaware of my job search, I trust that you will hold this correspondence in strict confidence and consult with me before releasing my materials to a prospective employer.

Sincerely,

James Swift

James Swift

Enclosure

'Cold' cover letter to employment industry professional (senior network control technician/administrator)

James's goal is to move from a network administrator/tech to a senior position.

JAMES SWIFT

18 Park Street • London X1 0BB • jswift@sbcglobal.net. • 020 8123 4567

January 20, 20–

I regard network downtime as unacceptable, yet realize it sometimes happens due to powers beyond my control. I always have contingency plans. —James Swift

ABC Services, Ltd
Industry Square, London X2 2EF

RE: SENIOR NETWORK CONTROL TECHNICIAN/ADMINISTRATOR, LONDON AREA

Dear Personnel Recruiter,

As I consider career options that offer new and challenging opportunities to expand my growth, I am excited by your job posting for a Senior Network Control Technician/ Administrator. My qualifications and technical background, as well as fieldwork, marketing, and customer service experience, match your requirements for this position. The enclosed CV reflects the experience and technical training/expertise to provide customized network and hardware/software solutions to meet remote customer needs.

The following key strengths also exemplify highly marketable skills and characteristics. I possess:

- *An accommodating attitude and willingness to work hard at any level to accomplish tasks and meet deadlines.*

- *The ability to effectively prioritize tasks and job assignments to balance customer needs with company goals.*

- *Strategic planning to head off downtime and restructure company systems to realize major improvement.*

- *Aptitude for troubleshooting problems, while respecting customers and explaining problems/solutions in simple, illustrative language.*

- *Consultative, straightforward communication techniques that promote development of strong and lasting rapport and trust.*

- *A work ethic that honours integrity and excellence to enhance company distinction.*

- *A persuasive, take-charge style seasoned with a sense of humour for a pleasant work environment.*

- ***Psychological insight and a talent for motivating others to work at higher levels to increase productivity.***

An interview to further investigate your needs and my qualifications would be mutually beneficial. I look forward to hearing from you. In the meantime, thank you for your time and consideration.

Sincerely,

James Swift

James Swift

Enclosure: CV

'Cold' cover letter to employment industry professional (accountant)

JANE SWIFT

18 Park Street • London • X1 0BB
swift_accountant@email.net

Emily _____   (Date)
(Title)
ABC Corporation
1 Industry Square
London X2 2EF

Dear Ms _____,

As I am just completing the requirements for my MBA in Accounting at City Institute of Technology, I am exploring the potential opportunities with a well-established firm that will lead to a career as an accountant. I hope to join an organization where I can learn and grow within the accounting profession and build a long-term relationship. With these goals in mind, I have enclosed for your consideration and review a CV that briefly outlines my credentials.

Some of the key experiences I can bring to an entry-level position with your firm include:

- **Administering Accounts Receivable and Payroll for an engineering firm that was also engaged in construction and some customer manufacturing.**

- **Preparing individual tax returns as part of a volunteer programme.**

- **Serving as Treasurer of a voluntary organization, which encompassed maintaining financial records and providing financial reports to the auditors and to the national organization.**

- **Proficiency with basic Windows and Microsoft Office applications, as well as a keen interest in technology and high-tech businesses.**

I am confident that my education and experience to date provide me with the skills that would be beneficial to your firm and its clients. I would also enjoy speaking to you in person to discuss the possibilities that exist and how I can best serve the needs of your firm and your clients. Please call me at 020 812 4567 to arrange a convenient date and time for us to meet. I look forward to opening a dialogue with you soon.

Very truly yours,

Jane Swift

Jane Swift

enclosure

'Cold' cover letter to employment industry professional (quality assurance)

James Swift
18 Park Street
London X1 1OB
020 8123 4567/mobile: 07850 515536

(Date)

Philip _____
(Title)
ABC Corporation
1 Industry Square
London X2 2EF

Dear Mr _____,

Reliability. Problem Solving. Attention to Detail. These are a few of the many qualities I have developed as a Quality Assurance Technician. If you are looking for a topnotch Quality Assurance Technician, look no further. I have over 15 years of experience in quality assurance and quality control and have not only designed better consumer-friendly products but have improved sales of existing products.

Because delivering solid productivity has been the norm throughout my career in the electronics field, I have achieved superior results at ABCD Biomedical, EFG Technologies, HIJ Electronics, KLM Healthcare, NOP Magnetic, and QRS Electronics. As a result, you get a Quality Assurance Technician who is productive from day one. My commitment to you would be the same: simplify processes, improve products, develop workforce competencies, and boost output while completing projects ahead of time and under budget.

Qualifications I can bring to your clients are outlined on the enclosed CV. Given my technical skills, familiarity with the product line, and understanding of your clients' needs, I could step into the position and be of immediate assistance.

Please contact me at my home telephone number to arrange a convenient time to meet. Thank you for your time; I look forward to speaking to you soon.

Yours truly,

James Swift

James Swift

enclosure

'Cold' cover letter to employment industry professional (executive computer specialist)

James Swift
18 Park Street, London X1 0BB
020 8123 4567   james@anyaddress.co.uk

[Date]

Emily _____
[Title]
ABC Ltd
Industry Square
London X2 2EF

Dear Ms _____,

My experience installing and maintaining computer networks, hardware and software, along with my skills in training users and developing cost-saving applications, are the assets I would bring to the position of Executive Computer Specialist.

I am a Certified Novell Administrator. My technical skills include expertise in Novell Netware, MS DOS and Windows, as well as experience with hardware including Cabletron, and software including the Microsoft Office Suite.

My computer expertise has saved my employers production time and costs. As a Senior Computer Specialist, I installed a Personal Computer LAN using the Novell Netware Networking System. I saved £20,000 and used the savings to upgrade the equipment installation. Also in that position I designed and implemented a system to cut printing costs. The system is projected to save the government £2.5 million over four years.

I have also developed software packages, including 'point of sale' software and mortgage software, which was for commercial sale.

I believe my skills and experience would make me succeed in the position of Executive Computer Specialist. Kindly review my CV, then contact me to arrange a professional interview.

Yours sincerely

James Swift

James Swift

enclosure

'Cold' cover letter to employment industry professional (director)

Jane Swift
18 Park Street, London X1 0BB
020 8123 4567   jane@anyaddress.co.uk

[Date]

Mr _____
[Title]
ABC Ltd
Industry Square
London X2 2EF

Dear Mr _____,

In the course of your search assignments, you may have a requirement for an organized and goal-oriented Director. My present position provides me with the qualifications and experience necessary to successfully fulfil a Director's position. Key strengths which I possess for the success of an administrative position include:

- Direct line operations responsibility improving gross margin to 8.0%.
- Planning and developing over £10 million in new construction projects.
- Reduction of departmental operating expenses to 1.1% below budget.
- Negotiating and developing contractual arrangements with vendors.

I have the ability to define problems, assess both large-scale and smaller implications of a project, and implement solutions.

The enclosed CV briefly outlines my administrative and business background. My geographic preferences are the South and Southeast regions of the country. Relocating to a client's location does not present a problem. Also, I possess an MBA degree from _____ University, and a BSc in Business Administration from _____ University. Depending upon location and other factors, my salary requirements would be between £80,000 and £100,000.

If it appears that my qualifications meet the needs of one of your clients, I would be happy to discuss my background further in a meeting with you or in an interview with the client. I will be contacting your office in the near future to determine the status of my application.

Yours sincerely,

Jane Swift

Jane Swift

enclosure

'Cold' cover letter to employment industry professional (senior manager)

James Swift
18 Park Street, London X1 0BB
020 8123 4567   james@anyaddress.co.uk

[Date]

Mr _____
ABC Ltd
Industry Square
London X2 2EF

Dear Mr _____,

Mentored by Bob _____, founder of _____, I successfully progressed within his privately held organization for twelve years, serving on the **Board of Directors of 13 separate companies** and holding positions including **Treasurer**, **Director of Finance** and ultimately **CEO**. During my tenure the company grew from 7 employees to more than 1,000 while **revenues increased from £2 million to £65 million**. My enclosed CV gives further details.

My reason for contacting you is simple. I am interested in exploring any senior management opportunities that may be available through your organization and would also be interested in interim or consulting roles. Geographically speaking, I have no limitations and am available for relocation throughout the UK and abroad. Due to the level and quality of my performance I feel it pertinent to state that I am only willing to consider positions consistent with my current income level. I have the experience, the talent and the energy to turn around, create or grow a dynamic organization.

I have built my career on my commitment and ability to create open lines of communication between the Board of Directors and senior management to **protect the investments of my organization** and to **assure the attainment of the target return**.

I look forward to hearing from you in the near future to discuss any mutually beneficial opportunities. If you do not at present have a need for a professional with my experience but know of someone who may, please be so kind as to pass on my letter and CV to that individual, or simply ring me.

Yours sincerely,

James Swift

James Swift

enclosure

'Cold' cover letter to employment industry professional (international operations)

James Swift
18 Park Street, London X1 0BB
020 8123 4567   james@anyaddress.co.uk

[Date]

Ms _____
[Title]
ABC Ltd
Industry Square
London X2 2EF

Dear Ms _____,

Over the years, I have built a successful career in **international operations and project management** on my ability to assess situations accurately and quickly, identify problems and focus on strategies that obtain results. I am currently seeking a challenging opportunity with an internationally focused, growth-oriented organization. I am willing to explore interim assignments and consulting projects as well as senior management opportunities. My enclosed CV details some of my accomplishments and credentials.

I have extensive experience in **diplomacy and international public affairs** dealing with foreign government officials, Heads of State and Ambassadors as well as senior executives. Building effective teams and inspiring others to peak performance are among my strengths. I am particularly adept at living and working effectively in foreign countries and with individuals of various cultural backgrounds. As such I am interested in opportunities both in the UK and abroad.

Feasibility studies, **crisis resolution** and **international risk assessment** are areas where I excel. Unit construction and operations, mining/drilling and industrial equipment procurement, sales and distribution are areas where I may be of particular assistance, but my skills are transferable to virtually any industry.

I look forward to hearing from you to discuss any mutually beneficial opportunities that you may be aware of. Please feel free to send my CV to others who may have a need for a professional of my calibre.

Yours sincerely,

James Swift

James Swift

enclosure

'Cold' e-mail to employment industry professional (IT professional)

From: Jane Swift [smithITpro@mindspring.com
To: hr@corpotech.com
Cc:
Subject: Project management

Dear Sir or Madam,

Capitalizing on my success managing IT design and implementation projects for ABC Design in London, I am seeking a professional opportunity where my project management, customer relations and organizational skills could benefit your clients. With this goal in mind, I have attached for your consideration a CV outlining my qualifications.

Some of the experiences I would bring to a position with your firm include:

- Defining project parameters, including interviewing clients to assess goals and objectives, and developing specifications and project deliverables.
- Serving on leadership teams that have managed project budgets of up to £10 million to meet customer deadline requirements and budgetary constraints consistently.
- Coordinating activities of programmers, Web developers, software engineers, network engineers, graphic artists and customer representatives to meet project goals.
- Testing and validating applications during development stages and upon completion to ensure client objectives are met.

I am open to relocation anywhere in the United Kingdom and would eagerly accept either contract assignments or permanent employment. I believe that my capabilities would allow me to serve your needs and benefit your clients, and I would enjoy meeting you to discuss my qualifications in greater detail. Please contact me via phone or e-mail to arrange an initial interview.

Thank you for your time and consideration. I look forward to speaking to you soon.

Sincerely,

Jane Swift
020 8123 4567

'Cold' e-mail to employment industry professional (computer professional)

From: James Swift [computerpro@earthlink.net]
To: hr@comp.com
Cc:
Subject: Technology guru, plus global experience

Dear Human Resources,

My broad background in all aspects of computers, from design and installation through to user training and maintenance, coupled with my business operations expertise, are the assets I would bring to a position with one of your clients.

Currently I hold a management level position with ABC, a firm that designs and builds flight simulators for UK and foreign governments. I provide the electronics expertise in completing approximately 12 major projects annually, which means I conceptualize the simulators' computerized mechanisms, direct the design and manufacturing processes, and then install and test the systems at clients' sites around the globe.

In addition to providing technical expertise, the other major aspect of my job involves aggressively targeting new business. At a point when ABC was facing an essentially saturated UK market, I designed and implemented an Internet Web site, and then had it translated into several languages to target international clientele. The site generated 80% of our new business within one year.

Other assets I would bring to this position include skill in relocating entire company computer systems from existing facilities to new or expanded sites, as well as experience servicing all major brands of PCs. I am extremely familiar with nearly every computer-associated component, program and operating system on today's market.

Thank you in advance for taking a few moments to review my CV. I am confident that the experience you'll find outlined therein will be valuable to your firm. Kindly contact me to arrange a professional interview.

Best regards,

James Swift
020 8123 4567

'Cold' e-mail to employment industry professional (programmer/analyst)

From: James Swift [certifiedprogrammer@yahoo.com]
To: hr@techvibes.com
Cc:
Subject: REF: Programming assignments

Dear Sir or Madam,

My certification in computer programming, along with my professional background in electro-mechanical engineering, are among the primary assets I would bring to a programmer/analyst position with one of your clients.

As part of my training at Computer Institute in south London, I was required to design, write, code, edit and modify an e-commerce Web site. The project succeeded not only because of my skill in applying my technical knowledge, but also because of my strict attention to detail.

Currently I'm employed at ABC in London, executing experiments on electrical/ mechanical equipment I was involved in manufacturing to ensure conformance to customers' specifications.

I am also committed to furthering my professional education, which is essential for success in this field. I plan to augment my knowledge by attending and completing relevant courses.

I am confident this background equips me well for success with one of your clients. Kindly review my CV, then please contact me to arrange an interview.

Very truly yours,

James Swift
020 8123 4567

'Cold' e-mail to employment industry professional (IT management)

From: James Swift [ITexpert@aol.com]
To: hr@techjob.com
Cc:
Subject: Top productivity enhancement professional

Dear Human Resources,

Leading information technology projects for high-growth companies is my area of expertise. Throughout my career I have been successful in identifying organizational needs and leading the development and implementation of industry-specific technologies to improve productivity, quality, operating performance and profitability.

In my current position at XYZ company, I have initiated and managed the technological advances, administrative infrastructures, training programmes and customization initiatives that have enabled the company to generate over £3 million in additional profits in the past year. The scope of my responsibilities has included the entire project management cycle, from initial needs assessment and technology evaluations through to vendor selection, internal systems development, beta testing, quality review, technical and user documentation, and full-scale, multi-site implementation.

My technological and management talents are complemented by my strong training, leadership and customer service skills. I am accustomed to providing ongoing support and relate well to employers at all levels of an organization, including senior executives. Most notable are my strengths in facilitating cooperation among cross-functional project teams to ensure that all projects are delivered on time, within budget, and to specification.

Originally hired for a one-year contract at XYZ, I have been offered a permanent position within the company. However, I am interested in greater challenges and would welcome the opportunity to meet you to determine the contributions I can make to your client. I will call you next week to set up an appointment.

Sincerely,

James Swift
020 8123 4567

'Cold' e-mail to employment industry professional (systems integration)

From: Jane Swift [systemsintegrationpro@hotmail.com]
To: hr@sys.com
Cc:
Subject: Onstar engineer plus more

Dear Company Representative,

My solid background in electrical engineering supported by extensive management and product development experience are key assets that I can contribute to your client's future success.

Throughout my career I have worked with cutting-edge technologies, including **embedded microprocessors**, **RF**, **telecommunications** and **wireless**, in the development and manufacture of products for varied industries. In all of my positions, integrating software, firmware and hardware to create unique applications has been a key strength. Some of these applications that proved quite marketable include development of custom instrumentation and a PC-based network for tracking vehicles in transit. In addition, I have also played an important role in both the sales and customer support process, helping ABC Ltd win its largest municipal contract with the City of London.

Currently, I am exploring opportunities in the telecommunications industry where I can contribute significant expertise in systems integration. I would welcome the opportunity to meet you to explore areas of mutual benefit. Attached is my CV for your review.

In order to present my credentials more fully, I will follow up with a call to you to answer any questions you may have. Thank you for your consideration.

Sincerely,

Jane Swift
020 8123 4567

'Cold' e-mail to employment industry professional (systems administrator)

From: James Swift [systemsspecialist@mindspring.com]
To: hr@compjobs.com
Cc:
Subject: Sys admin/people skills/army background

Dear Sir or Madam,

If you seek a new Systems Administrator who is not only technically oriented but also people oriented, then we have good reason to meet. As you'll find on my attached CV, I possess extensive technical skills and experience. What are more difficult to portray in a brief CV are my people skills.

Several colleagues, supervisors, subordinates and end-users have commended me for my interpersonal skills. I am dedicated to helping others with their technical issues and sharing my knowledge to help them complete their work more efficiently. My job is to serve as a support person, there to keep the system operating smoothly for end-users, as well as to provide them with training. I also understand that most technical projects are a team effort. Again, I have been recognized for my abilities as a team player as well as a team leader. I have a proven track record in taking projects and running with them, but the successes are a result of the combined efforts of the whole team. Whether it's a matter of motivating others, coordinating tasks, or just doing my part, I can do it.

My technical skills speak for themselves. My primary focus has been on Windows NT. In fact, I am currently pursuing my Microsoft Certified Systems Engineer qualification. My plans are to attain this at about the time I leave the Army. I will be able to bring this added expertise to an employer.

A meeting would be greatly appreciated. Please feel free to contact me to arrange a time or to gain further information on my background. I am sure you will agree that I am right for the job after reviewing my CV and meeting me in person.

Thank you for your time and prompt reply. I look forward to meeting you in the near future.

Best regards,

James Swift
020 8123 4567

Power phrases

Consider using adaptations of these key phrases in your 'cold' letters to employment industry professionals.

I am an optimist, thrive on challenges, lead by example and readily adapt to situations. If your client – international or domestic – would benefit from these kinds of qualities, we should get to meet each other. If you would ring or write at a time convenient to you, I look forward to telling you more about my background.

As a dedicated listener, I am usually designated for client/customer relations and produce notable results in client/customer retention – even under the least favourable conditions.

An industry association referred to _____ as an active and selective executive search firm, and mentioned your name because of your work in logistics. I liked that referral and think our meeting would be mutually beneficial.

I would like to talk to you personally to further discuss our meeting. I suggest next week, the week beginning – October, when you have a free minute. I have asked my staff to forward your message immediately in case I am unavailable when you call. I look forward to hearing from you.

Please include my name in your job search database.

Including a mortgage loan benefit, I am currently earning £3,000 per month plus a car allowance. This should provide you with an indication of my present job level. Your suggestions or comments would be appreciated.

For 25 years, my family operated one of the most prestigious landmark inns/restaurants in Dorset. From the age of 6, I was a part of the family workforce – I couldn't wait to 'help.' That attitude pervades my work ethic and I'm grateful for the training that helped me to develop an attitude of service, teamwork and pride in performance and product.

One of your clients is looking for me, if not today then sometime in the near future. I know good people are hard to find because I've had to find them myself.

I have the depth of experience it takes to make a positive contribution.

Income is in the mid-five figures, but the right opportunity is the motivating factor. References and CV are available. With my well-rounded professional background I look forward to a new and interesting career opportunity through your firm.

I'm a natural 'enroller' because my enthusiasm is contagious and I personally project credibility – people are inclined to (1) cooperate and participate wholeheartedly on projects with which I'm involved, (2) favourably consider products I recommend, and (3) be open to my efforts on their behalf when they experience problems or dissatisfaction.

The following are some highlights of my track record for your consideration: ...

I understand your clients frequently ask you to locate senior operating executives with much higher than average ability to accomplish difficult jobs quickly and profitably.

It is my goal to play an integral part in the development, operation and success of a small to mid-sized company where the diversity of my experience and the level of my commitment can be used to their fullest advantage and I can have the satisfaction of seeing the results of my efforts ... a real impact on profitability!

Please call at a time convenient to you this week so we can explore potential opportunities more fully. Use the home number, please; our company's uncertain financial status is stirring up the office rumour mill. Thank you for your time and attention.

I am a motivated and dedicated leader. Many of my staff have worked for me for 10 to 30 years. My enthusiasm for meeting goals and accomplishing objectives has been contagious, and I know how to reward outstanding performance without disturbing a profit and loss balance. My employees and I thrive on a 'family' environment with no loss of respect or production.

As a former business owner, I am well aware of the needs, concerns and challenges facing management. By the same token, I am accustomed to operating with the best interests of the total business in mind – and at heart, as well. I operate expeditiously, constantly seeking the best use of time, effort, resources and money ... for my staff and myself.

My experience as an entrepreneur as well as an employee of a powerful, demanding employer gives me the unique ability to empathize with the needs of management as well as the assertiveness necessary to represent management effectively.

I'm seeking an opportunity to join an employer who can benefit from my expertise and experience while offering me the opportunity for challenge and continued professional growth, as well as commensurate compensation.

I'm a dedicated listener and an accomplished problem solver, always seeking to assist clients in achieving their mission. My clients experience and express a sense of trust and confidence in me and my recommendations because my sincerity and my efforts invested on their behalf are evident and consistent. They never have a doubt that I really care and will operate in their best interests.

Broadcast letter (teaching position)

This instructor was awarded the teaching position she aspired to.

Jane Swift
18 Park Street • London X1 0BB
jswift55@mindspring.com

May 3, 20–

Human Resources Offices
ABC College
Industry Square
London X2 2EF

I am interested in ideas, not merely visual products.
—Marcel Duchamp

Dear Human Resources Coordinator,

An instructor in good standing at XYZ College, I am very interested in moving from painting, design, and art appreciation instructor to your recently posted **Jewellery Repair and Design Faculty position**. I was thrilled to discover an **exceptional match between your requirements for this opening and my skills and qualifications**. The enclosed curriculum vitae reflects a progressive career path and a credible candidate for this position. Qualifications follow:

Your Requirements:	**My Qualifications:**
Diploma in Metal Working	Diploma in Jewellery/Metalsmithing from EFG Art College, 20–.
Bench work/experience with jewellery repair practices	Jewellery repair and bench work for local retail jeweller. Experience includes stone setting, soldering, pearl bead stringing, ring sizing, jewellery designing, and riveting. Consider value and safekeeping.
Teaching, jewellery design education, and curriculum development	Two years' teaching experience. Comprehensive knowledge of casting gained through education, freelance, and contract work includes wax carving, wax chasing, and mould making.
Excellent communication skills	Comprehend the English language. Excellent oral and written self-expression. Give clear instructions and relate well to students. Relaxed communication style fosters encouragement and support. Subscribe to open-door policy.

Page 1 of 2

Jane Swift
Page 2 of 2

Commitment to working with a diverse population	Successfully teach and interact with physically and mentally challenged individuals, as well as people of all ages from varied backgrounds and cultures.
Ability to manage projects and set specific objectives	Extremely goal-oriented, giving particular attention to planning and follow up for positive results. Day planner and 'to-do' lists spark productivity. Experience coordinating special events such as art shows, parties, and dinners.

Besides these qualifications, I am an avid photographer, have an interest in gemology, and produce an average of one large object a month. Personal qualities include a cheerful, energetic demeanour, positive attitude, dedication, self-sufficiency, and creative/innovative idea generation. I am passionate about art, teaching, and mentoring, and enjoy the two-fold return of the enthusiasm I bring to class.

Additionally, positive feedback from both peers and students precedes me:

- 'I have never seen painting so strong from the art department', and 'you are raising the bar.'
- 'I got more from this class (Painting I) than most others I've had.'
- 'This was the most exciting/stimulating class I've taken in 1½ years.'
- 'It was nice to see your work and know that it came from someone as normal as the rest of the world.'
- Your help contributed most to my learning. You were not afraid to help in any way you could.'

Comments like these are especially fulfilling. Other job satisfaction comes from observing facial expressions when students finally comprehend a theory or concept and helping students discover and expand their creativity.

I am willing to handle the responsibility and safety issues involved in running a jewellery/metals lab and believe properly taught techniques and procedures are of vital importance. The prospect of teaching in my field and being on the ground floor of future jewellery department development energizes me. I am confident I will continue to offer a fresh perspective to course and curriculum development at ABC College and look forward to a personal interview to further discuss your needs. Thank you for your time and consideration.

Sincerely,

Jane Swift

Jane Swift

Enclosure: CV

Broadcast letter (assistant director of student housing)

Used a side-by-side comparison to effectively illustrate her qualifications for the position.

Jane Swift

18 Park Road • London X1 0BB • 020 8123 4567

Miss Christine Timmons   January 12, 20–
Assistant Director of Student Housing
University of London
Industry Square
London X2 2EF

Re: Reference Code: TC-E-5556E2

Dear Miss Timmons,

In response to your ad for an Assistant Director for Student Housing advertised in Sunday's *Newsday*, I have enclosed my CV for your review. To further illustrate my qualifications, the following outlines the scope of my experience as it pertains to the position's requirements.

Your requirements	**My qualifications**
● Bachelor's degree or four years of experience in lieu of degree.	● Master's degree in Clinical Counselling. ● Eight years of combined experience in resident hall administration and counselling capacities.
● Promote and develop educational programming and maintain extensive budget.	● Plan, develop, and implement educational programmes, and manage an operational budget.
● Administration of three to five residence halls housing approximately 1,000 students.	● Administration of residence halls housing up to 500 college students.
● Supervised, develop, and evaluate three to five full-time resident hall directors.	● Supervise, develop, and evaluate 26 Resident Advisers with direct responsibility for four RAs and a Head Resident Adviser (HRA).
● Develop departmental policies and procedures, manage area office including billing, occupancy, and facilities records.	● Direct all aspects of front desk management and facilities maintenance operations.
● Assist in the development and leadership of departmental committees, and serve as a manager for student conduct cases.	● One year as Director of Committees and Organizations for the student body.

Thank you for your review and consideration. I look forward to hearing from you soon.

Sincerely,

Jane Swift

Jane Swift

Broadcast letter (financial planning professional)

The employer was so impressed with the detail of the letter that he offered a position to this applicant at the initial interview.

James Swift   18 Park Street • London X1 0BB
            Phone: 020 8123 4567 • Mobile: 07850 515536 • E-mail swifttown@juno.com

September 19, 20–

ABC Financial
David Borgrum, Manager
Industry Square
London X2 2EF

Dear Mr Borgrum,

The Rock. ABC is known internationally by this symbol of security and permanence, the assurance to their clients the company will always be there. The corporate slogan 'Growing and Protecting Your Wealth' can only be accomplished through principled management, effective investment strategies, and ethical financial planners.

The relationship. With corporate scandal and financial malfeasance perceived to be the norm, now, more than ever, a relationship built on integrity and mutual respect is paramount to success in the financial services industry. As a goal-oriented financial planning professional who possesses strong marketing and communication skills, I am confident upon review of my qualifications you will find I have the solid combination of experience and achievement that ABC looks for in its representatives.

My qualifications include:

✔ Registered Investment Adviser.
✔ B.A. in Economics.
✔ Commitment to client satisfaction and quality service through needs assessment.
✔ Demonstrated results in business development and execution of marketing strategies.
✔ Effective communication and presentation skills necessary to articulate product benefits clearly and accurately to clients.
✔ Outstanding time management and organizational ability.
✔ A willingness to 'go the extra mile' for client and corporation.

The consultation. Inherent to every successful consultation, is my obligation to obtain a comprehensive financial background in order to meet the clients' future needs and objectives. Performing an effective client needs assessment, gives me the decisive edge when the client makes their financial planning decisions. Furthermore, I am skilled at new business development, cold calling and seminar presentations. Employers and colleagues have consistently praised my attention to detail, hard work ethic, and ability to deal with the most complex client engagements.

Please contact me at your earliest convenience to set up an interview concerning employment opportunities within your company. I look forward to hearing from you.

Sincerely

James Swift

James Swift

Broadcast letter (heavy equipment operator)

Relocating to Scotland and wants to secure a position that could capitalize on his diverse range of skills.

JAMES SWIFT

Dear Sir or Madam,

Please accept the enclosed CV in application of your Heavy Equipment Operator position advertised in *The Times Journal*.

My diverse range of experience includes over ten years of experience operating and maintaining heavy equipment. In my current position, I operate backhoes, loaders, lulls, Gallion cranes, Ditch Witch trenchers (large and walk-behind), for lifts, street sweepers, and bucket trucks. In addition, I supervise the troubleshooting, maintenance, and repair of all of the department's equipment.

Of equal importance are my supervisory and leadership skills where I have managed multiple teams of up to 30 employees. Being extremely diligent, I have assumed responsibility for overseeing and monitoring various projects and issues which affect the daily operations, efficiency, and profitability of the company. I am recognized by senior management for consistently completing projects on time and within budget.

Working in several trades during my career has developed my strong multi-tasking abilities which have proven to be an asset in my current position. Additional areas of experience include plumbing, irrigation, landscaping, electrical work, fibre optics, and carpentry. In each of these areas, I have received training and have worked independently.

If you are in need of a person with my skills, I would welcome the opportunity to meet you to determine the contributions I can make to your company.

Thank you for your consideration.

Sincerely,

James Swift

James Swift

18 Park Street • London X1 0BB
Phone: 020 8123 4567 • Mobile: 07850 515536 • jswift@yahoo.com

Broadcast letter
(executive chef/hotel restaurant manager)

James started as a chef and went into the management side of the restaurant.
He is now looking to work for a multi-restaurant chain in a management capacity.

James Swift

18 Park Street
London X1 0BB
020 8123 4567

Dear Sir/Madam,

I am confident that my extensive experience as an executive chef and hotel/restaurant manager would serve as an asset to a position in your organization. My career began 23 years ago as an apprentice training under several notable internationally known chefs. Since that time I have been involved extensively in the area of food services management and marketing.

I am currently General Manager and Corporate Executive Chef of XYZ London. In 20–, I was hired to start up this 225-seat restaurant. The casual dining establishment is part of ABC Ltd. I am responsible for all financial reporting and instituted key control systems to meet the standards of the parent company. Additional achievements include gaining excellent media publicity, creative menu development, and directing on- and off-site catering for many London premieres. I was asked to coordinate all aspects of our new construction and assist in the design aspects of the kitchen.

As Director of Operations for DEF Catering and DEF Restaurant in Bristol, my staff and I expanded the business to accommodate parties ranging from 10 to 4,000 people and grossed over £1.5 million in sales.

Working as Director of Operations and Executive Chef for GHJ Country Club, I oversaw all profit and loss functions for a 165-seat à la carte restaurant and a 1,000-seat banquet facility. The club had an 18 hole Championship Golf Course that I managed, with an active membership of 1,000 members.

I gained extensive international experience working as Executive Chef for KLM's, a five-star-rated restaurant in New Zealand, I prepared food for the Prime Minister, various heads of state, and visiting dignitaries, I obtained my New Zealand Master Chef's Certification. In addition, I served as an Executive Pastry Chef and Chef for a Hawaiian hotel owned and operated by NOP Ltd.

Thank you for your consideration. I look forward to speaking with you personally regarding my qualifications and how I can contribute positively as a member of your management staff.

Sincerely yours,

James Swift

James Swift

Broadcast letter (maintenance mechanic)

Jane was a bus driver who moved into a warehouse position, and eventually into a higher-paying maintenance mechanic position. After a downsizing, she wishes to continue her career as a mechanic.

JANE SWIFT

18 Park Street • London X1 0BB
020 8123 4567 (H) 07850 515536 (M) E-mail:janeswift3@msn.com

RE: Maintenance Mechanic

Dear Sir/Madam,

As a professional Facilities and Maintenance Mechanic, I understand that success depends on several factors. These include timely upkeep of machinery maintenance and repair, supervision of maintenance programmes, and monitoring outside contractors. My extensive hands-on experience as a mechanic has allowed me to ensure timely completion of projects and adherence to corporate safety requirements.

Throughout my career I have been promoted and have acquired increasing responsibilities within every position. In my latest position as a Mechanic for ABC Foods, I had the reputation for excellent machinery knowledge and a keen attention to detail.

ABC Foods is downsizing the plant in Slough, and I have accepted a voluntary separation package from the company. I would like to continue my career with a new company offering me new challenges.

Thank you for your consideration. I possess excellent hands-on knowledge as well as supervisory expertise, and I look forward to meeting you personally so that we may discuss how I may make a positive contribution to your team.

Very truly yours,

Jane Swift

Jane Swift

Enclosure

Broadcast letter (database engineer)

Jane Swift
18 Park Street, London X1 0BB
020 8123 4567 jane@anyaddress.co.uk

[Date]
Phillip _____
[Title]
ABC Ltd
Industry Square
London X2 2EF

Dear Mr _____,

Empowering your employees with the information and tools necessary to make better strategic business decisions is very likely to improve your company's competitive advantage and profitability. I can do this through insightful strategic planning and the delivery of superior data warehouse and decision support systems.

My extensive career experience in data warehousing, database administration and business systems development, coupled with my commitment to exceed customer expectations and my focus on achieving sustainable strategic competitive advantage, are the primary assets I would bring to your Director of Database Engineering position. I have successfully delivered numerous data warehouse projects that were effectively aligned with company strategic objectives. I am also highly skilled at directing teams on complex initiatives and improving processes, communication, teamwork and quality.

As a senior-level employee of XYZ Information Technology Ltd, I have established an excellent track record for successfully managing large complex projects. Notably, I managed a £10 million development project for Business One, building and implementing their first enterprise data warehouse and certain downstream divisional data marts. So successful was this project that within three months of implementation it established itself as the recognized supreme source of accurate company data for all of Business One's North European business units. Additionally, it met tight service level commitments over 97% of the time and experienced no downtime due to programming error.

As a Project Leader/Manager for DEF Business Systems Ltd, I also managed the development of a large data warehouse. I led the design and development efforts for this data warehouse of sales information for their Speciality Products division. This was the first data warehouse developed at DEF that successfully met user expectations.

An additional asset I would bring to your organization is competency in correlating data warehousing functions with overall company goals. I am skilled in providing advice to senior managers and executives and adept at monitoring data warehouse systems to continually ensure their value and usefulness to an organization as a whole.

I am confident that this experience equips me well for success as your Director of Database Engineering. Kindly review my CV, then please contact me to arrange a professional interview.

Yours sincerely,

Jane Swift

Jane Swift

Broadcast letter (senior technical sales)

JAMES SWIFT
18 Park Street, London X1 0BB
020 8123 4567   james@anyaddress.co.uk

Emily _____
[Date]
[Title]
ABC Ltd
Industry Square
London X2 2EF

Dear Ms _____,

As a seasoned Technical Sales and Marketing Consultant, I've generated considerable new business for my previous employers, and now I'd like to do the same for you. For the past 15 years I have pursued an increasingly successful career in telecommunications sales and marketing. Among my accomplishments are:

SALES
Qualified to spearhead the entire sales cycle management process, from initial client consultation and needs assessment through to product demonstration, price and service negotiations, and final sales closings.

MARKETING
Success in orchestrating all aspects of developing a gainful marketing strategy, from competitive market intelligence and trend analysis, product development, launch and positioning, to distribution management and customer care.

TELECOMMUNICATIONS & NETWORK SOLUTIONS
Recognized for pioneering technology solutions that meet the needs of complex customer service, logistics and distribution operations. Able to test operations to ensure optimum systems functionality and availability, guide systems implementation across multiple platforms, and deliver user training and support programmes that outpace the competition.

I hope you will contact me in the very near future. You'll find my address and telephone number above. I would welcome the opportunity to contribute my skills to the success of your marketing team and look forward to learning about any available opportunities in your company.

Yours sincerely,

James Swift

James Swift

enclosure

Broadcast letter (telecommunications)

JAMES SWIFT

18 Park Street • London X1 0BB • telecompro@aol.com
Home: 020 8123 4567 • Work 020 8123 4567 • Mobile: 07850 515536

(Date)

Emily _____
(Title)
ABC Corporation
1 Industry Square
London X2 2EF

Dear Mrs _____,

If you need someone with proven international success who will really listen to your clients' needs and has leaped over cultural barriers to forge some of the most profitable technical opportunities in the telecommunications field, I am your #1 choice for any opportunity in international or domestic sales or marketing.

For the last ten years, my work in strategic partnering, developing alliances, creating new opportunities, and exceeding multinational clients' expectations has helped my employers more than double their sales. However, follow-up, tenacious attention to detail, and my ability to listen have critically solidified longstanding relationships with major players worldwide.

With a global leader in telecommunications, I received 3 promotions in 4 years due to my success in managing contacts, motivating staffs, and implementing marketing campaigns that delivered ROI threefold.

Since 20– I have …

- Marketed a full range of data and voice communication services to multinational corporations and Internet service providers in Japan, Southeast Asia, Canada, and Western Europe.
- Brought in 28 new global accounts representing up to a 250 per cent increase in business – currently handle brand management efforts for XYZ on pace to exceed annual goal; managed 20 accounts requiring broadband connectivity to international locations.
- Created the first transcontinental ATM circuit and earned one of the most prestigious awards in the company.
- Trained technical associates in ATM and employed knowledge of DWDM, SONET, SDMS, and TCP/IP technology to create some of the most cost-effective networks on the planet.

If these proven successes sound like the work of a go-getter you need on staff …

- Consider that, in just 2 years with a system software developer, I added £1.5M in new business, trained an all-Japanese staff in direct marketing principles, and launched direct sales campaigns that increased client awareness of our services.

Page 1 of 2

James Swift
Page 2 of 2

Additionally, my efforts with an international contractor …

- Partnered the parent company with Japan-based joint venture interests that enabled the first UK-built airport in Japan.
- Kept Japanese executives and high-ranking government officials apprised of progress – and landed 2 additional opportunities for a total of £10M in business in just a year.

Technically speaking …

- I have worked with ATM, Frame Relay, Private Line, SONET, DWDM, SNA/SDLE, SDMS and IP, and managed networks and a diverse array of hardware and software packages – in addition to holding numerous Novell and Windows specialized certifications.

I love calling on clients who have been abused by other reps, because I know my negotiating skills, ability to cross cultural barriers and generate win-win opportunities will get the decision-maker to sign every time.

Reviewing my attached CV, you will note doctoral, master's, and bachelor's degrees – and a host of quantifiable results and technical training that serve only to enhance my drive and enthusiasm. I will gladly set aside time to meet you and discuss how my knowledge of technology, client relations, and strategic partnering can become your biggest asset.

I will take the liberty of contacting you on Monday at 10 a.m. If you need to reach me, please feel free to contact me at 020 8123 4567. Thanking you in advance for the opportunity to meet you, I am,

Sincerely yours,

James Swift

James Swift

enclosure

Broadcast letter (senior R&D engineer)

Jane Swift

18 Park Street • London X1 0BB
020 8123 4567 •R&Dpro@email.com

SENIOR R&D ENGINEER ... patent holder ... launched x# new products ...
recognized worldwide ... created win-win alliances ... cornered global markets ...

(Date)

Philip _____
(Title)
ABC Ltd
1 Industry Square
London X2 2EF

Dear Mr _____,

If your R&D-to-market time needs a sense of urgency, creativity, and a seasoned coordinator of people and priorities, I am one individual you need to discuss the ABC Position with. Here's why:

- STRATEGIC PLANNING: Etched long- and short-term technological plans that kept a £2B manufacturer ahead of its competition since 20-

- COORDINATED RESOURCES: 20+ years in planning, reviewing, and benchmarking technical performance, meeting budgetary goals, and coordinating interlaboratory and interdepartmental efforts

- IGNITED STAFFS' CREATIVITY: Led efforts and piqued an in-house multidisciplinary R&D staff's synergy; got x# new products to market

- ENRICHED KNOWLEDGE: Trained sales, marketing, and technical staffs since 19–; well-known for abilities to communicate new ideas, selected for numerous assignments in product training worldwide.

- MOVED THE MARKET TO OUR PRODUCT: Recognized expert – created the need for cutting-edge technology in the cutting tool market by featuring results in technical articles for leading publications.

- INTEGRATED OPERATIONS: 1 of 2 individuals to integrate a newly acquired company's R&D with parent company's

- IGNORED STIGMAS: First person to involve marketing with R&D – created pathway between R&D and marketing, bringing projects to market in record time; landed £10 million+ in new accounts – only non-salesperson to get a one-of-a-kind annual sales award

- IMPECCABLE RECORD: Achieved 70 to 80 per cent first-time success rate in field testing for all products developed; hold x# UK patents; consulted worldwide by engineers and scientists; published; presenter at technical conferences since post-doctoral fellowship

Reviewing my credentials and past results, you will note they occurred in the XYZ field. However, I am confident the core *technical, interpersonal, and organizational expertise I bring to your staff and customers would easily retrofit at ABC Ltd.*

If you need a driven problem solver who can get your people moving to the work, I am readily available to discuss how I can channel my more than two decades of success as your ABD POSITION at ABC Ltd. I will be in the area next month, and would prefer to meet you then.

I am in a position to move to the London area, and *am ready to demonstrate how I can reignite your R&D efforts and create a flurry of opportunity.* Should you need added information, please do not hesitate to contact me on 020 8123 4567.

Sincerely,

Jane Swift

Jane Swift

enclosure

Broadcast letter (multilingual sales manager)

James Swift

---

18 Park Street – London X1 0BB
Mobile: 07850 515536 – Pager 020 8123 4568 – E-mail: jswift@hotmail.com

Fluent in Spanish … time management skills … 8 years front line experience … service-oriented positions … trainer … presentation expertise …

(Date)

Emily _____
(Title)
ABC Ltd
1 Industry Square
London X2 2EF

Dear Ms _____,

If you know your *customers and operations* deserve attention to detail, as well as a high-energy individual who is fluent in Spanish and makes people a #1 priority, I am the individual you need to interview for a ZYX position at ABC Ltd.

Reviewing my credentials, you will note I have taught in a secondary school for the past eight years. This exposure to daily planning, keeping people motivated and moving to the work can be an immediate asset at ABC, and here are some areas up-front that align with your needs:

- SUCCESS IN DIRECT COMMUNICATION: Whether the students, decision-makers or the general public, my presentation skills kept people interested, involved and properly served …

- MULTILINGUAL ABILITIES: Fluent in Spanish, Japanese, and Russian – despite having a Spanish-only background, mastered the dialects of Russian and Japanese and was teaching classes upon hire at a school district …

- ALWAYS LOOKING FOR IMPROVEMENTS: Successfully integrated technology with additional conversational strategies … working for a distributor as an undergraduate, took initiative to revamp routing – increased productivity and service … increased a student's competency from 31 per cent to 100 per cent while an undergraduate …

- FOCUS ON SERVICE: Made individual needs a priority as a teacher – adept in varying approach per individual personalities and priorities …

- MOTIVATED: Worked up to 30 hours weekly while pursuing degree … proven abilities to juggle diverse assignments opened door for additional assignments and leadership roles …

I seek to channel my communication, presentation, customer service, training and organizational skills, and the ZYX opportunity at ABC Ltd matches my goal for a transferable opportunity. You would benefit from someone with a *proven track record in front line positions, and your customers and operations will have a team player who knows how to set goals, meet goals, and keep customers' needs at the forefront.*

Page 1 of 2

I will take the liberty of contacting you on _____ at _____ to confirm your receipt of my information and briefly discuss how my energy and talents could be your asset. I would also like to arrange our meeting at that time. Should you need to reach me sooner, I can be contacted at 07850 515536 or jswift@hotmail.com.

Best regards,

James Swift

James Swift

enclosure

Broadcast letter (management)

Jane Swift
18 Park Street, London X1 0BB
020 8123 4567   jane@anyaddress.co.uk

[Date]

Phillip _____
[Title]
ABC Ltd
Industry Square
London X2 2EF

Dear Mr _____,

People will only give you what you're willing to accept. That's why my staff employed 'The Golden Rule' every day, treating customers the way they themselves would like to be treated.

If you need someone with a technical background who has hired and kept top talent challenged and on their toes to deliver exemplary service, then consider that in 20+ years:

— I translated my knowledge of physics and business into profits and operational success – for my staff, my employer and myself.
— I took on the lead engineering position in my second year with an industry giant, skipping over the traditional 12-year career path – I simply outworked everyone and never said I couldn't do something or get it done on time or within budget.
— I earned full latitude in decision making after proving my team's understanding of a new target market's needs – I introduced more products than my predecessors, improved processes, and cut manufacturing and warranty costs by roughly £1M the first year.
— Operations I had an impact on experienced extremely low employee turnover – and employees met or exceeded customer expectations 100 per cent of the time.

I've made sure my staff are so service-oriented that the customer doesn't have to ask for warranty repairs or 'the next step' – they have the answers or already have performed the warranty work.

And when my name is on a project, it is always on schedule within budget – and is a winner:

— When a relationship with a speciality manufacturer ended, I spearheaded development of an intake manifold line, analysed and negotiated manufacturing costs, and selected vendors – and launched an 18-unit product line in 18 months that led the industry.
— The first race manifold we developed took the first 5 finishes in the 1985 motorsport race without prior testing by participating teams.

Jane Swift
Page 2 of 2

If you seek someone with the work ethic of a business partner, then I am your top choice for the _____ opportunity with ABC Ltd. I fully understand the nuts-and-bolts of customer service, and certainly can combine my financial know-how with proven success in the field at ABC.

Right now I'm ready to step down from entrepreneurial management, simplify my role, and do 'one or three things' well for an organization that values integrity, hard work and creativity.

If I sound like the person you need at ABC , then contact me right away to discuss the _____ opportunity. I can be reached on 020 8123 4567 after 6 pm. Monday to Friday, or at my place of business on 020 8345 6789 during business hours. I will take the liberty of contacting you on Monday at 10 am to see when we can arrange an interview.

Yours truly,

Jane Swift

Jane Swift

enclosure

Broadcast letter (HR generalist)

Jane Swift
18 Park Street, London X1 0BB
020 8123 4567   jane@anyaddress.co.uk

HR GENERALIST
9 years advising senior decision-makers on employee matters...
5 years in benefits administration for £1B company and 5 affiliates...
15 years delivering HR presentations...
Open enrolment/benefits processing for professional employees...
13 years grievance/disciplinary meeting involvement...
10+ years training/development, entry through professional levels...
Worked through mergers and reorganizations...
Created award-winning concept for enrolment booklet...
Earned highest ratings throughout career...

[Date]

Phillip _____
[Title]
ABC Ltd
Industry Square
London X2 2EF

Dear Mr _____,

If your organization seeks someone to advance your human resources programmes, consider my proven track record. I am ready for a challenge with ABC Ltd, as your recent growth needs someone used to working with new subsidiaries and maintaining the bottom line. I am absolutely ready to step in as your Human Resources Director at ABC, as my commitment extends to all areas you seek to address.

I bring you and your employees objectivity, knowledge of policy/procedure implementation and interpretation, and hands-on work in an ever-changing climate. Here are some highlighted abilities that could be put to work immediately at ABC Ltd:

— MET THE CHALLENGE: With little notification, stepped in and was an asset in an HR Directorship capacity; administered £12M in health and pension benefits; initiated multi-tier healthcare plan to better suit regional product needs

— BENEFITS: 5 years working with open enrolment for all levels of employees – restructured benefits during 3 internal reorganizations

— REMAINED FLEXIBLE: Adapted to the needs of entrepreneurial organizations while continuing a career with conservative major utility company

— LEADERSHIP: Entrusted to step in for superiors due to track record in HR; number 1 person consulted by senior managers of a £1B parent company and its 5 affiliates regarding HR or benefits; met with bargaining unit leadership, discussed and resolved grievances and complaints

Jane Swift
2 of 2

— COMMUNITY INVOLVEMENT: Accepted leadership role in major charity organization, keynote speaker for regional fund-raising appearances

— TRAINING / DEVELOPMENT: Delivered HR and benefits presentations since 1995, safety training, 2 years

— OVER/ABOVE: Travelled over 3-year period to help a newly formed company whose explosive growth took them to 2,000 employees in 3 years (coordinated staffing and benefit enrolment while maintaining existing workload); singled out for HR support for special finance division structure, took on policy making/interpretation and HR

If you need someone seasoned in policy making who can interface with decision-makers and keep you 100 per cent compliant with regulations, I am awaiting your call for an interview.

I prefer to take the lead in contacting you, so I will call on Monday at 10 am to brief you on how my background could be an immediate asset and arrange our meeting. I can forward a CV for your review immediately. Should you need to reach me earlier, I am on 020 8123 4567.

Sincerely,

Jane Swift

Jane Swift

~ Benefits Enrolment ~ Multi-Tier Coverage ~ Labour Relations ~ Grievances ~
Arbitration ~ Job Bidding ~ CPP, CRS, PDS ~ Redundancy Compensation ~
Sexual Harassment ~ Safety Training ~ Background Investigations ~

Broadcast letter (operations manager)

JAMES SWIFT
18 Park Street ● London X1 0BB
020 8123 4567 james@anyaddress.co.uk

[Date]

ABC Ltd
Industry Square
London
Attention Ms Emily_____

Dear Ms _____,

Do you need an experienced, versatile individual who can improve bottom-line profits? I can offer innovative ideas to the position of Operations Manager – ideas that can benefit a service-driven, quality-oriented company like yours. No one has money to burn in a tough economy, which is why adding an already-skilled manager to your staff can reduce time and money.

The match between your needs and my talents is ideal. Why? Because my strengths lie in understanding the labour and manufacturing operations that design, build, install and manage equipment for environmental and production improvements. I am a leader both by example and through effective management of individuals and teams. In short, I have the drive and vision to make a positive difference in any organization.

Dozens of proposed projects have been successfully implemented due to my established reputation for the quality of work completed. The work performed under my direction has come in at, or below, budget and we meet project deadlines.

The enclosed CV summarizes my qualifications and achievements. I would be glad to discuss any of this information with you as an opportunity of employment. Because 'proven skills' are best explained in person, I look forward to our conversation and will ring early next week to arrange our meeting. Thank you for taking the time to review my CV and for your consideration.

Sincerely,

James Swift

James Swift

enclosure

Broadcast letter (information technology programme manager)

James Swift
18 Park Street, London X1 0BB
020 8123 4567   james@anyaddress.co.uk

[Date]

Mr Philip____
CIO
ABC Ltd
Industry Square
London X2 2EF

Dear Mr _____,

May I ask your advice and assistance?

As a result of XYZ's merger with DEF, I am confidentially exploring my opportunities. Although I am confident that I will be offered a role in the new organization, I am currently assessing where I can make the optimal contribution.

I am an Information Technology Programme Manager. In this role, I have led the development of key financial systems and strategic business plans, co-managed the seamless migration of two divisions to another site, and founded the City People Networking Group – delivering noteworthy cost savings and productivity gains. For the past 11 years, I've had dream jobs with leading firms like GHI and JKL. I have been entrusted with the direction of large-scale, global projects. Many times, I learned 'on my feet' – to implement new systems, design testing methods, manage resources, repair damaged vendor relations for mutual gain and to meet a wide array of challenges. My career has accelerated based on the results, as you'll note from the accomplishments in my enclosed CV.

I'm considering transferring my skills and experience to an organization where I can continue to be a team player and visionary leader for state-of-the-art technology programmes, and where I'll also continue to learn new functional and technical areas. My expertise and interests are in the financial service industry.

I would greatly appreciate a few minutes of your time to discuss my options and glean any suggestions you can offer. I'll phone you in a few days to see if we can arrange a brief meeting.

Thanks very much.

Yours sincerely,

James Swift

James Swift

enclosure

Broadcast letter (pharmaceutical sales)

Jane Swift

(Date)

ABC Laboratories
1 Industry Square
London X2 2EF

Ladies and Gentlemen:

ABC Laboratories is one of the fastest-growing companies in the UK. Your achievements are impressive, and I am eager to make a contribution to your professional team as a Pharmaceutical Sales Representative. Given a chance, based on my enthusiasm and desire to excel, I can make a positive difference in your company!

As a recent graduate, my professional job experience is limited. However, I believe that you will find that I exhibit intelligence, common sense, initiative, maturity, and stability. Various jobs over the last ten years have required a good attitude and keen interpersonal skills. These jobs, along with my education, life's experiences and extensive travels, have not only enlightened me intellectually, but have also given me a totally different paradigm compared with other candidates.

Analysing an audience is of utmost importance as a sales representative. As the daughter of a physician, I had great exposure to the medical environment. I strongly believe this gives me insight into the way physicians think – that patents' needs come first. Therefore, effective presentations of products must be made in a timely, succinct, and caring manner for successful sales in this industry. My desire is to stay close to the medical field, and working in a pharmaceutical company is exactly where I aspire to be!

After reviewing the enclosed CV, please contact me at 020 8123 4567 to arrange an interview. Because 'proven skills' are best explained in person, I look forward to discussing how my qualifications can meet your personnel needs and contribute to your company's important mission.

Sincerely,

Jane Swift

Jane Swift

enclosure

18 Park Street London X1 0BB • 020 8123 4567

Broadcast letter (director of operations)

James Swift
18 Park Street   ●   London X1 0BB
020 8123 4567   james@anyaddress.co.uk

[Date]

Philip_____, [Title]
ABC Ltd
Industry Square
London X2 2EF

Dear Mr _____,

Problem – Action – Results. It is a simple formula, and one that I have implemented successfully throughout my long career in manufacturing. A former business associate passed your name on to me after commenting that my business philosophy and style reminded him of a CEO he had heard speak at a conference in Manchester. That CEO was you.

It has been several years since I took my first job as a machinist back in Norwich, but I have never lost my enthusiasm for finding faster and better ways to accomplish goals while cutting costs. I have worked my way up through the ranks from Foreman, to Plant Supervisor, to Manufacturing Engineer, to Assistant Director of Operations, and finally Director of Operations. Taking a swing at every new idea that came my way, I may have missed a few, but overall my batting average has been good:

● led a £200M manufacturing firm to earning ISO 9002 certification on first attempt;
● revitalized operations at a plant site in Scotland by implementing a comprehensive employee training programme;
● increased profits by 200% by identifying and rectifying problems with production and delivery at a Sheffield manufacturing facility;
● spearheaded technological advances at an Oxfordshire plant which was converting from manual to CAD/CAM capabilities.

I believe strongly in teams and am comfortable working with R&D, engineering and marketing professionals. My colleagues have expressed appreciation for my direct and honest approach to people and problems.

Between jobs now, I am available on 20th March and would like to get together with you to explore potential opportunities with ABC. It would be great to meet over lunch. I will give you a ring on the morning of the 18th to see if that can be arranged.

I'm sending along my CV to lay a foundation for our discussion. I look forward to meeting you and exchanging ideas.

Sincerely,

James Swift

James Swift

enclosure

Broadcast letter (consultant)

JAMES SWIFT
18 Park Street, London X1 0BB
020 8123 4567   james@anyaddress.co.uk

[Date]
Philip _____, [Title]
ABC Ltd
Industry Square
London X2 2EF

Dear Mr _____,

- **Is your organization fully prepared to safeguard its technology services, information and facilities in the event of a disaster?**

- **Are you taking full advantage of high-value and cost-effective vendor agreements?**

- **Do you benefit from high team performance and low turnover?**

If you have answered 'No' to any of the above questions, then allow me to introduce myself and the expertise I can offer your organization. With a proven and award-winning track record of achievement, I offer a unique combination of expertise in disaster recovery/business continuity planning, vendor management/negotiations, and team leadership. I am currently offering my services to organizations within the London area, and would like to draw your attention to the value I offer.

Put simply, my expertise is delivering results. In previous positions, I have designed, implemented and optimized comprehensive world-class disaster recovery and information security procedures, saved millions in vendor negotiations and third-party service agreements, and led a variety of cross-functional teams to consistently achieve and exceed organizational mandates.

If the following interests you, I invite you to review the attached CV which further illustrates my experience, achievements and expertise:

- **Expert in Disaster Recovery, Information Security and Business Continuity** – expertise includes planning, protection and offsite recovery of technology services, databases and facilities

- **Superior contract procurement, negotiation and vendor management capabilities** – proven record for negotiating agreements that improve service quality and save millions in vendor costs

- **Strong, decisive and motivating leader** – reputation for building and leading high-performance teams to breakthrough achievement

- Available for **full-time, part-time, contract and consulting opportunities**

If you believe that you could benefit from a highly motivated and talented professional with a reputation for generating results, then I would welcome the opportunity to meet and discuss the specific value I can offer your organization.

I thank you for your consideration and I look forward to speaking to you soon.

Sincerely,

James Swift

James Swift

enclosure: CV

Broadcast letter (project manager)

JANE SWIFT
MBA, PMP
18 Park Street, London X1 0BB
020 8123 4567   jane@anyaddress.co.uk
– WILLING TO RELOCATE –

[Date]

Dear Employer:

Because of current market conditions and high unemployment, I am sure you have many candidates and few *Project or Training Manager* positions to fill. With this letter and CV, please allow me to add to your group; but, may I also give a few reasons why you might want to call me ahead of other qualified candidates should an appropriate position become available?

You will note that my educational and professional *background is broad* and includes experience in post-secondary organizations, community colleges, business and the armed forces. Because of this range of experience, I am able to bring *insight and the ability to relate well to individuals at all levels and from diverse backgrounds.*

Working within for-profit organizations has enabled me to develop an *eye for the bottom line*. Whether it be budgetary or profit-enhancing, I am continually evaluating systems and methods to make them more efficient and productive.

Incredible as it may sound, I appreciate and welcome change. I am *known for my abilities as a change agent*. However, while I may embrace change – technological or otherwise – I recognize that many do not. Therefore, from a management standpoint, I look for ways to make transitions more tolerable for the people in my charge.

While my CV is comprehensive, it does not fully demonstrate the manner in which I have achieved success. My character, personality and the ability to effectively lead a project or team could be best seen in a personal meeting. Therefore, I would welcome an interview to further discuss your needs and my qualifications. Thank you for your time and consideration.

Yours faithfully,

Jane Swift

Jane Swift

enclosure

Broadcast e-mail (senior buyer/purchasing agent/purchasing manager)

From: James Swift [purchasing@earthlink.net]
To: hr@abc.com
Cc:
Subject: Smart Purchasing Choice

Dear Mr / Ms / HR,

SENIOR BUYER * PURCHASING AGENT * PURCHASING MANAGER

Do you cringe at the high costs your company incurs for goods and services?

Do you need someone who will maximize vendor resources, working hard to secure lower-cost, longer-term contracts?

Do you need someone on board who will immediately slash supply costs and streamline purchasing operations?

   With more than 20 years in purchasing, retail sales management, store expansions, and new product research and market launch, I believe I may offer just what you're missing.
   In my esteemed career with ABC, a premier auto parts and accessories distributor, I have:

- Directed procurement of over £100M of goods and services, accounting for 60% of ABC's total purchasing budget.
- Launched 3 private label programmes, garnering £500k in additional profits during the first year of distribution.
- Recouped £300k in stolen merchandise and prosecuted the employees responsible.
- Generated £3M in savings by cultivating partnerships and negotiating long-term contracts with key suppliers.

   With the right opportunity, I'd be perfectly willing to relocate. With regard to salary, I understand that flexibility is essential and would consider a compensation package appropriate for a person with my outstanding qualifications and dynamic track record of accomplishments.
   If you're tired of seeing your company's profits slip through your fingers, ring me today to arrange a business meeting. I can't wait to discuss how I could benefit your purchasing operation right away. I can be reached at the number below to arrange our interview.

Yours faithfully,

James Swift
020 8123 4567

Broadcast e-mail (logistics)

From: James Swift [logisticspro@earth.ink.net]
To: careers@ryder.com
Cc:
Subject: A logical choice for your client

Dear Careers,

An industry association referred to your organization as an active and selective executive search firm, and mentioned your name because of your work in logistics. I liked that referral and think our meeting would be mutually beneficial.

I have a successful career in using logistics to cut costs and improve profits, usually in concert with other parts of the business. For example:

● I supervised the start-up of several remote offices to assist our plants in improving their distribution operations. By offering customized service, and through sharp negotiations, we saved over £500 million in various operations and warehouse costs.
● I directed the efforts of sizeable computer resources in the design and installation of a major application that saved £2.5 million in carrier costs. The application became the standard throughout the company's forty-six locations.
● Working with International Sales, I have established various Quality Control programmes that have improved the timeliness and accuracy of product and paperwork delivery. Customer complaints plummeted to virtually zero, and remain there today.

A recent reorganization has reduced the number of senior management positions available within my company. I have concluded that another firm may offer a position and career advancement more in line with my personal expectations.

I would like to talk to you further. I suggest next week, the week of October 29, when you have a free minute. I have asked my staff to forward your message immediately in case I am unavailable when you call. I look forward to hearing from you.

Sincerely,

James Swift
020 8123 4567

Broadcast e-mail (new product marketing)

From: James Swift [marketing export@ad.com]
To: jsmith@recruitment.com
Cc:
Subject: Real Marketing Savvy

Dear Mr Smith,

If you are looking for a successful executive to take charge of new product marketing, you will be interested in talking to me.

Ten years of experience in every aspect of marketing and sales in different industries give me the confidence to be open to opportunities in almost any field. My search is focused on companies that innovate, because I am particularly effective at new product marketing. I have successfully managed new product-marketing research, launch planning, advertising, product training and sales support, as well as direct sales. In my current position with XYZ Company, I created several products and marketing approaches on which other operating divisions in the company based their programmes.

My business education includes a Marketing MBA from _____ University's School of Management, and provides me with a variety of useful analytical tools in managing problems and maximizing opportunities. My superior sales track record guarantees that I bring the reality of the marketplace to each business situation; I know what sells and why.

Currently, my total compensation package is in the low forties; I am looking for a company that rewards performance consistently.

Since I am currently weighing several interesting opportunities, please contact me immediately if you are conducting any searches that might be a good fit. Relocation is no problem.

Thank you in advance for your consideration.

Yours sincerely,

James Swift
020 8123 4567

Broadcast e-mail (senior marketing executive)

From: Jane Swift [marketingexec@yahoo.com]
To: hr@marketingpros.com
Cc:
Subject: Ref: Your Marketing Executive Search

Dear Mr Sir or Madam,

I recently learned of your firm's excellent record of matching senior marketing executives with top organizations. I have also learned that you have an officer-level marketing assignment in process now – I am a serious candidate for your client's vacancy. Please consider some successes:

■   After joining _____ as Marketing Director, I revitalized a declining processed-meat product category in less than a year, introducing better-tasting formulas and actually reducing product costs by over £100,000. Dramatic new packaging enhanced customer appeal, and fresh promotion strategies doubled previous sales records.
■   I have carefully crafted and fine-tuned many new product introductions and line extensions, such as _____ turkey, _____ processed meats, and _____'s deodorant maxi-pads.
■   My sales/marketing experience dates from 1990, when I formed a direct sales company to pay for my _____ MBA (now the top-rated programme in the UK, I'm proud to say). Much of my subsequent success springs from strong working relationships with sales management and joint sales calls with field reps and marketing brokers. I have designed events like the _____ programme, and _____'s sponsorship of the City football team.
■   I have a strong personal and professional interest in consumer electronics. I consult professionally and have successfully adapted marketing techniques for home and commercial satellite systems, 'high-tech' audio/video, and radio communications equipment.

Please inform your client I am fluent in French and I quickly absorb other languages. If your client challenges executives with the greatest of responsibilities and rewards them for remarkable performance, please contact me as soon as possible. I'll quickly repeat my past successes.

Sincerely,

Jane Swift
020 8123 4567

Broadcast e-mail (director, asset liquidation)

From: James Swift [assetliquidationpro@mindspring.com]
To: hr@careermaster.com
Cc:
Subject: Asset liquidation challenge? Get this guy!

Dear Human Resources,

In recent years, as the Director of Lease Asset Liquidation with XYZ UK, I successfully engineered the recovery of £23 million in assets, almost three times the original buyout offer of £8 million. Throughout my career I have been instrumental in developing and implementing workout and liquidation strategies and as such I have earned a strong reputation as a professional who gets the job done.

My reason for contacting you is simple. I am interested in project opportunities that will serve both to challenge and to make use of my abilities in asset liquidation management. My current project will be completed within the next four to six weeks. I am currently considering offers and intend to make a decision by 1st February.

The attached summary details some of my accomplishments. I look forward to hearing from you to discuss any mutually beneficial opportunities. Please feel free to pass along my CV to others who may have a need for my professional assistance.

Sincerely,

James Swift
020 8123 4567

Power phrases

Consider using adaptations of these key phrases in your broadcast letters.

I hope this summary describes my experience and provides you with a better understanding of my capabilities. Thank you for your help.

If you feel that any of the strengths outlined in my CV could make a valuable contribution to your organization, please contact me to let me know of your interest.

Recently I read about the expansion of your company in the _____. As the _____ industry is of great interest to me, I was excited to learn of the new developments within ABC Ltd.

I feel confident that a short conversation about my experience and your growth plans would be mutually beneficial. I will be ringing you early next week to follow up this letter.

Currently, my total compensation package is in the low £40Ks; and I am looking for a company that rewards performance consistently.

I'm a responsive and responsible listener, maintaining a gracious and empathetic attitude, creatively troubleshooting, thoroughly researching options and making well-thought-out recommendations designed to establish and enhance customer/client relationships.

I am available for relocation and travel and am looking for compensation in the £30K range.

I fervently request more than your cursory consideration; I request your time to verify my claims. YOUR TIME WILL NOT BE WASTED.

Superior recommendations from industry leaders as well as verifiable salary history are available.

I hope you will not think me presumptuous in writing directly to you; however, in view of your position, I believe that you are more aware of your organization's telecommunications personnel requirements than anyone else.

I am confident that with my experience I can make a significant contribution to your organization.

Throughout my career, I've been fortunate to represent quality merchandise and services and have learned just how to present them in their most favourable light. I know how to evaluate competition, to assess consumer/market needs, exploit a market niche, maximize profit margins, and create and maintain a reputation for dependability and excellent service.

I am a self-starter looking to join a reputable firm, one that could benefit from an individual who is ready to give 110 per cent. With over three years of sales experience, I have developed excellent interpersonal, organizational and communication skills. I am a hard-working individual who is motivated by the knowledge that my earnings are directly related to the time, energy and effort that I commit to my position.

I am personable, present a highly professional image, and deal effectively with both peers and clientele. I am confident you will agree that I should be representing your firm and not your competition. My salary requirements are negotiable. I will ring you this week to set up a mutually convenient time for an interview.

Since beginning with ABC Company, my average commission has progressed from £250 to £400 a week. My current salary or commission requirement would range upward of the mid-£20ks, with specifics flexible and negotiable.

I look forward to hearing from you in the near future to arrange an interview with you, during which I hope to learn more about the position, your company's plans and goals, and how I can contribute to the success of your team.

I am grateful for that environment and the faith that was demonstrated in my capabilities. I automatically moved into the role of Executive Assistant, constantly seeking ways to limit expenses, cut costs and generate additional profit for the company. I was exceptionally successful in that endeavour – while managing 5 operations, 3 warehouses, 6 Warehouse Managers and a staff of 60.

I appreciate the time you've spent reviewing this letter (and the accompanying material). I hope to hear from you in the very near future to arrange to meet in person and discuss just how my qualifications may be of value to your organization.

Networking letter (managerial/administrative position)

A colleague that James hasn't spoken to in several months has been nominated for a prestigious award. He decides to capitalize on an opportunity to renew the acquaintance and enlist her help in his job search.

James Swift
18 Park Street
London X1 0BB
0208 123 4567

January 12, 20–

Ms Philippa Consodine, Managing Director
ABC Ltd
Industry Square
London X2 2EF

Dear Philippa,

Congratulations on your nomination for the Athena Award. Even though you were not the ultimate winner, the nomination itself demonstrates the high degree of professional excellence you have achieved.

It's been a while since we chatted, and I wanted to bring you up to date on what I've been doing. After leaving The Highlands, I explored several options before accepting a position as Director of Human Resources for XYZ. Unfortunately, the daily drive to Anytown, among other factors, proved to be untenable – particularly during the winter months – and I have left that position.

This puts me back in the job market, and I am writing to enquire if you are aware of any managerial/administrative positions that would capitalize on my skills. I have enclosed for your reference an updated CV that includes my recent experience.

Reiterating some of the key capabilities that I can bring to a position, consider the following:

- **Excellent team building and leadership skills**
- **Superb interpersonal skills and supervisory experience**
- **Developing and implementing human resource policies**
- **Extensive knowledge and experience in the healthcare arena**

I am convinced that my experience and professional diligence could be an asset to one of ABC's member companies, and would appreciate any referrals you may be able to give me for potential employment opportunities. I will contact you to arrange a convenient date and time when we might renew acquaintances. In the meantime, feel free to pass my CV on to anyone who may have an appropriate opportunity, or give me a call on 020 8123 4567.

Thank you in advance for your assistance. I look forward to talking to you soon.

Sincerely,

James Swift

James Swift

Enclosure

Networking letter (administrative assistant)

This 'insider' networking letter positions well for an administrative assistant, especially since this firm values foreign language proficiency in German and French.

Jane Swift
18 Park Street, London X1 0BB • 020 8123 4567

April 26, 20–

Mr Tom O'Kane
Head of Human Resources
ABC Ltd
Industry Square
London X2 2EF

Dear Mr O'Kane,

Kirsten Alexander of Human Resources suggested that I contact you in regard to applying for a position as an Administrative Assistant. If you have need of a well-qualified professional with German and French language skills and experience in office administration, customer service, sales, training, and marketing, then we have good reason to meet.

My CV is enclosed for your review. Highlights include:

✔ Over eight years' experience in organization, coordination, communication, and customer service. Consistently focus on creating and maintaining excellent client relationships, and training others in successful techniques to do the same.
✔ A resourceful problem-solver with a track record of getting positive results, such as a 75% collection rate on accounts 90 days past due.
✔ Ability to build confidence and trust at all levels, and demonstrated experience in supporting cooperative, results-oriented environments.
✔ Proven communication skills, including fluency in French and German.

My career success has been due in large part to supporting teams, as well as internal and external customer relationships, and tackling persistent problem areas with creative approaches. I am seeking the opportunity to use my experience, skills, and enthusiasm in a new organization where I can continue to contribute to bottom-line results while growing professionally.

Should my qualifications meet with your needs, I would be available to schedule a meeting immediately. I will call your office next week to answer any questions you may have and to set up a mutually convenient appointment. Thank you for your consideration.

Sincerely,

Jane Swift

Jane Swift

Enc. CV

Networking letter (creative media)

A letter from a Japanese exchange student pursuing either work experience or employment in a new education programme.

Jane Swift

November 14, 20–

Ms Deborah Marks
Chairman, Creative Media Dept.
University of London
Industry Square
London X2 2EF

Dear Ms Marks,

Since meeting you earlier this year at the Korean Film Festival we have exchanged e-mails and met several times. We have discussed our mutual interest in the Japanese film industry and its future in the global entertainment business. You know well my vision of integrating Japanese gaming and animation technologies into filmmaking.

Over the course of our conversations, you have mentioned that there might be an opportunity for employment in the Creative Media Department. I am very interested.

I offer negotiation, persuasion, and liaison abilities; and management, leadership, and communication skills. I have also proven that I can use my bilingual proficiency to enhance international relations. Please see my CV for examples of how I have used these abilities in the past.

I believe that my unique strengths can contribute to the growth of the Creative Media programme, particularly if you are able to secure departmental status. I welcome the opportunity to discuss my continued involvement in your programme.

Sincerely,

Jane Swift

Jane Swift

Enclosure: 2-page CV
Addendum of Completed Coursework

---

18 Park Street London X1 10BB
020 8123 4567 • jane@hotmail.com

Networking letter (management)

JANE SWIFT
18 Park Street, London X1 0BB
020 8123 4567   jane@anyaddress.co.uk

[Date]

Philip_____, [Title]
ABC Ltd
Industry Square
London X2 2EF

Dear Mr _____,

It has been said, *'in today's world there are two kinds of companies – the quick and the dead'.* I propose the same is true of managers. I am a dynamic management professional with extraordinary team-building and interpersonal skills, and thrive in a fast-paced environment that is constantly moving and producing solid bottom-line results. I relish a challenge and will never run from a difficult situation. In fact, if you want a successful completion, you can count on it, accurately, timely and right the first time.

In addition to solid people skills, I possess an extensive management background in International Affairs. While living in Germany for five years, I had the opportunity to study the language and culture. Bilingual with excellent comprehension of both German and English, my translation skills are strong in both languages. I also have conversational knowledge of French. Having held direct responsibility for commercial dealings with the UK, Ireland, and Germany, my knack for capturing key client relations with diverse cultures and people is intense. I would like to bring my business savvy and management/marketing skills to your firm.

My experience spans industries such as Property Development, International Affairs and Procurement; however, I am an ideal candidate for a company that values a well-rounded person who can step in wherever needed and isn't afraid to learn. Dedicated to doing whatever it takes to achieve outstanding results, I would lead your team to meet tight deadlines. In short, I would not let you down.

My CV is enclosed for your consideration. I look forward to meeting you to discuss your needs and the immediate impact I would make on your organization.

Yours sincerely,

Jane Swift

Enclosure

Networking letter (computer and information systems manager)

A letter sent to follow up a meeting with a medical school dean.

James Swift

18 Park Street • London X1 0BB
020 8123 4567 • jswift@alohanet.com

January 14, 20–

John Jones, M.D.
Dean, Faculty of Medicine
University of London
Industry Square
London X2 2EF

Dear Dr Jones:

Perhaps you remember our chance meeting at the Bio Asia-Pacific Conference at the XYZ Hotel Waikiki on August 18 and 19, 20–. In our brief conversation, I shared with you the idea of using Web Development as an administrative tool. You expressed interest in the possibility of implementing such a system within the Faculty of Medicine.

May I suggest a formal meeting to explore the idea?

I have some exciting and creative ideas, which may encourage you to take the next step toward realizing the positive impact a content management system would have in the Faculty of Medicine. This would also be a great opportunity for us to discuss your goals and how an administrative intranet would help you reach them in a more timely and cost-effective manner.

In addition, there has recently been spirited discussion within the IT community on the topic of organizational continuity and its potential vulnerability due to advances in technology. I think you'll find the specific strategies I have to share with you worthy of consideration.

If you recall, my background is in Web Planning and Developing, with specific skills in developing administrative intranets and public Web sites, and designing Web-based software to address the internal and external reporting needs of organizations.

Enclosed is my CV attesting to my experience and specialities. I will contact you within the next few days to discuss the possibility of meeting you.

Respectfully,

James Swift

James Swift

Computer and Information Systems Manager
Enclosure: CV

Networking letter (chief financial officer)

JAMES SWIFT
18 Park Street ● London X1 0BB
020 8123 4567 james@anyaddress.co.uk

Dear _____,

Perhaps your company could benefit from a strong chief financial officer with a record of major contributions to business and profit growth.

The scope of my expertise is extensive and includes the full complement of corporate finance, accounting, budgeting, banking, tax, treasury, internal controls and reporting functions. Equally important are my qualifications in business planning, operations, MIS technology, administration and general management.

A business partner to management, I have been effective in working with all departments, linking finance with operations to improve productivity, efficiency and bottom-line results. Recruited at The XYZ Company to provide finance and systems technology expertise, I created a solid infrastructure to support corporate growth as the company made the transition from a wholesale-retail distributor to a retail operator. Recent accomplishments include:

- **Significant contributor to the increase in operating profits from under £400k to more than £4M.**
- **Key member of due diligence team in the acquisition of 25 operating units that increased market penetration 27% and gross sales 32%.**
- **Spearheaded leading-edge MIS design and implementation, streamlining systems and procedures that dramatically enhanced productivity while cutting costs.**

A 'hands-on' manager effective in building team work and cultivating strong internal/external relationships, I am flexible and responsive to the quickly changing demands of the business, industry and marketplace. If you are seeking a talented and proactive finance executive to complement your management team, I would welcome a personal interview. Thank you for your consideration.

Yours sincerely,

James Swift

Enclosure

Networking letter (general)

JAMES SWIFT
18 Park Street, London X1 0BB
020 8123 4567   james@anyaddress.co.uk

[date]

Mr Philip_____
ABC Ltd
Industry Square
London X2 2EF

Dear Philip,

Congratulations on your re-election. I hope this letter finds you and your family well and that you have an enjoyable Christmas.

I am writing to update you on my job search. You may recall from our last discussion that I am now focusing on obtaining a position that will sustain me until such time as I am ready for retirement (in three to five years).

As you recommended, I have applications on file with ABC for various hourly-paid positions and have corresponded with various department heads, in each case indicating my flexibility and strong interest in making a meaningful contribution to smooth operations within one of their departments.

I genuinely appreciate the advice and assistance you have offered to date. Once again, I am requesting that if you are aware of any other avenues I should be pursuing, please let me know. I believe I have skills and experience to offer and can be an asset to someone in just about any position requiring maturity, reliability and dedication.

Thank you, again, for all you help, and 'Merry Christmas'.

Sincerely,

James Swift

Networking letter (accounting)

James Swift
18 Park Street • London X1 0BB • 0208 123 4567
accountingpro@aol.com

(date)

Mr Philip _____
ABC Manufacturing Ltd
1 Industry Square
London X2 2EF

Dear Mr _____,

As a motivated accounting professional with proven capabilities in financial analysis and accounting management, I believe that my education and experience could benefit your company. For this reason, I have enclosed a CV for your review, which outlines my relevant experiences. Some key qualifications that may be of interest to your firm include:

● Extensive experience in providing timely and accurate financial reports using a variety of applications and procedures. I have managed accounting functions for a manufacturing firm with over £100 million sales. I advanced quickly in the finance department and have gained a wide range of experience, primarily focusing my efforts on analysing, reporting, and planning.
● Absolute reliability and dedication to efficiency. As key financial analyst, I have worked closely with controllers and managers in monitoring financial input/output, streamlining financial reporting processes, and meeting aggressive deadlines for delivering information and analyses. I am also knowledgeable and current on legislative and regulatory requirements.
● Long-term vision. I have participated in both strategic planning for long-term marketing, and in annual budget preparation. My analyses and input have contributed to the successful outcomes of external audits, annual reviews, and budgeting processes in domestic operations.
● Proficiency in current business applications, including CODA, DCS, 4TH Shift, FAS1000, MP 2, FOCUS, and Microsoft Office.

I have a strong desire to move into a business environment where my skills can be fully used effectively furthering a leading firm's business objectives. I am confident that my knowledge and expertise, along with my dedicated professionalism, would allow me to make a significant contribution to your company's ongoing success. I would enjoy meeting you to discuss the possibilities further. Please contact me to arrange a convenient date and time for an interview. Thank you for your time and consideration. I look forward to speaking to you soon.

Sincerely,

James Swift

James Swift

Enclosure

Networking e-mail (HR administration)

From: James Swift [hrspecialist@hotmail.com]
To: hr@careers.com
Cc:
Subject: Great to talk to you again!

Dear _____,

It was a pleasure to speak to you on the telephone recently and, even more so, to be remembered after all these years.

As mentioned during our conversation, I have just recently re-entered the job market and have ten years of experience with a 3,000-employee retail organization in the area of human resources administration. My experience includes recruitment and selection, human resources planning and employee relations. I have been responsible for all facets of management of the company personnel, including development and training, and liaison with both staff and training providers.

My goal is to become an HR Manager in a larger organization with the possibility of advancement in the human resources area. My preference is to remain in the South East.

For your information, my CV is attached. If any situations come to mind where you think my skills and background would fit or if you have any suggestions as to others to whom it might be beneficial for me to speak, I would appreciate hearing from you. I can be reached on the telephone number shown below.

Again, I very much enjoyed our conversation.

Yours truly,

James Swift
020 8123 4567

Networking e-mail (publishing)

From: James Swift [publishingpro@aol.com]
To: hr@jobsprofessional.com
Cc:
Subject: Thanks for all the help :-)

Dear _____,

It was a pleasure to meet you for lunch today. I am grateful for the time you took out of your busy schedule to assist me in my job search.

It was fascinating to learn about the new technology which is beginning to play a major role in the publishing field. I have already been to the book shop to purchase the book by _____ which you highly recommended. I look forward to reading about his 'space age' ideas.

I will be contacting _____ within the next few days to set up an appointment. I will let you know how things are progressing once I have met her.

Thanks again for your help. You will be hearing from me soon.

Yours sincerely,

James Swift
020 8123 4567

Power phrases

Consider using adaptations of these key phrases in your networking letters.

It was good talking to you again. As promised, I am enclosing a copy of my CV for your information. If any appropriate opportunities come to your attention, I would appreciate it if you would keep me in mind.

After you have had a chance to look over the CV, please give me a ring.

I am beginning to put some 'feelers' out in advance of the completion of my degree in December.

I do not intend to target any specific type of job. I am open to almost anything that my qualifications will fit. My only criteria are the following:...

I would appreciate any advice and/or referrals you might be able to give me.

I am looking for a position in management and would appreciate any assistance you could provide.

As always, it was good to talk to you. Your positive outlook is catching. I've been called the eternal optimist, but I always feel more upbeat after a conversation with you.

Many thanks for the words of encouragement and taking the time from your busy schedule to help me. It is truly appreciated. I have never faced an unemployment situation like this before.

It was a pleasure to speak to you on the telephone recently and, even more so, to be remembered after all these years.

For your information, enclosed is my CV. If any situations come to mind where you think my skills and background would fit, or if you have any suggestions as to others to whom it might be beneficial for me to speak, I would appreciate hearing from you. I can be reached on the telephone numbers listed above.

He assured me that he would pass my CV along to you; however, in the event that it has not reached you yet, I am enclosing another.

Perhaps you know of a company that could use this scope of experience. In this regard, I enclose a copy of my CV outlining a few of my more significant accomplishments.

My objective is to find a _____ level position at a marketing-driven company where my skills can contribute to the firm's growth and profitability.

I am not limited by location and would consider the opportunity wherever it presented itself.

First of all, let me thank you sincerely for taking the time and trouble to return my call last Monday. I found our conversation informative, entertaining and (alas) a little scary. Needless to say, I genuinely appreciate your prompt response and generous, helpful advice.

Again, a thousand thanks for your time and consideration. If I might ask you one last favour, could you please give me your opinion of the revision? A copy is enclosed.

I am writing to you in response to our recent conversation over the telephone. I thank you for your time and your advice. It was most generous of you and sincerely appreciated. Please accept my apologies for invading your privacy. I anticipated an address for written correspondence from an answering service.

I look forward to hearing from you on your next visit to _____.

I hope you'll keep me in mind if you hear of anything that's up my street!

I recently learned that your firm is well-connected with manufacturers in the _____ area and does quality work. We should talk soon, since it's very likely we can help each other. I'll be in the office all next week and look forward to hearing from you. I have alerted my secretary; she'll put your call right through.

_____ suggested that I contact you regarding employment opportunities.

After many years in the _____ community, I have decided that a career change is due in order to use my interpersonal skills to their fullest.

Follow-up letter (after telephone contact) (fundraising consultant)

From an applicant who has had too many jobs in too few years, this letter was designed to get two competing 'partners' to bring her on board.

Jane Swift

02 May 20–

Ms Patty Martineau
Director
ABC Associates
Industry Square
London X2 2EF

Dear Ms Martineau,

Thank you for making time to explore how I could help ABC Associates as your newest Fundraising Consultant.

I've already starting thinking about how I might be most productive – right from the start. Of course, my ideas must be preliminary; I don't know exactly how your organization works. Nevertheless, I would value your reactions to the preliminary thoughts you'll find in the next paragraphs.

I want each of your clients to see the tailored solutions we provide as a rapid, seamless, continuing operation that guides them through the complex world of modern fundraising. In fact, I want them to think of us as their 'sole source' for the resources they must have to grow financially and operationally. If we are to speak with the one voice the clients should demand, then our business model requires close teamwork between Ms O'Neill, you, and me.

In the meantime, I am modifying my own continuing professional development programme to concentrate on fundraising from a consultant's perspective. I've begun to look through the literature and contact professional organizations to hear about the latest trends directly from industry leaders. Later, I'll use what I learn to re-evaluate my own successes in campaigns done with and without consultants.

I appreciate your vote of confidence in recommending that I meet with Ms O'Neill. And I want to make that interview just as useful for her as possible. Toward that end, may I call in a few days to get your reactions to the preliminary thoughts I've outlined above?

With many thanks for all your help…

Sincerely,

Jane Swift

Jane Swift

18 Park Street • London X1 0BB
020 8123 4567 (home) • js@randomc.com

Follow-up letter (after telephone contact)
(adult education)

JANE SWIFT

---

18 Park Street
London X1 0BB
020 8123 4567

EDUCATOR/ADVOCATE/MENTOR
'Every leader a teacher, every teacher a leader, every student a success.'

Emily _____
(Title)
Anytown Community College
1 Industry Square
London X2 2EF

Dear Ms _____,

   I enclose my CV in follow-up to our conversation last week regarding the adult education position currently available at Anytown Community College. I appreciate very much your offer to forward my credentials to the appropriate individual.
   With a master's degree in Education Administration, plus four years of cumulative experience in the classroom, I believe I possess the expertise and qualifications that are critical to leading your organization's adult students to successfully achieve their educational goals.
   What do I offer your students?

- Effective listening and communication skills – a demonstrated ability to provide individualized instruction based on students' interests and needs.
- Encouragement and motivation – a creative, inviting atmosphere, no matter what age, skill level, or cultural background.

   I am excited at the opportunity to work with adult students, because I recognize that they are in that classroom because they want to be there. The adult population brings a unique flavour of enthusiasm and motivation that energizes and inspires me as an instructor and makes me eager to go above and beyond expectations to help them reach their goals.
   In terms of salary, I realize that flexibility is essential and am therefore open to discussing your organization's compensation package for an individual with my distinctive talents. If you believe that I could play an important role on your educational team, please call me at 020 8123 4567 to arrange an interview.

Sincere regards,

Jane Swift

Jane Swift

enclosure

Follow-up letter (after telephone contact)
(legal assistant)

JANE SWIFT
18 Park Street, London X1 0BB
020 8123 4567   jane@anyaddress.co.uk

[Date]

Phillip _____
[Title]
ABC Ltd
Industry Square
London X2 2EF

Dear Mr _____,

Thank you for returning my telephone call yesterday. It was a pleasure speaking to you and, as promised, a copy of my CV is enclosed. As I mentioned, I have been working in law firms since the end of February, as well as working on weekends and in the evenings for over one year. At present, I am looking for a second or third shift to continue developing my word-processing and legal skills.

Although the majority of my positions have been more managerial and less secretarial, I have developed strong office skills over the years. While I was attending both undergraduate and graduate courses, I worked as an Administrative Assistant to Faculty and Department Heads, in addition to working in other professional capacities.

_____ speaks very highly of me, and if you need to confirm a reference with him, please feel free to contact him at _____. In addition, I would be happy to supply you with names of people I have worked for within law firms over the past year.

Within the next day, I will be contacting you to arrange a convenient meeting time to discuss the position you now have available. However, if you would like to speak to me, feel free to contact me on 020 8123 4567.

Thank you again for calling yesterday. I look forward to speaking to you on the telephone, and meeting you in person.

Sincerely,

Jane Swift

Jane Swift

enclosure

Follow-up letter (after telephone contact) (purchasing)

James Swift
18 Park Street, London X1 0BB
020 8123 4567   james@anyaddress.co.uk

[Date]

Bob _____
[Title]
ABC Ltd
Industry Square
London X2 2EF

Dear Mr _____,

In reference to our telephone conversation, enclosed is my _____ CV. I believe the one you have is written with a purchasing position in mind.

Since we last spoke I have been working as a business consultant for the _____ group of companies on projects in a number of different areas outlined below.

- Spearheaded and supervised upgrading of the _____ companies' communications systems, including printing and copy machines, telecommunications systems, computer hardware and software systems, computer scanning system, computer filing system, and fax and modem transmission systems.
- Set up and implemented an auto and entry floor mat marketing programme for _____ including pricing and product displays for retail sales outlets.
- Researched, purchased and installed a bar code labelling programme for the companies' products, including label set-up and printing systems to allow them to sell their products to _____.
- Participated in the design and layout of a new logo for _____ division including specifications for all letterheads, forms and printed communications materials.
- Provided major input for a factory-paid _____ point-of-sale system to display custom automotive floor mats.

Most of my projects should be wrapped up by the end of November, and so I will be looking for another company that could make use of my broad range of experience. Please let me know if you think you might have something for me.

Sincerely,

James Swift

James Swift

enclosure

Follow-up letter (after telephone contact) (manager)

James Swift
18 Park Street, London X1 0BB
020 8123 4567   james@anyaddress.co.uk

[Date]

Bob _____
[Title]
ABC Ltd
Industry Square
London X2 2EF

Dear Mr _____,

THANK YOU for allowing me to tell you a little about myself. I have just completed my MBA (December, 20 —) and would appreciate the opportunity to talk to your client companies who are in need of an experienced and seasoned manager. Whether the need is for general (operational) management, products, marketing or sales, my substantial background in management, marketing and technical products should be very valuable to your clients.

I have enclosed two CVs (marketing-oriented and operational-oriented) with some other information which you may find useful. With eyes firmly welded to the bottom line, I offer: the ABILITY to manage, build and quickly understand the business; EXPERIENCE in domestic and international corporate cultures; INTELLIGENCE and the capacity to grasp essential elements; and the WILLINGNESS to work hard, travel and relocate.

Realizing that most of your clients aren't looking for Directors, I'm not necessarily looking for fancy titles (but I am promotable). What I am looking for is that special position which will offer not only a challenge but a career opportunity with long-range potential. I know my successes will bring them (and me) rewards.

CVs and letters are brief by their very nature and cannot tell the whole story. I would be happy to discuss with your client and you how my commitment to them will help solve their needs or problems and will definitely make good things happen! After all, isn't that the bottom line?

May we work together?

Yours sincerely,

James Swift

James Swift

enclosures

Follow-up e-mail (after telephone contact) (general)

From: Jane Swift [swift@earthlink.net]
To: hr@ltdcompany.com
Cc:
Subject: Glad we finally met

Dear Ms _____,

I appreciate the time you took yesterday to discuss the position at _____. I recognize that timing and awareness of interest are very important in searches of this type. Your comment regarding an attempt to contact me earlier this summer is a case in point.

Attached, as you requested, you will find an outline CV. I also believe that my experiences as a director of physical plant services are readily transferable to a new environment. I believe that I can contribute a great deal to the satisfaction of your client's needs.

Realizing that letters and CV are not an entirely satisfactory means of judging a person's ability or personality, I suggest a personal interview to discuss further your client's needs and my qualifications. I can be reached directly or via message on 020 8123 4567, so that we may arrange a mutually convenient time to meet. I look forward to hearing from you. Thank you for your time and consideration.

Sincerely,

Jane Swift
020 8123 4567

Follow-up e-mail (after telephone contact) (arts management)

From: Jane Swift [promotionspro@yahoo.com]
To: jsmith@artsmanagement.com
Cc:
Subject: Thanks from a motivated fanatic

Dear Ms Smith,

As per yesterday's conversation, I am forwarding a copy of my CV and am looking forward to our meeting in the very near future.

As we discussed, the positions which interest me are as follows:

     Event/Arts Management
     Promotions/Advertising/Public Relations
     Corporate Training

I am a fanatic about image, excellence and attention to quality and detail. As my academic and career background reveal, I have the tenacity of a terrier when it comes to task accomplishment.

I have never held a '9 to 5' job and would most likely be bored to death if I had one. Therefore, I am looking for something fast-paced and challenging to my grey matter that will allow growth and advancement and an opportunity to learn. I am in my element when I am in a position to organize … the more details the better!

I'll give you a call on Tuesday, — th March to try to arrange an appointment for further discussion.

Sincerely,

Jane Swift
020 8123 4567

Power phrases

Consider using adaptations of these key phrases in your follow-up letters after phone calls.

As you requested in our telephone conversation this morning, I am enclosing a copy of my CV for your review.

As you can see from my CV, I have some excellent secretarial experience.

I'll give you a ring on Tuesday, —th March to arrange an appointment for further discussion.

In reference to our telephone conversation, enclosed is my sales and marketing CV; I believe the one you have is written with a purchasing position in mind.

I am a bright, articulate and well-groomed professional with excellent telemarketing skills, sales instincts and closing abilities. I am seeking a dynamic position with a reputable firm. I would like to meet you in person to discuss how I could contribute to the effectiveness of your clients' operations.

Again, thank you for your flexibility and for arranging this at a time convenient to me.

Please remember me if something arises that would tie in with my background.

My many long-term professional relationships would benefit any employer in this area.

I'd like to meet you to tell you more about my background and to show you some of the training and marketing materials I've developed. This would give you a better picture of my capabilities.

As you suggested when we spoke last week, I have enclosed my CV for your review and consideration. I contacted you on the recommendation of _____ of _____, who thought that you might have an interest in my qualifications for a position in the near future.

I have long admired _____ for its innovations in the industry, and I would consider it a tremendous career opportunity to be associated with your organization.

Follow-up letter (after face-to-face meeting)
(library system director)

Jane was genuinely impressed with the facility she visited, but also recognized she could help them improve by applying her management experience.

Jane Swift
18 Park Street • London X1 0BB • 020 8123 4567

January 12, 20–

Ms Louisa May Prescott
County Library Services
Industry Square
London X2 2EF

Dear Ms Prescott,

Thank you for the opportunity to visit your facilities and discuss the Director's position with you. I enjoyed meeting you and the other trustees, as well as Sylvia Morrison and members of the library staff. I was impressed with your outline of the position and believe that I possess the capabilities to successfully lead the County Library system well into the 21st century.

My tour of three of your branches and my conversations with several staff members made it easy for me to understand how you have achieved your national ranking. As someone with over 20 years in the library field, and experience visiting literally hundreds of library branches in the course of a year, I was favourably impressed with the design and space of your branches. The cordiality of your staff members and the good way in which the facilities are maintained are also quite impressive. Your 'Friends' organization also appears to be a real asset to the library.

Some key talents that I can bring to this leadership position include:

- *Establishing a strategic vision and motivating staff to pursue that vision.*
- *Maintaining productive rapport with advisory boards, and successfully interacting with governmental entities and the community at-large to achieve library goals.*
- *Developing information technology plans that have prepared libraries for the 21st century and that anticipate the changing technological landscape.*

I remain most interested in this position and am confident that my knowledge and expertise would allow me to exceed your expectations in this leadership role. I look forward to discussing my application further with you soon.

Sincerely,

Jane Swift

Jane Swift

Follow-up letter (after face-to-face meeting) (sales)

A two-point letter: (1) reinforces the point that he was successful in sales, even though he hadn't ever worked in pharmaceutical sales, and (2) moves the hiring official to make a decision.

JAMES SWIFT

18 Park Street • London X1 0BB • 020 8123 4567 • jswift72@aol.com

July 20, 20–

Mark Pugh
Area Manager
ABC Pharmaceuticals
Industry Square
London X2 2EF

Dear Mr Pugh,

Thank you for making time to meet me this morning. Even during our interview, it struck me how good a match I think I am for ABC. And on the way home, I began to formulate a plan to be productive for you from the first day, based on how I might meet your special needs. Here's what I've come up with so far:

Your needs	My capabilities
● Good track record	● Bringing in twice my sales quotas for four consecutive years. ● Being my organization's top producer in those same four years.
● Communication skills that build sales	● Capturing sales with presentations before busy decision makers.
● Good work ethic	● Turning around a market that had been stagnant for 15 years. ● Regularly overcoming strong sales resistance.

I can offer everything you see above because I show the benefit of what I sell – not just to the end user, but to the people who deliver those benefits. That's a direct parallel with an ABC strength.

I've already spoken with your London representative. And I'm looking forward to my 'ride along'.

At this point, most applicants would ask you to contact them if you have questions. I want to do something different. Please consider this question: What additional information do you need from me to choose me as the best applicant for the position?

Sincerely,

James Swift

James Swift

Follow-up letter (after face-to-face meeting)
(loan processor)

James had to overcome the effects of a prolonged slowdown in his industry – portfolio management – and convince the decision maker that his skills were transferable and he could master the intricacies of new product lines he had never worked with before.

James Swift

18 Park Street
London X1 0BB

020 8123 4567 (Home)
020 8345 6789 (Office)
jswift@hotmail.com

13 June, 20–

Malcolm S McLeod
Director
ABC Finance
Industry Square
London X2 2EF

Dear Mr McLeod,

Thank you for meeting me this afternoon. I think ABC Finance and I are a good match if I can be your newest loan processor.

In fact, as I was driving back to Laindon, I began to plan how I might be productive for you right from the start. My ideas are, of course, preliminary. But I would value your reactions to this tentative plan:

- I would start by introducing myself to every 'player'. I want them to think of me as ABC Finance. And I want to find out what their special needs are before any rush requirements come up. When they need answers, I want them to remember two things: my name and my phone number.

- I have already started my plan to master your requirements. As a first step, I'm jotting down the kinds of questions I must have the answers to so I can process mortgage loans fast and right the first time. I want ABC Finance to be the 'provider of choice' in the eyes of buyers and agents – in short, anyone who wants quality loan processing services. If I am successful, I hope our percentage of revenue for mortgage loan processing grows steadily.

As you asked me to, I plan to call on Friday. And I've already thought of the question I would most like to ask. Here it is: Will the plan I've outlined above work for ABC Finance faster and better than any plan suggested by the other candidates you've interviewed?

Sincerely,

James Swift

James Swift

Follow-up letter (after face-to-face meeting)
(hospitality manager)

Lacking professional experience as a concierge, Olivia was sure to remind her interviewers of her related volunteer work, enthusiasm, education, international travel experience, and multi-lingual communication skills. Notice how she copied ('cc') her interviewers.

Jane Swift

18 Park Street
London X1 0BB
020 8123 4567
worldtraveller@sky.net

February 19, 20–

Ms Janet Berlinger
Human Resources
ABC Hotel
Industry Square
London X2 2EF

Dear Ms Berlinger,

Thank you for the opportunity to participate in a follow-up interview with you and your supervising managers, Mr Sean Johnson and Mrs Rita Bronson, to discuss further the possibility of my joining your hospitality team as Hospitality Manager.

As discussed during our meeting, The ABC Hotel is the ideal work environment for me to express my enthusiasm for working with people as well as put to use my education in psychology and business administration. I feel strongly that my work experience at The XYZ Hotel and my personal experience acquired over the years while travelling worldwide will prove especially valuable in this highly visible position. Combined with an ability to communicate effectively in Spanish, French, and Italian, I feel I would make a significant contribution to The ABC Hotel.

Please note that my availability is immediate. If you need to contact me, I can be reached at the above telephone number. Thank you again for your time and consideration. I hope to speak to you soon.

Sincerely,

Jane Swift

Jane Swift

cc: Mr Sean Johnson
     Mrs Rita Bronson

Follow-up letter (after face-to-face meeting) (merchandise manager)

This thank-you letter capitalizes on reinforcing the 'fit' between the potential job and her qualifications, as well as introducing some areas overlooked in the interview.

Jane Swift

18 Park Street • London X1 0BB
020 8123 4567 Home • Email: jswift@bol.com

November 9, 20–

Ms Melinda Newby, Director
Human Resources
ABC Limited
Industry Square
London X2 2EF

Dear Ms Newby,

Thank you for the opportunity to interview for the **Merchandise Manager** position. You were extremely generous with your time and I was impressed with the warmth and efficiency of your office, and your genuine interest in acquainting me with the company's concepts and goals.

My background is unique – it does not fit into a traditional career mould – yet it encompasses a very diverse exposure in Home Furnishings and Ready-to-Wear. As we discussed, my extensive experience with the type of clientele your company targets has prepared me to quickly 'come on board' your team. My sales record of £279,000 (20–) demonstrates that I can produce immediate value, as well as train new sales reps in highly effective merchandising and closing techniques.

What I did not stress is that I have also built an arsenal of skills around quantitative, technical processes involved in merchandising planning. For example, I have developed six-month merchandising plans for the south west division of XYZ Apparel, and classification planning which established the focus on merchandise categories, prices, styles, sizes, and colours.

I have always strived to achieve high quality results by knowing the customer well, anticipating profitable market trends and never forgetting the store image. Offering wide, but well-edited, assortments of multiple classifications so that one-stop shopping can easily occur has been my hallmark. Such high standards have been central in all of my work, whether with a major retail department store, London wholesale showroom, or upmarket home furnishings boutique. Your corporate environment and company goals appear to reflect those same high standards and I am eager to join your team.

I am very interested in this position and would like to get in contact with you next week to check on the progress of your search. Thanks again for the opportunity to attend the interview.

Sincerely,

Jane Swift

Jane Swift

Follow-up letter (after face-to-face meeting) (manufacturer representative)

James Swift

18 Park Street   London X1 0BB
Home Phone: 020 8123 4567 • Mobile Phone: 07850 515536

February 28, 20–

Ms Kathleen McMann
General Manager
ABC Imaging
Industry Square
London X2 2EF

Dear Ms McMann,

Thank you for interviewing me on Friday, February 23rd, for the Manufacturer's Representative position. Everything I learned from you about ABC Imaging leads me to believe that this is a progressive company where I could fully use my skills and make a valuable contribution. In fact, I have not been this determined or excited about a job since I started my business 25 years ago.

As I mentioned to you, I am sales oriented and have a solid technical background in printing. I relate well to printers at any level. In my sales activities with John Watkins when he was a printing buyer at XYZ Industries, I found him to be very demanding and hard to please. One of the reasons why I was successful in acquiring and retaining his business was my constant commitment to customer service. Whenever there were any questions, I never failed to answer them promptly.

During our discussion, you seemed to express a concern about my lack of experience with dealers. Although I had not mentioned it at the time we spoke, I have had long-term relationships with dealers like DEF, and have bought approximately £1 million worth of equipment from them, starting with my first press and expanding to 20 over the years. I am certain that with my persistency and follow-through, I know I can handle dealers at the sales and service end. Rest assured that I would keep you informed of my progress on a daily basis. Nothing would be done without you knowing about it. My first priority will be to make you look good.

Among my major strengths, I am goal-driven, self-motivated, have a strong work ethic, and an ability to learn quickly. My training period would be brief, and I would use my own time to familiarize myself with your equipment and product line. In addition, I am accustomed to long hours and have no objection to the travel requirements throughout the UK or being away from home four days a week.

Coming from a medium-sized company, it would be an honour to work at ABC Imaging, and I am hopeful that I would have the chance to be a member of your team. Please do not hesitate to call me if you have any further questions or need additional information from me.

I look forward to your positive decision about my application.

Sincerely,

James Swift

James Swift

Follow-up letter (after face-to-face meeting) (general)

JANE SWIFT
18 Park Street, London X1 0BB
020 8123 4567   jane@anyaddress.co.uk

[Date]

Phillip _____
[Title]
ABC Ltd
Industry Square
London X2 2EF

Dear Mr _____,

Thank you very much for taking the time to meet me today. I enjoyed our discussion, and I'm now even more excited about the possibility of working for ABC and with your team.

It was great to learn that you are embracing technology as it relates to your business – both in terms of day-to-day operations and the future delivery of ABC's programmes (eg, on-the-spot training). I am very interested in, and have an affinity for, computer technology and would love to be a part of your efforts in this area.

I am confident that I could make a strong contribution to the continued growth of ABC. As we discussed, I have related experience in all of the required areas for the position. In addition, I look forward to taking a project management approach to establishing the new system for the delivery of the assessment workshops to your key client. This process would allow me to ensure that I am meeting your objectives and getting a system 'up and running' within an established time frame. Having done this, I would continually review for improvement and focus on managing the enhancement of customer service.

I remain very interested in the position, and I look forward to hearing from you soon. If you require additional information in the meantime, I may be reached on 020 8123 4567.

Sincerely,

Jane Swift

Jane Swift

Follow-up letter (after face-to-face meeting) (librarian)

JANE SWIFT
18 Park Street, London X1 0BB
020 8123 4567 jane@anyaddress.co.uk

[date]

Mr Philip_____
ABC Library Service
Industry Square
London X2 2EF

Dear Philip,

Thank you for the opportunity to meet you and the selection committee on Monday. I enjoyed our discussion of the Director for Library Development opening. I was impressed with your vision for this individual's role.

Based on our conversation, I believe that I possess the capabilities to successfully meet your expectations for this key position with the Library Service.

To reiterate the experiences I bring to this opportunity, please note the following:

- *Promoting programmes and fostering working relationships with over 1,000 member libraries in all major segments of the field. These activities also encompass extensive community outreach.*
- *Providing strategic vision and mission, and motivating staff to pursue visionary goals. In two leadership assignments, I have recognized staff for their efforts and given them the guidance and direction that has delivered exceptional programme results.*
- *Managing capital projects and spearheading information technology initiatives. These encompassed upgrades to comply with disabled access requirements, renovations that improved space utilization, and leading efforts to incorporate technology into library settings.*
- *Supervising departments in urban and suburban settings to address a broad range of competing priorities. Among these experiences was the supervision of an Interlibrary Loan department serving 100 individual branches in a five-county area.*

I am most interested in this position and am confident that my track record at XYZ demonstrates my capacity to 'hit the ground running', and apply my leadership, enthusiasm, and expertise to furthering the mission of the Library Service in this development role. I look forward to continuing our discussions in the near future.

Sincerely,

Jane Swift

Jane Swift

Follow-up letter (after face-to-face meeting)
(construction manager)

James Swift
18 Park Street, London X1 0BB
020 8123 4567   james@anyaddress.co.uk

Emily _____   [Date]
[Title]
ABC Ltd
Industry Square
London X2 2EF

Dear Ms _____,

   We had the opportunity to speak briefly at last week's Chamber of Commerce meeting concerning the Construction Management position you are seeking to fill in Plymouth. I appreciate you filling me in on the details of the project and have enclosed my CV as you suggested.

   As we discussed, I am well acquainted with ABC's brand and store concept, and I am excited to learn of the company's expansion plans over the coming decade. With my background in construction, maintenance and project management as well as operations and strategic leadership, I believe I am primed to play a key role in this growth.

   As Chief Executive Officer of XYZ Landscape Design, I have been instrumental in leading the company to phenomenal success within a very short time, building the organization from start-up into a solid revenue generator known throughout the North West as an aggressive competitor in markets crowded by multimillion-pound, nationally recognized companies.

   I am currently in the process of selling the company and have been exploring opportunities with dynamic, growth-oriented organizations like yours that could benefit from my broad-based expertise in operations, organizational management, finance and business development. Complementing my diverse leadership background is expertise in all the fundamentals of construction management, including the ability to see projects through to completion while exceeding quality standards.

   Perhaps one of my strongest assets is my ability to cultivate long-lasting relationships with clients through attentive, direct communication. I have been highly successful at defining complex project plans, establishing budgets, outlining scope of work, and directly soliciting qualified contractors using the bid process. I also offer extensive experience navigating through the paperwork and bureaucracy, forging productive alliances with key regulatory agencies to streamline permitting and licensing and to facilitate expedited project starts.

   I would enjoy the opportunity to speak to you again in greater detail. Could we meet for lunch on Friday? I'll call your assistant in a few days to confirm the appointment.

Best regards,

James Swift

James Swift

Follow-up letter (after face-to-face meeting) (executive assistant)

JAMES SWIFT
18 Park Street, London X1 0BB
020 8123 4567   james@anyaddress.co.uk

[Date]

Phillip _____
[Title]
ABC Ltd
Industry Square
London X2 2EF

Dear Phillip _____,

The time I spent being interviewed by you and Sandra gave me a clear picture of your company's operation as well as your corporate environment. I want to thank you, in particular, Phillip, for the thorough picture you painted of your CEO's needs and work style.

I left our meeting feeling very enthusiastic about the scope of the position as well as its close match to my abilities and work style. After reviewing your comments, Phillip, I think the key strengths that I can offer your CEO in achieving his agenda are:

● Experience in dealing effectively with senior staff in a manner that facilitates decision-making.
● Proven ability to anticipate an executive's needs and present viable options to consider.
● Excellent communication skills – particularly the ability to gain feedback from staff and summarize succinctly.

Whether the needs at hand involve meeting planning, office administration, scheduling or just serving as a sounding board, I bring a combination of highly effective 'people skills' and diversified business experience to deal with changing situations.

With my energetic work style, I believe that I am an excellent match for this unique position. I would welcome an additional meeting to elaborate on my background and how I can assist your CEO.

Sincerely,

James Swift

James Swift

Follow-up letter (after face-to-face meeting) (assistant)

Jane Swift
18 Park Street, London X1 0BB
020 8123 4567   jane@anyaddress.co.uk

[Date]

Emily _____
[Title]
ABC Ltd
Industry Square
London X2 2EF

Dear Ms _____,

Thank you for the opportunity to discuss the position of Assistant.

ABC Ltd is involved in one of the most pressing concerns of today: environmentally safe methods of disposing of solid waste materials. The challenge of creating proper disposal systems is paramount. I look forward to being a part of an organization that is focusing on furthering the technology needed to enhance our environment.

At ABC I would be able to:

- Be a productive assistant to management
- Be a part of a technologically developing industry
- Be in a position to learn and grow with the opportunities presented by your company
- Be involved in the excitement of a new expanding company

The skills that I have to offer ABC Ltd are:

- Professionalism, organization and maturity
- Excellent office skills
- Ability to work independently
- A creative work attitude
- Research and writing skills
- Varied business background
- Willingness to learn

Again, thank you for considering my qualifications to become a part of your organization.

Sincerely,

Jane Swift

Jane Swift

Follow-up letter (after face-to-face meeting) (management information systems)

JAMES SWIFT

---

18 Park Street • London X1 0BB • 020 8123 4567

(Date)

Bob _____
(Title)
ABC Consultants
Industry Square
London X2 2EF

Dear Mr _____,

Thank you for meeting me this morning. Our associate, _____, assured me that a meeting with you would be productive, and it was. I sincerely appreciate your counsel, insight, and advice.

I have attached my CV for your review. I would appreciate any feedback you may have regarding effectiveness and strength. I understand you may not have any searches under way that would be suitable for me at this time, but I would appreciate any future considerations.

As we reviewed this morning, I seek and am qualified for senior MIS positions in a medium to large high-tech manufacturing or services business. I seek compensation in the £150,000-and-above-range and look to report directly to the business CEO. These requirements are somewhat flexible depending on a number of factors, especially potential, of a new position. My family and I are willing to relocate to any area.

Please consider any associates, customers, or friends who may have contacts that would be useful for me to meet. I have learned how important networking is, and will really appreciate some assistance from a professional like you.

Thanks again, Mr _____, and please let me know if I can be of service to you. I wish you and your colleagues continued success and look forward to a business relationship in the future.

Best regards,

James Swift

James Swift

enclosure

Follow-up letter (after face-to-face meeting) (sales)

James Swift
18 Park Street, London X1 0BB
020 8123 4567 james@anyaddress.co.uk

[Date]

Philip_____
[title]
ABC Ltd
Industry Square
London X2 2EF

Dear Philip,

First of all, thank you. I thoroughly enjoyed our meeting last Wednesday, and greatly appreciate your insight and the time taken to discuss where I might best fit in to the ABC team. Your professionalism and willingness to share what you know put me instantly at ease, and I am now even more motivated to be part of ABC's success.

Let me begin by restating how flattered I am that you saw such potential in me. I likewise feel confident that I have the management and leadership expertise, marketing skills and business development experience to be successful, and I see tremendous opportunities for ABC in the future.

However, as we discussed, I understand that my first step is to make my mark as a member of the Road Crew and am equally excited at the opportunity to make an impact on the front line. I realize that you are not currently in a position to make such an offer, but I want to re-emphasize my enthusiasm to join the ABC team wherever you feel I could add value.

If you don't mind, I'd like to take a moment of your time to re-state a few key points:

- I possess the drive, commitment and strong people skills required to make an impact in this industry.
- I offer proven business development, sales and revenue building experience.
- I know what it takes to get results, both out of myself and from others, and have proved again and again to be the 'go to' person when results are expected.

I hope that you and I have the opportunity to continue our discussions and, once again, I appreciate the time you spent with me. I wish you continued success in all your efforts and look forward to seeing you at the *Sales Excellence* seminar at the end of July.

Sincerely,

James Swift

James Swift

Follow-up e-mail (after face-to-face meeting) (general)

From: James Swift [j-swift@hotmail.com]
To: smith@alphjobs.com
Cc:
Subject: Great meeting! Can we talk again on Tuesday?

Dear Mr Smith,

I appreciate the time you took today interviewing me for the position. I hope our two-hour meeting did not throw off the rest of the day's schedule. I trust you will agree that it was time well spent, as I sensed we connected on every major point discussed.

Your insight on e-commerce was intriguing. My history in hi-tech, manufacturing and biomedical industries and background in technology solutions seems to be a good match with the opportunities available in your company. As I mentioned, at XYZ Biomedical I initiated the marketing strategies that opened our markets to the USA. What I failed to mention is that I also have contacts with some e-commerce investors developing online portals targeted to Americans.

I am very interested in the position and would like to contact you on Tuesday to see where we stand.

Sincerely,

James Swift
020 8123 4567

Follow-up e-mail (after face-to-face meeting)
(sales manager)

From:	James Swift [salespro@aol.com]
To:	jsmith@abc.com
Cc:	
Subject:	Thanks for an exciting meeting. Next steps?

Dear Mr Smith,

I thoroughly enjoyed our meeting on Wednesday. After learning more about ABC and its goals, the prospect of joining the organization as the Western Region Sales Manager is even more exciting.

One of the most important things I have learned in my 20+ years in sales is to listen to what the customer needs. I have always taken pride in designing customized solutions that not only meet the clients' objectives, but also are competitive in price. This philosophy has enabled me to exceed corporate expectations for 17 consecutive years. In addition, I have managed to convert about 65% of my clients to 'repeat order' accounts, an objective you indicated was a high priority for your sales team in ensuring the company's continued growth.

ABC's Western Region Sales Manager position is an important cornerstone in the company's overall growth plans for the new fiscal year. The company is poised to make significant strides to gain ground on the competition and the West of England territory will be instrumental in making the corporate goals a reality. I am excited about contributing my expertise, meeting ABC's customers, and building long-term client relationships.

Thanks again for your time. I am certain that I can be a valuable asset to your sales team, and I look forward to having the opportunity to contribute to ABC's growth.

Sincerely,

James Swift
020 8123 4567

Follow-up e-mail (after face-to-face meeting) (management)

From: James Swift [jsmith@yahoo.com]
To: jsmith@xyz.com
Cc:
Subject: The right choice for programme development

Dear Mr Smith

The position we discussed on Friday is a tremendously challenging one. After reviewing your comments about the job requirements, I am convinced that I can make an immediate contribution towards the growth and profitability of ABC Ltd.

Since you are going to reach a decision quickly, I would like to mention the following points, which I feel qualify me for the job we discussed:

1.   Proven ability to generate fresh ideas and creative solutions to difficult problems

2.   Experience in the area of programme planning and development

3.   Ability to successfully manage many projects at the same time

4.   A facility for working effectively with people at all levels of management

5.   Experience in administration, general management and presentations

6.   An intense desire to do an outstanding job in anything which I undertake

Thank you for the time and courtesy extended to me. I will look forward to hearing from you.

Sincerely,

James Swift
020 8123 4567

Follow-up e-mail (after face-to-face meeting) (senior counsellor)

This e-mail shows how her skills and experience in counselling matched this particular job opening and would be an asset to the agency and its clients.

From: Jane Swift [skilledcounsellor@earthlink.net]
To: cpatterson@couns.edu.msu
Cc:
Subject: Looking forward to next week

Dear Ms Patterson,

I would like to thank you for affording me the opportunity to meet you to discuss the Senior Counsellor position with your organization. I have long been an admirer of your services and commitment to the community. I am very confident that my education, experience and counselling skills will enable me to make an immediate and long-term contribution to your mental health programme.

The position we discussed seems well suited to my strengths and skills. My counselling and teaching background includes an emphasis on the family unit and its influence and relationship to each clients' needs and therapy.

I am looking forward to seeing you, again, next week. If you require any additional information before then, please feel free to call. Thank you for your time and consideration.

Sincerely,

Jane Swift
020 8123 4567

Follow-up e-mail (after face-to-face meeting) (graphic design)

From: James Swift [graphicdesignpro@earthlink.net]
To: jsmith@graphics.com
Cc:
Subject: Let's keep in touch

Dear Mr Smith,

It was a pleasure speaking to you regarding my search for a position in ABC Graphic Design. Thank you for your initial interest.

The position I am looking for is usually found in a corporate marketing or public relations department. The titles vary: Graphic Design Manager, Advertising Manager and Publications Director are a few. In almost every case the job description includes management and coordination of the company's printed marketing materials, whether they are produced by in-house designers or by an outside advertising agency or design firm.

I would like to stay in the _____ area; at least, I would like to search this area first. My salary requirement is £_____ a year.

My professional experience, education, activities and skills uniquely qualify me for a position in ABC Graphic Design. My portfolio documents over eight years of experience in the business, and includes design, project consultation and supervision of quality printed material for a wide range of clients.

I hope you will keep me on your files for future reference. I will telephone your office next week to discuss my situation further.

Sincerely,

James Swift
020 8123 4567

Follow-up e-mail (after face-to-face meeting) (general)

From: Jane Swift [jswift@hotmail.com]
To: hr@bigcom.com
Cc:
Subject: I listened …but here's the result

Dear Ms _____,

It was a pleasure meeting you last week in your office. I appreciate the time you spent with me, as well as the valuable information you offered. As we discussed, I have adjusted my CV in regard to my position with _____. I have attached the new CV with this e-mail so that your files can be updated.

_____, please allow me to thank you again for the compliment on my ability to handle an interview well. Please keep this in mind when considering me for placement with one of your clients.

Sincerely,

Jane Swift
020 8123 4567

Follow-up e-mail (after face-to-face meeting) (entry-level)

From: Jane Swift [jswift@mindspring.com]
To: djackson@allianz.com
Cc:
Subject: Thanks from a quick study

Dear Mr Jackson,

I would like to take this opportunity to thank you for the interview on Wednesday morning at Allianz, and to confirm my strong interest in an entry-level position with your company.

As we discussed, I feel that my education and background have provided me with an understanding of business operations which will prove to be an asset to your company. Additionally, I have always been considered a hard worker and a dependable, loyal employee. I am confident that I can make a valuable contribution to your Group Pension Fund area.

I look forward to meeting you again in the near future to discuss your needs further.

Sincere regards,

Jane Swift
020 8123 4567

Follow-up e-mail (after face-to-face meeting) (auditing)

From: Jane Swift [auditpro@earthlink.com]
To: hr@star.com
Cc:
Subject: Very motivated by meeting you

Mr _____,

Thank you for allowing me the opportunity to meet you to discuss the EDP Audit position currently available at ABC. The position sounds very challenging and rewarding, with ample room for growth. I feel my background and qualifications prepare me well for the position we discussed.

I have a great willingness and eagerness to learn more about EDP auditing, and feel that I am the type of individual who would blend in well with the EDP audit staff at ABC. I look forward to hearing from you.

Sincerely,

Jane Swift
020 8123 4567

Power phrases

Consider using adaptations of these key phrases in your follow-up letters after face-to-face meetings.

Thank you for meeting me this morning. Our associate _____ assured me that a meeting with you would be productive, and it was. I sincerely appreciate your counsel, insight and advice.

I have attached my CV for your review. I would appreciate any feedback you may have regarding effectiveness and strength. I understand you may not have any searches under way that would be suitable for me at this time, but I would appreciate any future considerations.

Please consider any associates, customers or friends who may have contacts whom it would be useful for me to meet. I have learned how important 'networking' is and would really appreciate some assistance from a professional like you.

Thanks again, _____, and please let me know if I can be of service to you. I wish you and your colleagues continued success and look forward to a business relationship in the future.

In addition to experiencing a very enjoyable and informative interview, I came away very enthusiastic about the position you are seeking to fill.

I hope _____'s consideration of candidates will result in our meeting again soon.

During my drive home I savoured the possibility of working for _____ in the _____ area, and I must say it was an extremely pleasing thought.

I look forward to meeting you again and hope our discussion will precede a long-term working relationship.

I am looking forward to meeting _____ on — August at 10.00 am, at which time I will convince her of my abilities and prove I am the best qualified person for the position.

It was a pleasure meeting you last week in your office. I appreciate the time you spent with me, as well as the valuable information you offered.

I hope you will take a few moments to review my CV and place it in your files for future reference. I will telephone your office next week to discuss my situation further.

Gone but not forgotten ...

Thank you for our time together this afternoon. What I lack in specific experience in your business I more than make up for with my people skills and my proven record of achievement, energy and pure tenacity.

Given the opportunity, I can succeed in your office. That makes you and me both successes. Is that worth the investment in training me?

I would like to take this opportunity to thank you for the interview this morning, and to express my strong interest in the position with _____.

I would welcome the opportunity to apply and to develop my talents further within your company.

Through my conversations with you and Mr _____, I felt that the company provides exactly the type of career opportunity that I am seeking, and I am confident that I would prove to be an asset to your organization.

I trust our meeting this morning helped you further define the position. First and foremost, however, I hope that you came away from our meeting with a vision that includes my filling one of the many offices in _____. I certainly did.

I would like to take this opportunity to thank you for the interview on Thursday morning. I was very impressed with the operation, and I am enthusiastic about the prospect of joining your team.

Since we spent so much time discussing the subject, I have enclosed ...

I look forward to hearing from you again to further discuss the position. Through my conversations with you and _____, I felt ...

After reviewing your comments about the job requirements, I am convinced that I can make an immediate contribution to the growth and profitability of _____.

Since you are going to reach a decision quickly, I would like to mention the following points, which I feel qualify me for the job we discussed: ...

The position in the _____ area is very attractive to me.

The interview confirmed that I want this career opportunity. Specifically, I want to work in the _____ department for you and _____. That is the simplest way to say it. I will ring you this week to see what the next step is in the process.

Again, thank you for your time and interest.

It was indeed a pleasure to meet you after working with you by telephone several years ago.

Thank you for taking time out of your busy schedule to meet me on Tuesday, — December, 20—. I left the interview with an extremely favourable impression of your company.

I would like to take this opportunity to thank you for the interview on Friday morning, and to confirm my strong interest in the _____ position.

A career opportunity with _____ plc is particularly appealing because of its solid reputation and track record in research and development. I am confident that the training programme and continued sales support will provide me with the background that I need to succeed in a _____ career.

I look forward to discussing my background and the position with you in greater detail.

I want to take this opportunity to thank you for the interview on Tuesday afternoon, and to confirm my strong interest in the position of _____ with XYZ Healthcare Agency.

From our conversation, I feel confident in my ability to reach and exceed your expectations.

I am looking forward to spending a day in the field with a _____ representative. I will telephone you later this week to set up an appointment for my second interview.

Thank you for your time during my visit to _____ yesterday. I enjoyed our conversation at lunch and learned more about personal trust and investment services.

Thank you for your time and interest today. As I indicated, I am very new to this game of searching for employment and it is nice to start this effort on a positive note.

I am eager to hear from you concerning your decision; I know that you have several other candidates to meet, so I will wait patiently. Good luck to you in your interview process; I know it must be difficult. Again, thank you so much for your time and consideration. I would welcome the opportunity to work for your company.

_____, my visit to your office left me feeling positive about the possibility of working for _____. I would appreciate an opportunity to join your staff, and look forward to hearing from you.

'Resurrection' letter (HR position)

James knows this decision maker personally. Although he didn't get the job, he wants to keep the lines of communication open and hopes to be considered for other positions in the future.

JAMES SWIFT

January 13, 20–

Mr Eric Pedersen, Supervisor
ABC Ltd
Industry Square
London X2 2EF

Dear Eric,

Congratulations on the selection of your new Director of Human Resources! I hope this new person meets your expectations and I wish you every success.

I appreciate the chance to apply for the position and am grateful for the consideration you have given me throughout this process. Although I am obviously disappointed at not being the successful candidate, I remain interested in potential opportunities with ABC Ltd. If for any reason you decide it is necessary to reopen the search at any time, please be aware that I am still interested in the position on either an interim or permanent basis.

In the meantime, should there be openings for support positions within the HR Department, or positions in other departments, I would like to be considered for such opportunities.

Eric, as we have discussed in the past, I am a team player and believe that I have a contribution to make. At this stage of my career, I would be happy to accept something other than a managerial position and am convinced that my organizational skills, communication skills, and flexibility would make me an asset to any organization. If you know of other openings, either within governmental agencies or the private sector, I would be most appreciative if you could pass that information on to me.

Thank you for all your time and consideration. I look forward to speaking to you again soon.

Sincerely,

James

18 Park Street • London X1 0BB • 020 8123 4567

'Resurrection' letter (stevedore)

This is a follow-up letter to several telephone conversations with the best contact within the target company, the company managing director.

JAMES SWIFT

18 Park Street • London X1 0BB
Home: 020 8123 4567 • Mobile: 07850 515536

November 14, 20–

Mr Gregory Roberts
Managing Director, ABC Shipping, Ltd.
Industry Square
London X2 2EF

Dear Mr Roberts,

First, I want to thank you for the time you spent with me in recent telephone conversations. I know you are a very busy person.

On August 4 I attended the stevedore recruiting event at the City Convention Centre. I submitted my CV and spoke very briefly with a representative. In the short time I chatted with her I did my best to communicate my interest in, and qualifications for, the job. However, due to the overwhelming number of applicants there wasn't sufficient time to convey how qualified I really am.

With that in mind, I have enclosed my brief CV for your review. To summarize:

● I have an extensive history of working safely around heavy equipment.
● I am in outstanding physical condition.
● I am a very reliable and dedicated employee.
● I have received first aid, CPR, and terrorism awareness training.

This CV is only a hint of who I am – words on paper cannot replace a personal conversation. Therefore, would you please consider my request for a face-to-face interview so that you may evaluate my qualifications, abilities, drive, and enthusiasm for yourself?

I will make myself available for any time that you can take out of your schedule. Thank you for your consideration, and I look forward to possibly meeting you in the near future.

Respectfully,

James Swift

James Swift

Enclosure: CV

'Resurrection' letter (social worker)

Having already been interviewed by Mr Thornson, Jane started the letter in an upbeat, informal manner to re-establish a rapport. The indication that he thought she was well suited at the time of their initial interview was an effective way to sell herself.

JANE SWIFT
18 Park Street
London X1 0BB
020 8123 4567
jswift@4kidsake.net

February 16, 20–

Mr William Thornson
Foster Care and Adoption Coordinator
BAAF
Industry Square
London X2 2EF

Dear Mr Thornson,

Talk about small coincidences. I bumped into Mr O'Brien and learned that St. Mary's is opening a new foster care division this coming March. One word led to another, and he informed me that BAAF is in desperate need of social workers and foster/adoptive care counsellors to fill several positions.

You might not recall my name, but hopefully I can help you to remember our meeting. I participated in an interview with you in early March of 20– for the position of Foster Care Counsellor with BAAF's Brentwood facility. We discussed my involvement with St. John's Youth & Family Counselling Programme at great length, and agreed I would be well suited for a similar position with BAAF as an Adoptive Care Counsellor. Unfortunately, funding was reduced that month leaving BAAF with no other choice but to put a freeze on recruiting.

As you can imagine, I am thrilled to learn of BAAF's new foster care programme, and would welcome the opportunity to meet again to pick up where we left off. For your convenience, I am enclosing my updated CV for your review.

Thank you for your reconsideration. I look forward to speaking to you soon.

Sincerely,

Jane Swift

Jane Swift

'Resurrection' letter (wholesale market manager)

Jane Swift
18 Park Street, London X1 0BB
020 8123 4567   jane@anyaddress.co.uk

[Date]

Phillip _____
[Title]
ABC Ltd
Industry Square
London X2 2EF

Dear Mr _____,

I understand from _____ of _____ that the search is continuing for the Wholesale Market Manager position at _____ Bank. As you continue your search, I would like to ask that you keep in mind the following accomplishments and experiences that I would bring to the job:

1. Maximized relationships and increased balances through the sale of trust and cash management products.

2. Captured largest share of public funds market in _____ within three years and captured a disproportionate market share of insurance companies in

   _____.

3. Developed cash management and trust products tailored to the needs of my target market.

4. Marketed services through mass mailings and brochures, through planning and conducting industry-specific seminars, and through active participation in target market's industry professional organization.

5. Direct experience in all phases of wholesale commercial banking, including: market segmentation, prospecting, building and maintaining customer relationships, lending, and the sale of non-credit products and services.

Sincerely,

Jane Swift

Jane Swift

P.S. I will call you next week, after you have seen the other candidates, to continue our discussion. In the meantime, please be assured of both my competency and commitment.

'Resurrection' letter (construction manager)

JAMES SWIFT
18 Park Street, London X1 0BB
020 8123 4567 james@anyaddress.co.uk

[Date]

Alice _____
[Title]
ABC Ltd
Industry Square
London X2 2EF

Dear Ms _____,

I am writing to you to follow up on the initial enquiry I wrote to you on —th July, 20—.
At that time I forwarded you a job search letter and CV. I am in the construction
management and business management fields. Since I have not had a response I can
only assume that you do not have any vacancies at present that meet my qualifications
or that my file has been deactivated.

I am still in the market for an executive position that matches my qualifications and
abilities. I am open to relocating throughout the United Kingdom and overseas. If any
positions become available, I would be interested in hearing from you. If you need an
updated CV, please write or ring me and I would be most happy to forward you any
information required.

Sincerely,

James Swift

James Swift

PS. I'll ring in a couple of days to follow up this letter.

'Resurrection' letter (entry-level)

Jane Swift

18 Park Street • London X1 0BB
020 8123 4567

(Date)

Bob _____
(Title)
ABC Consultants
Industry Square
London X2 2EF

Dear Mr _____,

I feel I should explain more thoroughly why I am willing to take even an entry-level position considering all my past experience. And that's just it – past experience.

For the past three years I ran my own small business, which, of course, kept me out of the job market. Meanwhile, computers took over the world! Fortunately, since moving here and doing temp jobs, I have had hands-on experience in data entry. I have also taken and finished a private course in Microsoft Word. So I believe that makes me computer literate, if not entirely experienced.

Nevertheless, I'm in no position to be proud or disdainful of clerical jobs, as I realize I must start somewhere. Fortunately, I enjoy all facets of office work (even filing), so that would not be a problem. I have enough faith in myself and my ability to learn quickly to know that some form of promotion would be possible for me … eventually.

Incidentally, even though I am on a temp job this week and possibly next, I do have an answering machine I check every couple of hours during the day. So please leave a message and I'll return your call soon after.

Thank you, and I look forward to hearing from you. I have enclosed another copy of my CV for you.

Sincerely,

Jane Swift

Jane Swift

enclosure

'Resurrection' e-mail (account executive)

From: Jane Swift [accountexecutive@aol.com]
To: hr@goodjobs.com
Cc:
Subject: Thanks from Jane, I'll be the next one

Mr _____,

I wanted to thank you for the interview on —th March, 20—. The position that was being offered sounds like something I would be interested in. However, I do understand your reasons for not choosing me for the position, and I thank you very much for your honesty.

Perhaps when you are looking for an account executive with five years of experience instead of ten, you will bear me in mind. I am determined to be your choice. I hope the fact that I came in a close second to someone with twice my chronological experience will help you keep me in mind.

I look forward to hearing from you, and thank you again for your time. With your permission I will stay in touch.

Sincerely,

Jane Swift
020 8123 4567

'Resurrection' e-mail (programmer)

From: James Swift [programmerpro@yahoo.com]
To: ht@hotjobs.com
Cc:
Subject: Oh the software we could create!

Dear Ms _____,

I must have been one of the first people you spoke to about the job, because at the time you seemed very interested in me. However, when I called you back, you had received so many calls for the position, you didn't know one from the other. That's understandable, so I hope I can stir your memory and, more importantly, your interest.

When I spoke to you I got the feeling we could both benefit from working together. I am a computer enthusiast, always looking for new applications and ideas to implement on the computer. I have a solid programming and project development background in both the Windows and Macintosh worlds. What's even better is my hobby: my work. I spend countless hours in one way or another doing things which concern computing.

You had asked if I had children and I do: a four-and-a-half-year-old daughter and a four-and-a-half-month-old daughter. You had some ideas for children's software and thought having kids would help when working on such software. My oldest uses _____ on my Macintosh at home and double-clicks away without any assistance from my wife or myself. She has learned a great deal from 'playing' with it and is already more computer literate than I ever expected. We need more software like _____ to help stir the minds of our kids.

I have attached a CV for your perusal. But in case you don't want to read all the details, here it is in short:

- I have 6 years programming and development experience in Windows.

- I have 3 years programming and development experience on the Macintosh.

- I am currently the Senior Developer for Macintosh programming here at _____ Ltd.

I look forward to speaking to you again, so please don't hesitate to call me, either at home (020 8123 4567) or at work (020 8234 5678) any time.

Regards,

James Swift
020 8123 4567

'Resurrection' e-mail (product manager)

From: Jane Swift [jswift@hotmail.com]
To: jkline@activeproducts.com
Cc:
Subject: We will work together!

Dear Ms Kline,

Four months ago you and I discussed an opportunity at Active Products, and you were kind enough to set up meetings with _____ and _____. Shortly thereafter, as you know, I accepted a position with _____, where I am now.

For reasons I will go into when we meet, I would like to reopen our discussions. If you think such a conversation would be mutually beneficial, I hope we can get together. I'll call next week to see when you have a half hour or so of free time.

Sincerely,

Jane Swift
020 8123 4567

Power phrases

Consider using adaptations of these key phrases in your resurrection letters.

I turned down your job offer, but for reasons I will go into when we meet, I would like to reopen our discussions. If you think such a conversation would be mutually beneficial, I hope we can get together. I'll ring next week to see when you have a half hour or so free.

As you continue your search, I would like to ask that you keep in mind the following accomplishments and experiences that I would bring to the job.

I am still in the market for an executive position that matches my qualifications and abilities. I am open to relocating throughout the United Kingdom and overseas. If any positions become available, I would be interested in hearing from you.

I look forward to hearing from you, and thank you again for your time. With your permission I will stay in touch.

I hope I can stir your memory and, more importantly, your interest.

I look forward to speaking to you again, so please don't hesitate to ring me either at home or at work any time.

Rejection of offer letter (head librarian)

Jane has decided to take another position. As a courtesy, she wants to tell Anytown that she's no longer interested in the position, while keeping her name alive for any future opportunities.

Jane Swift

18 Park Street • London X1 0BB • 020 8123 4567

January 12, 20–

Mr Henry O Felix, Director of Services
Anytown Library Services
Industry Square
London X2 2EF

Dear Mr Felix,

Thank you for taking the time to meet me recently to discuss the position of Head Librarian. I genuinely appreciated the opportunity to meet the Committee to learn about the position. I was very favourably impressed with the Anytown Library System and believe that if selected, my contributions would have significantly enhanced your organization's success.

However, I am writing to ask that my name be withdrawn from further consideration for the position at this time. I have recently been offered another challenging and rewarding opportunity. The relative time frames involved have made it necessary for me to render a decision without further delay, and I have chosen to accept the offer.

Had circumstances permitted, I believe that it would have been productive to continue our discussions and am confident that we could have arrived at a mutually beneficial arrangement. I would be most interested in applying and interviewing for the position should there ever be another search for a Head Librarian at some future date.

I wish you the best of luck in your current search, and much success in the future. Thank you, again, for your time and consideration.

Sincerely yours,

Jane Swift

Jane Swift

Rejection of offer letter (team supervisor)

This candidate interviewed for a position that turned out to be below his level of experience and at a salary well below his expectations. He didn't want to slam the door shut on other opportunities, but couldn't accept the position offered.

Ms Lucretia A Selander
Programme Director
ABC Ltd.
Industry Square
London X2 2EF

Dear Ms Selander,

Thank you for your e-mail message updating me on the status of the telecommunications project we discussed in our recent telephone conversation.

Although I genuinely appreciate your consideration for the Team Supervisor position, at this time, I feel it is in my best interest to seek a position more closely aligned with my level of experience and demonstrated managerial skills.

I remain most interested in opportunities with ABC, and would ask that you keep my name in consideration for other positions that would more fully capitalize on my knowledge and expertise.

Thank you for your time and interest.

Sincerely,

James Swift

James Swift

Rejection of offer letter (general)

Jane Swift
18 Park Street, London X1 0BB
020 8123 4567   jane@anyaddress.co.uk

[Date]

Phillip _____
[Title]
ABC Ltd
Industry Square
London X2 2EF

Dear Mr _____,

It was indeed a pleasure meeting you and your staff to discuss your needs for a
_____. Our time together was most enjoyable and informative.

As we have discussed during our meetings, I believe a purpose of preliminary interviews
is to explore areas of mutual interest and to assess the fit between the individual and the
position. After careful thought, I have decided to withdraw my application for the
position.

My decision is based upon the fact that I have accepted a position elsewhere that is very
suited to my qualifications and experiences.

I want to thank you for interviewing me and giving me the opportunity to learn more
about your facility. You have a fine team, and I would have enjoyed working with you.

Best wishes to you and your staff.

Sincerely,

Jane Swift

Jane Swift

Rejection of offer e-mail (department manager)

From: James Swift [managementpro@earthlink.net]
To: hr@jobs.com
Cc:
Subject: With regret for the present and sincere hope for the future

Dear Ms _____,

I would like to take this opportunity to thank you for the interview on Thursday morning, and to express my strong interest in future employment with your organization.

While I appreciate very much your offer for the position of Department Manager, I feel that at this stage of my career I am seeking greater challenges and advancement than the Department level is able to provide. Having worked in _____ management for over four years, I am confident that my skills will be best applied in a position with more responsibility and accountability.

As we discussed, I look forward to talking to you again in January about how I might contribute to ABC plc in the capacity of Unit Manager.

Sincere regards,

James Swift
020 8123 4567

Power phrases

Consider using adaptations of these key phrases in your rejection of offer letters.

It was indeed a pleasure meeting you and your staff to discuss your needs for a _____.

Our time together was most enjoyable and informative.

After careful thought, I have decided to withdraw my application for the position.

As we discussed, I look forward to talking to you again in _____ about how I might contribute to _____ in the capacity of _____.

Acceptance letter (marketing research manager)

JANE SWIFT
18 Park Street, London X1 0BB
020 8123 4567   jane@anyaddress.co.uk

[Date]

Ms Emily_____
ABC Ltd
Industry Square
London X2 2EF

Dear Ms _____,

Thank you for your positive response to my application for the Marketing Research Manager position. I am delighted to accept your offer of employment and look forward to getting 'stuck in' on the various projects we discussed during our meetings, especially sales forecasting and strategic market planning for ABC's core product line.

I am honoured that your organization feels that I am the right person to lead your marketing research efforts, and am confident that I can deliver the results ABC wants. As I mentioned in our telephone conversation yesterday, I am constantly in touch with what the competition is doing with the goal of placing my team's effort higher in the marketplace to yield maximum results.

As per your instructions, I will contact Mary Smith, Human Resources Manager, on Monday morning to arrange an orientation appointment. I look forward to meeting you after that to discuss in detail my ideas for meeting the objectives we explored in our interviews.

Sincerely,

Jane Swift

Jane Swift

Acceptance letter (director)

JAMES SWIFT
18 Park Street, London X1 0BB
020 8123 4567   james@anyaddress.co.uk

[Date]

Emily _____
[Title]
ABC Ltd
Industry Square
London X2 2EF

Dear Ms _____,

This letter will serve as my formal acceptance of your offer to join your firm as Director of _____. I understand and accept the conditions of employment which you explained in your recent letter.

I will contact your personnel department this week to request any paperwork I need to complete for their records prior to my starting date. Also, I will schedule a physical examination for insurance purposes. I would appreciate your forwarding any reading material you feel might hasten my initiation into the affairs of _____.

Yesterday I tendered my resignation at _____ and worked out a mutually acceptable notice time of four weeks, which should allow me ample time to finalize my business and personal affairs here, relocate my family, and be ready for work at _____ on schedule.

You, your board and your staff have been most professional and helpful throughout this process. I eagerly anticipate joining the ABC team and look forward to many new challenges. Thank you for your confidence and support.

Yours truly,

James Swift

James Swift

Acceptance letter (managing consultant)

Jane Swift
18 Park Street • London X1 0BB
020 8123 4567 Home • managingconsultant@comcast.com

(Date)

Dear Philip,

I want to thank you for the privilege of joining your staff as Managing Consultant. Your flexibility and cooperation in the counter negotiations were encouraging. Thank you for making every effort to make the pending transition a smooth one.

As per your requests, I am providing this letter, for my official file.

'In that your organization is a competitor of my previous employer, and in that this organization seeks to maintain goodwill and high levels of integrity within the industry, it should be duly noted, that neither you nor any representative of your organization, sought me as a prospective employee. It was my identification of a possible position, and solely my pursuits toward your company, that resulted in my resignation as Senior Director, to join your firm as Managing Consultant.'

If I can provide additional clarification on this matter, or assist in protecting the ethics of your company, notify me at your convenience. I look forward to starting with your team on the 15th of July. Until then …

Respectfully yours,

Jane Swift

Jane Swift

Acceptance e-mail (general)

From: James Swift [jswift@aol.com]
To: jsmith@anycompany.com
Cc:
Subject: Yes! Absolutely! I accept!

Dear Mr Smith,

I would like to express my appreciation for your letter offering me the position of _____ in your _____ Department at a starting salary of £30,000 per year.

I was very impressed with the personnel and facilities at your company in Derby and am writing to confirm my acceptance of your offer. If it is acceptable to you I will report to work on 20 November, 20—.

Let me once again express my appreciation for your offer and my excitement about joining your engineering staff. I look forward to my association with ABC Ltd and feel my contributions will be in line with your goals of growth and continued success for the company.

Sincerely,

James Swift
020 8123 4567

Power phrases

Consider using adaptations of these key phrases in your acceptance letters.

I am delighted to accept _____'s generous offer to become their _____. All of the terms in your letter of 13th October are acceptable to me.

My resignation was submitted to the appropriate managers at _____ this morning, but we are still working out the terms of my departure.

I am eagerly anticipating starting my new position, particularly at a company with _____'s reputation. During the interim, I will stay in direct contact with _____ to assure a smooth induction at _____. Thank you again for this opportunity.

We are still working out the terms of my departure from _____, but it is safe to say that I will report to _____ no later than —th November. It should be possible to confirm a starting date early tomorrow morning. I will telephone you directly when my former managers and I have a departure schedule completed.

_____ has scheduled my pre-employment physical for _____, and I do not expect any problems to arise. I have found several possible housing options that I will be investigating and I do not expect any problems here, either.

I appreciate the confidence you demonstrated by selecting me to be _____.

I am confident that you made an excellent choice.

I feel that I can achieve excellent results for your company, and I am looking forward to working with you. I am also anxious to get to know you and your organization better.

This letter will serve as my formal acceptance of your offer to join _____. I understand and accept the conditions of employment that you explained in your recent letter.

I will contact your personnel department this week to request any paperwork I might complete for their records prior to my starting date. Also, I will schedule a physical examination for insurance purposes. I would appreciate your forwarding any reading material you feel might hasten my initiation into the affairs of _____.

Yesterday I tendered my resignation at _____ and worked out a mutually acceptable notice period of four weeks, which should allow me ample time to finalize my business and personal affairs here, relocate my family, and be ready for work at _____ on schedule.

You, your board, and your staff have been most professional and helpful throughout this process. I eagerly anticipate joining the _____ team and look forward to many new challenges. Thank you for your confidence and support.

I look forward to making a contribution as part of your team.

I look forward to the challenges and responsibility of working in this position.

Negotiation letter (general)

Jane Swift
18 Park Street, London X1 0BB
020 8123 4567   jane@anyaddress.co.uk

[date]

Mr Philip _____
[Title]
ABC Ltd
Industry Square
London X2 2EF

Dear Philip,

I want to thank you for your invitation to join the ABC family. I have reviewed the offer of position and compensation, as presented in your letter dated _____. I would like to ask for clarification on a few items prior to providing you with a 'formal acceptance'. While none of these items is necessarily a 'deal breaker', I believe they will enable both parties to begin the partnership more informed of mutual goals and expectations.

As per the breakdown provided:

- I accept the bonus scheme as proposed

- I accept the paid holiday and personal days plan as proposed

- I accept the company car plan as proposed

- I accept the Direct Payroll Deposit plan as proposed (if elected)

- I accept the Medical, Dental, Pension and Life Insurance benefits as proposed, contingent on factors clarified below.

Points of clarification:

- What is available with regard to 'Share Options'?

- What are the 'standard hours of operation' for ABC employees?

- Would it be possible to have a 'Performance Evaluation' at the end of 6 months?

- I would like to structure the holiday entitlement as follows: 3 days in the remainder of the year _____, One week during the calendar year _____, Two weeks during the calendar years _____ – _____, Three weeks beginning January of _____.

- In light of the 'out of pocket expenses' anticipated, how might we agree to get the annual base salary to £35,000? I am open to a number of different options to achieve this goal, including profit sharing, commission, or percentage annual bonus arrangement.

I am excited about the long-term possibilities that exist at ABC. As you can see by my level of interest, I intend to be with you for a long tenure of success. I believe my skills will be an enhancement to the existing leadership. My presence will enable you and others to focus on new aspects of business development and achieve corporate goals and objectives that will be beneficial to us all. Again, I want to thank you for the gracious offer. I look forward to finalizing these minor details very soon.

Sincerely yours,

Jane Swift

Jane Swift

Negotiation letter (sales)

James Swift
18 Park Street, London X1 0BB
020 8123 4567   james@anyaddress.co.uk

[Date]

Dear Mr _____,

I have reviewed your letter and the specific breakdown regarding compensation. I believe there to be a few items to clarify, prior to providing you with a formal acceptance. I do not consider any of the items to be 'deal breakers' in any way. I also do not perceive them to be issues that cannot be discussed, as we are in fact moving ahead.

The primary concern has to do with the commission structure, as opposed to salary plus commission, to which I have grown accustomed. I am therefore asking for a one-off initial payment to me of £5000. I am trying to diminish some of the 'exposure' that I may experience in the transition from one office to another. I also believe exposure will be felt as a shift occurs from receipt of compensation on a monthly basis, as I am currently accustomed to a bi-weekly system. Lastly, I am hoping to afford your company the opportunity to share some of the 'risk' in this process and show some 'short-term good faith' towards what I hope will be a long-term relationship of success, productivity and increased profitability.

The second clarification revolves around the bonus scheme: the percentages, time frames and terms. This is something we can discuss over the course of the next weeks. You may even be able to pass on something specific to me in writing.

With these two concerns articulated, I want you to know that I will be meeting the owner of our company tomorrow morning, to discuss my plans for departure. In fairness to him and to my current client load, I could not start full time with you for 21 days.

I would like to set a time for us to have dinner one evening next week, so you can meet my wife and we can talk a little less formally.

Looking forward to what lies ahead,

James Swift

James Swift

Negotiation letter (senior lab specialist)

JAMES SWIFT
18 Park Street, London X1 0BB
020 8123 4567   james@anyaddress.co.uk

[date]

Philip _____
ABC Ltd
Industry Square
London X2 2EF

Dear Philip,

I want to thank you for the time that we were able to spend together last week. I was encouraged by the invitation to join the ABC family as Senior Lab Specialist. The position, responsibility and geography are consistent with my career goals and objectives. Based on the information that you gave to me, there are a number of items that need clarification prior to my providing you with a formal acceptance. None of the items listed is necessarily a 'deal breaker', but they are essential to our beginning this tenure with full disclosure of mutual expectations and responsibilities. Items for clarification are as follows:

- Detailed description of pension benefits
- Realistic analysis of the company shares and bonuses
- Written explanation of the car allowance
- The mobility plan seems very reasonable, but I would like specifics
- Relocation (Is it an allowance or reimbursement of actual expenses incurred in the move?)
- Detailed explanation of the Variable Pay Plan

This final item is significant, as it will have an impact on the 'full compensation potential' and modify the suggested salary. In our conversations, I informed you that I was earning £20k while working part-time and going to college. The salary offer is substantially lower and represents a pay cut. My goal is to discern how feasible it will be for me to meet my financial obligations.

I am interested in your company and this position, but am finding it difficult to give serious consideration to anything less than a £25k salary plus benefits. I am hoping to discover a variety of means that will enable you to help me achieve that goal, so that I can help you accomplish your growth and profit targets.

I look forward to discussing these issues with you in the very near future and trust that we will soon be working together in the best interest of Philip _____, James Swift and ABC Ltd.

Respectfully Yours,

James Swift

James Swift

Negotiation letter (product specialist)

JANE SWIFT

07850 515536 (Mobile) • 020 8123 4567 (Home)
productspecialist@email.com
18 Park Street • London X1 0BB

(Date)

Philip _____
(Title)
ABC Ltd
1 Industry Square
London X2 2EF

RE: Product Specialist/ABC Team

Dear Philip:

Thank you for your offer of employment with ABC Ltd. Your state-of-the-art company would afford me the opportunity to make a contribution while continuing to grow professionally in an ever-evolving industry. I am confident that my strong work ethic would enhance the ABC Team.

As you know from our previous conversations, I have outstanding skills and abilities that I can bring to ABC. First and foremost is my hands-on experience in the medical field. I have a proven track record of relating well to other medical professionals and accommodating their needs. It is my understanding that as Product Specialist, my expert communication skills will be tantamount to performance success. With my experience in troubleshooting technical problems, I know that technology can be learned but becomes useful only when it can be translated into user effectiveness. My expertise integrates both of these critical components that are key in the Product Specialist role.

The Product Specialist position promises challenge and a high level of professional commitment that I am prepared to embrace. However, based upon the value I can bring ABC, plus the knowledge that the annual salary range for this type of position in our industry normally falls between £34,000 and £46,000, I must request that you reconsider your starting offer of £35,000. I am more than happy to assume all of the responsibilities necessary to meet the expectations of the Product Specialist position at a starting salary of £40,000. Of course, I appreciate the generous benefits package that you provide.

I look forward to your response, and hope that we can reach an agreement that will enable me to begin my career with ABC on June 4.

Sincerely,

Jane Swift

Jane Swift

Resignation letter (ITU nurse)

This situation was sensitive. A lot of names and dates were needed to explain the events leading to the decision to resign. Notice how Jane apologises so she doesn't burn her bridges.

Jane Swift, RN
18 Park Street • London X1 0BB • 020 8123 4567

April 26, 20–

Ms Dorothy Powell
Director of Special Care
ABC Hospital
Industry Square
London X2 2EF

Dear Ms Powell,

As requested by Joan Larson, Nursing Manager, I am submitting this letter as written confirmation of my resignation as a per-diem on-call ITU nurse with ABC Hospital.

My employment with ABC was scheduled to begin April 7th as a permanent part-time ITU nurse; however, in the interim, I accepted a permanent full-time position with XYZ Hospital to begin May 1st. On April 3rd I met with Gretchen Miller, Human Resources Administrator, to inform her of my decision. I expressed a desire to honour my commitment with the understanding that the need for flexibility in my schedule would be taken into consideration. Ms Miller contacted Joan Larson to discuss an alternative employment arrangement. Subsequently, my status from permanent part-time was changed to per-diem on-call.

Immediately upon completion of the mandatory two-week orientation period, I was faced with a schedule conflict. As a result of an apparent miscommunication, I was scheduled to do my floor orientation from April 21st through 25th. I approached Diane Willis, Nursing Manager, to resolve the conflict and learned that she was completely unaware of both my situation and agreement between Joan Larson, Human Resources, and myself. As a result, my resignation seemed to be the logical solution.

Ms Powell, it was never my intention to cause problems within your administration; therefore, please accept my apology for any inconvenience experienced. Thank you for the opportunity to be a part of your staff.

Sincerely,

Jane Swift

Jane Swift

Resignation letter (care coordinator)

Jane was offered a new position with another organization, and this letter helped her make a positive exit from her current employer.

Jane Swift

18 Park Street
London X12 0BB
020 8123 4567

April 9, 20–

Ms Karen Lawrence, RN
Patient Care Manager
Community Care Centre
Industry Square
London X2 2EF

Dear Karen,

This letter will confirm my resignation from the position of Care Coordinator. I have accepted a new position as Supervisor of Client Services at a growing medical centre in London.

My last day of employment will be on Friday, May 9, 20–, which should provide sufficient time to complete existing projects and assist with the transition to a new coordinator.

The past 10 years at the Centre have been both professionally and personally rewarding. Thank you for your trust and support over the years. I have appreciated the opportunity to expand my skills and work with many talented individuals.

Thank you, sincerely

Jane Swift

Jane Swift

Resignation letter (management)

A very firm resignation, where a company needs encouragement to live up to obligations.

James Swift
18 Park Street
London X1 0BB

home: 020 8123 4567
mobile: 07850 515536
jamesswift@crpm.com

November 11, 20–

Tim Johnson, President
ABC Ltd
Industry Square
London X2 2EF

Dear Mr Johnson,

I am writing this letter as a follow-up to the resignation notice I submitted on Wednesday, November 5, 20–. Given the sensitive nature of the events leading to my resignation, I feel it is in everyone's best interest to resolve any issues remaining as quickly as possible.

In this respect, I hope that you will demonstrate swift compliance in delivering to me the management severance package guaranteed as a result of my employment with your firm. I wish to move ahead in my career and put the past several months behind me, as I am sure you can understand; therefore, I am certain you will act upon this request in a professional and forthright manner.

Please be advised that, in the event there is an attempt to withhold or deny this severance package to me, I will have no other alternative but to seek legal remedy for this situation. **Again, I believe that you will act as a man of integrity concerning this issue**, and I only mention the possibility of legal action in the unlikely event that my request is rejected or delayed.

I can assure you that I, like you, would like this to be resolved without further complications or additional steps – and as quickly as possible.

Mr Johnson, I thank you in advance for your swift attention and cooperation in this matter.

Sincerely,

Jane Swift

Jane Swift

Resignation letter (sales representative)

JAMES SWIFT
18 Park Street, London X1 0BB
020 8123 4567   james@anyaddress.co.uk

[Date]

Phillip _____
[Title]
ABC Ltd
Industry Square
London X2 2EF

Dear Mr _____,

Please accept my resignation from my position as Sales Representative in the
_____ area, effective — January, 20—. I am offering two weeks' notice so that
my territory can be serviced effectively during the transition, with the least amount of
inconvenience to our clients.

While I have very much enjoyed working under your direction, I find now that I have an
opportunity to develop my career further in areas that are more in line with my long-
term goals. I thank you for the sales training that I have received under your supervision.
It is largely due to the excellent experience I gained working for ABC Ltd that I am now
able to pursue this growth opportunity.

During the next two weeks, I am willing to help you in any way to make the transition as
smooth as possible. This includes assisting in recruiting and training my replacement in
the _____ region. Please let me know if there is anything specific that you would
like me to do.

Again, it has been a pleasure working as a part of your group.

Best regards,

James Swift

James Swift

Resignation letter (director)

JANE SWIFT
18 Park Street, London X1 0BB
020 8123 4567   jane@anyaddress.co.uk

[Date]

Emily _____
[Title]
ABC Ltd
Industry Square
London X2 2EF

Dear Ms _____,

As of this date, I am formally tendering my resignation as _____. I have accepted
a position as Director of _____ at a university medical centre in _____.

My decision to leave ABC Ltd was made after long and careful consideration of all
factors affecting the company, my family and my career. Although I regret leaving many
friends here, I feel that the change will be beneficial to all parties. My subordinate is
readily able to handle the company's operations until you find a suitable replacement. I
intend to finalize my business and personal affairs here over the next few weeks and will
discuss a mutually acceptable termination date with you in person.

Finally, I can only express my sincere appreciation to you and the entire board for all
your support, cooperation and encouragement over the years. I will always remember
my stay at ABC for the personal growth it afforded and for the numerous friendships
made.

Yours truly,

Jane Swift

Jane Swift

Resignation e-mail (general)

From: James Swift [systemsoperator@hotmail.com]
To: jsmith@abc.com
Cc:
Subject: With regrets but many thanks

Dear Mr Smith,

This is to notify you that I am resigning my position with ABC Ltd effective Saturday, 26 March, 20–.

I have enjoyed my work here very much and want to thank you and the rest of the MIS Department for all the encouragement and support you have always given me. In order to achieve the career goals that I've set for myself, I am accepting a higher level Systems Operator position with another company. This position will give me an opportunity to become more involved in the technical aspects of setting up networking systems.

I am more than happy to help with any staff training or offer assistance in any way that will make my departure as easy as possible for the department. I want to wish everyone the best of luck for the future.

Sincerely,

James Swift
020 8123 4567

Power phrases

Consider using adaptations of these key phrases in your resignation letters.

I am offering two weeks' notice so that my territory can be serviced effectively during the transition, with the least amount of inconvenience to our clients.

While I have very much enjoyed working under your direction, I now find that I have an opportunity to develop my career further in areas that are more in line with my long-term goals. I thank you for the sales training that I have received under your supervision. It is largely due to the excellent experience I gained working for ABC that I am now able to pursue this growth opportunity.

During the next two weeks, I am willing to help you in any way to make the transition as smooth as possible. This includes assisting in recruiting and training my replacement in the _____ region. Please let me know if there is anything specific that you would like me to do.

Again, it has been a pleasure working as a part of your sales force.

I have thoroughly enjoyed the work environment and professional atmosphere at _____. Your guidance and counselling have been the source of great personal and career satisfaction, and I am grateful.

These _____ years have made a considerable contribution to my career and professional development and I hope that I have likewise contributed during this time to the growth and development of ABC Ltd. I am grateful for the kinds of associates I have had the opportunity to work with and the substantial support I have consistently received from management.

Thank-you letter (after appointment) (general)

JAMES SWIFT
18 Park Street, London X1 0BB
020 8123 4567   james@anyaddress.co.uk

[Date]

Phillip _____
[Title]
ABC Ltd
Industry Square
London X2 2EF

Dear Mr _____,

I want you to be among the first to know that my job search has come to a very successful conclusion. I have accepted the position of _____ at _____, located in _____.

I appreciate all the help and support you have provided over the last few months. It has made the job search process much easier for me. I look forward to staying in contact with you. Please let me know if I can be of any assistance to you in the future. Thank you.

Sincerely,

James Swift

James Swift

Thank-you e-mail (after appointment)
(software manager)

From: James Swift [softwarespecialist@yahoo.com]
To: hr@abc.com
Cc:
Subject: Great news! Thanks for the help :-)

Dear Ms _____,

I am happy to inform you that I received and accepted an offer of employment just after Christmas. I am now employed by _____.

I would also like to thank you for all your help in recent months not only in my search for employment but also for your understanding and friendly words of encouragement.

My duties include responsibility for all accounting software (General Ledger, Accounts Payable, Accounts Receivable, and Fixed Assets) for _____ worldwide plus the first-year training of several entry-level employees.

I am enjoying my new responsibility and being fully employed again, although at times I feel overwhelmed with all I have to learn.

If there is ever anything I can do for you please ring me. I hope you and your family have a wonderful Christmas and wish you much luck and happiness in the new year.

Sincerely,

James Swift
020 8123 4567

Power phrases

Consider using adaptations of these key phrases in your thank you letters.

I am writing to share this good news with you and to thank you for your efforts on my behalf. If there is ever anything that I can do for you, please do not hesitate to ring me.

Thank you for all your help. I have accepted a position as a _____ for _____.

I want you to be among the first to know that my job search has come to a very successful conclusion.

I appreciate all the help and support you have provided over the last few months. It has made the job search process much easier for me. I look forward to staying in contact with you. Please let me know if I can be of any assistance to you in the future.

I would like to extend my sincere thanks to you for your kind help and encouragement during my job search. If I can be of any assistance to you in the future, please do not hesitate to contact me. I was often reminded during the past few months that we too easily lose contact with old friends. Let's try to stay in touch.

If you ever get a chance to visit _____, on business or pleasure, please be sure to let me know.

If there is ever anything I can do for you, please ring me. I hope you and your family have a wonderful Christmas and wish you much luck and happiness in the new year.

Just a quick note to bring you up to date with what I am doing.

Appendix: how to jump-start a stalled job search

Jerry has been out of work now for a year. His redundancy package was really lousy – a week for every year of service, which amounted to seven weeks for him. The house, two cars and three kids should have provided enough pressure to get Jerry's backside into gear, but they didn't.

Jerry told me that no one was phoning him. No one would return his calls. It was a bad time of year, he would say, or his contacts were all stale. Often, he would just express amazement and bewilderment as to how he could be in such a predicament.

There was no mystery here. He wasn't getting calls because he wasn't making calls in the right way. When he did dial a headhunter or a personnel department, his tone was so negative that he rarely got through the first screen. He was mailing out CVs, but just a handful each week, and he didn't even follow up on these. Jerry was scared and frightened of the search process, and the financial pressures made him so anxious that he wasn't able to do what he needed to do to land a job. Jerry became terrified by what he saw as his failure.

For Bob, the story is different. He has a job. It's not yet 9 o'clock, but Bob is already complaining about what a lousy place this is to work. His boss is a moron – can you believe what he did last week? The pay is low, the benefits poor, and the cafeteria serves inedible rubbish. He winds up with 'I've got to get out of here'. You'd guess that good old Bob is mounting a huge job search campaign, and that he's got one foot out the door. You'd guess wrong. Bob's not going anywhere, at least not under his own steam.

He is frightened of making an effort, taking the plunge, and then finding that he can't make the grade. So, instead, he hides out in a dead-end job, with a going-nowhere company, letting his fears conquer the soul of his work life. Bob and Jerry have both allowed their fear to stall their job search.

For Bob and Jerry, or for you, if your job search is stalled, there is hope – if you are prepared to take very small but very important steps to change your work–life situation. Write down all of your thoughts about yourself, your career and your job situation. All of them. Just put everything down on paper; don't edit anything. Then read them aloud. First to yourself, and then to a trusted friend or colleague. Ask for feedback. Ask the other person to tell you whether they agree or disagree with what you've written. Start to understand your negative thoughts and begin to discover who you *really* are.

When failure feels like forever

Fear of failure is so hateful to us, so threatening, that we'll do whatever we possibly can to avoid it. As bad as your job situation is right now, your fear of failure is even worse. So you stall, you procrastinate and you point the finger of blame, but you don't see the other three fingers pointing right back at you.

You can tell me that you are actually doing everything you can to get a job – everything you can imagine. You can be working like the devil on a search, but doing all of the wrong things. You might tell yourself and the world that, yes, you are trying to get a job. But in your heart of hearts, you may have doubts about the way you are going about it. Don't feel distraught; lots of people feel the same way. Job hunting and career management are not skills you were taught in school or anywhere else.

Evaluate your search. Are you being realistic? Are you working intelligently at your job search? Are you really doing all of the right things, or are you rationalizing doing what is comfortable? Or are you avoiding failure by making dumb decisions and then hiding behind them?

If your job search seems hopeless, try to understand what you get out of not doing what it takes to get a good job. How do you feel when that rejection letter comes? Do friends or relatives pester you by asking how the search is going, or whether you got the job? If you have to tell them that no, you didn't get the job, do you feel like a failure?

However, if you are stalling about getting your search in gear, think about what that will get you. What are you getting out of not looking for a job? Are you avoiding the rejection that is a big part of every job search? Are you escaping from the many *nos* you will have to hear before you hear *yes* from the lips of an employer?

If you are engaged in a genuine job hunt, I can guarantee that you will fail along the way. I hope that you will fail many, many times. If you don't, then you're not looking hard enough. Every job search involves failure and rejection. If you are networking, making phone calls, doing your research, sending out CVs, going to interviews with prospective employers and responding to ads, then you are creating hundreds of chances for rejection, hundreds of opportunities to hear the word *no*. This rejection must happen if you want to get out of your present situation! I can't tell you that it's a lot of fun to get rejection letters, or to have people hang up on you. It's never an enjoyable thing. It is a fact of life, and you can develop the ability you need to overcome rejection.

Lock and load

OK. You've been out of work for a while. You're low on ideas, and your petrol tank reads 'empty'. You don't know which way to turn. The things you've done so far just haven't worked out. It's time to take it from the top.

Believe it or not, you can start over again, and you have certain advantages in doing so. At least some of the people who screened you out so many months ago have, in all likelihood, moved on to another place. Sure, most of the jobs you applied for have been filled, but a whole new batch has now opened up. And, if there were ill economic winds blowing through an industry you took a fancy to, perhaps things are now looking up for some of the companies on your list.

With a few adjustments here and there, and a bit more attention to a few points, you can rescue a faltering job search and get yourself back to work.

Getting unstuck

If you are stuck, if your search is not working well, it's time to try things that may have seemed unnecessary or gimmicky earlier in your search. It's time to get unstuck – by any means necessary:

- Send copies of your job search activity list, including names of companies to phone, numbers of CVs to be sent out each week, etc, to two or three colleagues or friends. Have them ring you on key dates to check up on you. Don't say you don't need supervision, and don't worry if it's embarrassing. Chances are, you do need help, and chances are, your friends would love to have a concrete way to help you. This is the time to put peer pressure and shame to work for you. If your friends can't help you, join a local job-hunting group; your peers can help you, and you can help your peers.

- Reward yourself for progress in your search. Keep an account of your activities. When you reach a target (say 25 CVs sent out this week, and 25 follow-up calls made on the 25 CVs you sent out last week), then you can cash them in for a fun activity. At this point, that fun activity may be a morning of not having to do something you hate to do, like making follow-up calls on CVs.

● Don't get overwhelmed by irrelevant details. Create a personal 'parking space' for non-essential activities. A good meeting facilitator puts up a piece of paper in the front of the meeting room. When someone makes a comment that is off the topic, the facilitator writes it down on that paper. If there's time, or if the topic comes up again, the idea is pulled out of the 'parking space' for discussion. The meeting stays focused, and the person with the idea hasn't forgotten about it. Don't throw out your non-essential ideas. Park them instead. When you have time, after you achieve your most essential objectives, visit the 'parking space' and take an old idea out for a spin.

● Break up major tasks into small steps. Don't write 'find a job' on your to-do list. Instead, make a list of the many steps you need to find a job, using this book. As you complete each step, tick it off. Save the ticked-off list so that you can see yourself making progress.

Sometimes, being a procrastinator is due to not knowing any better. There are many books and courses on priority management. They can help you give some order to your to-do list, and help you avoid the feeling of being overwhelmed. Managing priorities is a very learnable behaviour!

Get a new CV

White collar or blue collar, executive director or electrician, you should throw out whatever you've got and start again from scratch, because the current version obviously isn't working. Write at least two new drafts. One should be in chronological format; the other should be in either functional or combination format.

Don't pooh-pooh the idea of rewriting your CV by claiming that getting your foot in the door hasn't been the problem. It is entirely possible that your CV is strong enough to get you in the race, but doesn't pack enough punch to push you over the finishing line. Your CV must get your foot in the door, set the tone for the interview and, after all the interviewing is done, act as your last and most powerful advocate when the final decision is being made. Build one from the ground up that does this.

Rewrite your job search letter

Adhering to a single, bland, 'one-size-fits-all' job search letter is a common mistake. Remember, different circumstances require different letters.

I would advise you to make a commitment to sending follow-up letters with religious zeal, if you are not already doing so. This may seem like a minor detail, but it is one of the most important – and easiest – ways for you to stand out from the competition.

When it comes to job search and follow-up letters, the whole really is greater than the sum of its parts. Employers maintain dossiers on every candidate during the selection process; your coordinated written campaign makes you stand out from the other contenders as someone who pays a little bit more attention to detail and who goes a little further to get the job done. Don't worry about sending your new CV to companies you've already contacted. A new CV means a new you.

Work as a temporary

Get hold of a temporary employment directory or check the Yellow Pages for temporary agencies. Contact every appropriate agency listed for your area and offer your services.

There are two benefits to working with a temporary agency. First, while you can retain time to pursue a structured job hunt, you also get some work and get paid – thereby keeping your skills current and, just as important, the wolf from the door. Second, you may be able to upgrade that temporary job into a full-time position. (At the very least, you can expand your contact network.)

Today, there are temporary agencies that represent professionals at virtually all levels. Some even specialize solely in management people, and high-level ones at that, because companies are increasingly inclined to 'test-drive' executives before making a permanent commitment to them.

Check your references

Do it now. You'd be surprised how many otherwise qualified candidates eventually learn that they were taken out of the running by failing the 'tie-breaker' test. Two or more people are under final consideration; management decides to call your referees to help them decide who will get the job. If you have not attended to this area, you should: mediocre (or worse) references can undo months of preparation on your part.

Widen the scope of your job search

Under what other job titles could you work? Can you commute an extra 20 minutes for the right job? Consider relocation to another city, but bear in mind that, for most of us, this is an extremely costly proposition and that you should not depend on a firm's picking up your moving expenses. On the other hand, if you are single and can fit all your earthly possessions in the back seat of your car, some far-flung operation may be worth serious consideration.

Incorporate job hunting as part of your daily routine. Stop in and see what firms are in that office building you pass every morning. Perhaps there are opportunities there for you.

Of course, you are not going to get far by simply appearing at the reception desk and demanding an interview. Be a little more circumspect. Ask – politely – about the firm in question. What does it do? Who is in charge of recruitment? Are there any circulars, advertisements or company reports you can take home with you? After your initial visit, you can incorporate this information into a new research file for the company and add the firm to your database of leads.

This, by the way, is the job hunting technique I personally loathe more than any other; but it was also the technique that landed the job that – 22 years later – has obviously given me a buoyant career. The fact that you don't like a particular job hunting technique doesn't mean it won't work for you.

Body check

If you find yourself running into brick walls on the job search front, it's a good idea to look at the most important points more thoroughly. Remember, your personal friends often have trouble bringing up this subject; people in a position to employ simply move on to the next applicant.

If you do not brush and floss regularly, and have bad breath, this will not aid your candidacy. If you eat a lot of spicy foods (onions, garlic), you may be aware of the importance of keeping your breath fresh after a pungent meal but this is not, alas, your only worry. These foods typically sour your sweat and taint your clothing. Change your diet and have your interview clothes cleaned before every wearing. (But note that polyester and other synthetic fabrics are notorious for retaining body odours even after cleaning – one of many reasons to avoid them.)

Have you put on a few pounds while looking for work? Many people use eating as a response to stress. Turn off the TV once a day and get some exercise. Couch potatoes don't make good candidates. Regular physical activity will improve your appearance and your mindset, so don't skip it.

These suggestions may be difficult for you to implement if they run counter to long-established patterns, but being in a permanent job search mode is, you must admit, a much more daunting prospect than change. If you need motivation, recall the statistical truth that overweight and malodorous people are always the last to be employed or promoted.

Prepare, prepare, prepare

It may seem obvious, but all too often this is the step that people take for granted. When you walk into the interview, you should be ready to answer all the questions you could ever be asked, as well as all the ones you couldn't. Don't make the mistake of preparing only for the questions you want to hear!

Follow up

I worked for some years as a headhunter and corporate personnel director. I can't count the number of times managers told me that there was really nothing to distinguish Candidate A (who got the job) from Candidate B (who didn't) – *except that Candidate A showed an unusual level of determination and attention to detail*. The way Candidate A conveyed this, of course, was usually through a dogged follow-up campaign.

Stepping stone jobs

Even though this has been touched on earlier in this book, it bears repeating in this context. If you have been unemployed for a significant period of time, you might find it fiscally prudent to accept that less-than-perfect job. That's OK. By the same token, there is a big difference between settling for less than your dreams and making the wrong job your life's work. If circumstances force you to take a temporary detour from your ultimate career goal, give an honest day's work for an honest day's pay, and continue to pursue other opportunities.

Remember: you're the most important part of this

Maintain ongoing motivational input. Reading this book and its companion book, *Ultimate CV* is a good start. You should also consider going online or visiting the library to check out motivational tapes and related materials. You're worth it.

You are not a loser; you got knocked off course. The trick is to get back in the saddle. If you climb up and grip the reins, tomorrow you'll see all kinds of opportunities you didn't see before. You can get back on track, and you can get back to work.

Index

Note: CVs, e-mails and letters for individual jobs are listed under job title, eg teacher

acceptance responses
  e-mail 262
  letters 259–61
  power phrases 263–64
account executive 250
accountant
  employment industry professional, 'cold'
    cover letter to 148
  networking letter 204
accounting manager 104
administrative assistant 198
adult education 211
advertisements 51–53
  cross-checking categories 52
  hidden job market 52
arts management 216
ASCII text 80–81
assembling a job search letter
  checklist 41–43
  contact information 41–42
  gathering information 31–35
  length 40–41
  objectives 42–43
  punchy sentences 35–38
  sentence structure 35–36
  simplicity 38–39
  voice and tense 39–40
  writing style 43
assessment coordinator 101
assistant 229
assistant director of student housing 165
attention, gaining 3, 7, 22
auditing 239

banking 136
benefits of job search letters 6

Best Writer's Guide 89
brevity 27–28
broadcast job searches
  e-mails 189–93
  letters 163–88
  power phrases 194–96
business magazines 60

care coordinator 271
checklists
  appearance/style 48–49
  assembling a job search letter
    41–43
  what goes in, what stays out 29–30
chief financial officer 202
computer and information systems manager
  201
computer professional 155
construction manager
  follow-up letter after face-to-face meeting
    227
  resurrection letter 248
consultant 186–87
content of letter
  brevity 27–28
  checklist 29–30
  professional behaviours 22–26
  salary information 28–29
  telephone/e-mail 29
contract tracker 65–66
creative media 199
credit account specialist 130
customer service representative 98
CV online banks 50–51
  see also internet, how to use for your job
    search

database engineer   170
department manager   257
direct research contacts
   alumni/ae associations   58
   associations   58
   e-mail blasts and mailing lists   58
director
   acceptance letter   260
   employment industry professional, 'cold'
      cover letter to   151
   potential employer, 'cold' cover letter to
      133
   resignation letter   274
director of operations   185
director, asset liquidation   193

e-mail
   address   68–69, 70–73
   alerts   50–51
   stationery   87–88
employment industry professionals, 'cold'
   cover letters to
   e-mails   154–59
   letters   145–53
   power phrases   160–62
entertainment industry   121
entry-level librarian   113
entry-level network administrator   112
executive assistant
   follow-up letter after face-to-face meeting
      228
   newspaper advertisements, response to
      106
executive briefing letter   15–17
executive chef   168
executive computer specialist   150
[#]
failure, dealing with fear of   283
   starting again   284
final product   see style
financial planning professional   166
follow-ups
   after face-to-face meetings
      e-mails   232–39
      letters   219–31
      power phrases   240–43
   after telephone contact
      e-mails   215–16
      letters   210–14
      power phrases   217–18
fundraising consultant   210

graphic design   236

head librarian   254
headhunters   20–21
health care   145
health care management   95

heavy equipment operator   167
hospitality manager   222
hotel/restaurant manager   168
Hotmail   71–72, 83, 85–86
Houghton Mifflin   89
HR administration   205
HR generalist   180–81
HR position   244
Human Resource Management, Society for
   72, 82
hydrogeologist   97

information technology programme
   manager   183
international operations   153
international sales   138
international sales manager   105
internet, how to use for your job search
   accuracy   88
   benefits of using Internet   67
   computer access   68
   conversion to ASCII/text-based format
      80–81
   customizing/sending electronic
      letters/CVs   82–87
   differences, electronic v paper letters
      74–77
   electronic signatures   87–8
   e-mail stationery   87–88
   free e-mail accounts   70–71
   job search letter   73–74
   multiple electronic letters
      77–78
   online job-hunting   73–74
   online privacy   68–69
   organization   68–69
   organizing job-hunting e-mail account,
      71–73
   protecting privacy   69–70
   reaching the right person   87
   spam/reverse spam   69
   subject line, e-mail   81–82
interview, preparation for   288
investment banker   91
IT management   157
IT professional   154
ITU nurse   270

jargon   38
job search letters, types of
   broadcast letter   17–19
   executive briefing   15–17
   general   12–14
   recruitment agencies   20–21
job search, jump-starting a stalled
   fear of failure   283
   follow-up   288
   irrelevant details   285

jobs as stepping stones   288
personal hygiene   287–88
preparation for interview   288
priority management   284–85
references   286
rewriting CVs   285
rewriting job search letters   285–86
widening job search area   286–87
working as a temp   286
job search, re-evaluating   282–88
jobs as stepping stones   288
junk mail   6, 69

legal administrator   92
legal assistant   212
legal secretary   103
librarian   226
library systems director   219
loan processor   221
logistics   190

mailing lists   58
maintenance mechanic   169
management
  broadcast letter   178–79
  follow-up e-mail after face-to-face
    meeting   234
  networking letter   200
  potential employer, 'cold' cover letter to
    122
  resignation letter   272
management information systems
    230
manager
  follow-up letter after telephone contact
    214
  potential employer, 'cold' cover letter to
    114–15
managerial/administrative position
    197
managing consultant   261
manufacturing   93
manufacturing representative   224
marketing research manager   259
mass mailing   47
media   132
mental health   116
merchandise manager   223
Microsoft Outlook,   72, 86, 87
multilingual sales manager   176–77

negotiation
  letters   265–69
  e-mails   205–06
  letters   197–204
  power phrases   207–09
networking   53–56
new product marketing   191

newspaper advertisements
  power phrases   107–11
  response letters to   95–106

office administrator   102
online job postings, response e-mails to
    90–94
operations manager   182
Outlook Express   72, 87

Parkinson, M   59
personal hygiene   287–88
personal recommendations   54
personal trainer   119
pharmaceutical sales
  broadcast letter   184
  potential employer, 'cold' cover letter to
    134
planning
  approaches   62–64
  business magazines   60
  contact tracking   65–66
  direct-research contacts
    alumni/ae associations   58
    associations   58
    e-mail blasts and mailing lists   58
  follow-up calls   65
  job advertisements   50–53
  networking   53–56
  online job postings   50–51
  recruitment agencies   59
potential employer, 'cold' cover letter to
  e-mails   139–41
  letters   116–38
  power phrases   142–44
power phrases
  acceptance   263-64
  broadcast e-mails/letters   194–96
  employment industry professional, 'cold'
    enquiries to   160–62
  follow-up after face-to-face meeting
    240–43
  follow-up after telephone contact
    217–18
  networking   207–09
  newspaper advertisements, responses to
    107–11
  potential employers, 'cold' enquiries to
    142–44
  rejection   258
  resignation   276–77
  resurrection   253
  thank you letters   280–81
product manager   252
product specialist   269
production supervisor
  online job postings, response e-mail to
    94

potential employer, 'cold' cover letter to 128
programmer 251
programmer/analyst 156
project manager
  broadcast letter 188
  potential employer, 'cold' cover letter to 139
publishing
  networking letter 206
  potential employer, 'cold' cover letter to 137
purchasing 213
purchasing agent 189
purchasing manager 189

quality assurance 149

radiation safety officer 123–24
recruiter 135
recruitment agencies 59
references 286
registered nurse 120
rejection
  e-mail 257
  letter 254–56
  power phrases 258
relocating 286–67
research professional 118
resignation
  e-mail 275
  letters 270–74
  power phrases 276–77
resurrection
  e-mails 250–52
  letters 244–49
  power phrases 253
rewriting CVs/job search letters 285–86

salary/salaries 28–29
sales
  follow-up letter after face-to-face meeting 220, 231
  negotiation letter 267
  potential employer, 'cold' cover letter to 131
sales associate 99
sales manager 233
sales professional 129
sales representative 273
senior buyer 189
senior counsellor 235
senior customer service specialist 117
senior lab specialist 268
senior manager 152
senior marketing executive 192

senior network control technician/ administrator 146–47
senior R&D engineer 174–75
senior technical sales 171
simplicity 38
skilled labourer 100
social worker 246
software development 140
software manager 279
speech therapist 96
spell-checking 23, 44, 88
stevedore 245
style
  appearance 48–49
  brightening the page 44–45
  envelopes 47–48
  fonts 44
  layout 44
  mail merge 47
  proofing and printing 45–47
  stationery 45–47
systems administrator 159
systems integration 158

teacher
  broadcast letter 163–64
  potential employer, 'cold' cover letter to 127
team supervisor 255
technical sales representative 90
telecommunications 172–73
temporary work 286
thank you (after appointment)
  letters 278–79
  power phrases 280–81

veterinary surgeon 125

websites
  Hotmail 71–72, 83, 85–86
  Monster.com 72
  Yahoo! 72
wholesale market manager 247
widening job search area 286–87
work experience 141
work placement 126
writing job search letters, steps
  gaining attention 7
  generating interest 7–8
  turning desire to action 8–9
  turning interest to desire 9–11

Yahoo! 72
Yellow Pages 57, 59
Your Job Search Made Easy 59